MW00669192

THE BERKLEE BOOK OF
JAZZ HARMONY

To access audio visit:
www.halleonard.com/mylibrary

4047-0694-5646-5183

JOE MULHOLLAND & TOM HOJNACKI

To the memory of my father, Joseph J. Mulholland, who always believed in me. This one's for you, Dad.
—Joe Mulholland

To the memory of my parents Edward and Miriam Hojnacki.
—Tom Hojnacki

Berklee Press

Editor in Chief: Jonathan Feist
Vice President of Online Learning and Continuing Education: Debbie Cavalier
Assistant Vice President of Operations for Berklee Media: Robert F. Green
Assistant Vice President of Marketing and Recruitment for Berklee Media: Mike King
Dean of Continuing Education: Carin Nuernberg
Editorial Assistants: Matthew Dunkle, Amy Kaminski, Sarah Walk
Cover Design by Dzenita Hajric

Piano: Tom Hojnacki and Joe Mulholland
Bass: Bob Nieske
Drums: Bob Tamagni
Engineer: Peter Kontrimas, PBS Studios in Westwood, MA

ISBN 978-0-87639-142-6

 **Berklee** Press

 **Berklee Online**

Study music online at
online.berklee.edu

DISTRIBUTED BY

 HAL•LEONARD®
7777 W. BLUEMOUND RD. P.O. BOX 13819
MILWAUKEE, WISCONSIN 53213

1140 Boylston Street
Boston, MA 02215-3693 USA
(617) 747-2146

Visit Berklee Press Online at
www.berkleepress.com

Berklee Press, a publishing activity of Berklee College of Music, is a not-for-profit educational publisher.
Available proceeds from the sales of our products are contributed to the scholarship funds of the college.

CONTENTS

AUDIO TRACKS iv

ACKNOWLEDGMENT v

INTRODUCTION vi

CHAPTER 1   Major Key Harmony 1

CHAPTER 2   Secondary Dominants, Extended Dominants,
and the "II V" Progression 38

CHAPTER 3   Substitute Dominants: "SubV's" 63

CHAPTER 4   Minor Key Harmony: A Sea of Options 83

CHAPTER 5   Modal Interchange 116

CHAPTER 6   Blues in Jazz 132

CHAPTER 7   The Diminished Seventh Chord 147

CHAPTER 8   Modulation 166

CHAPTER 9   Modal Harmony in Jazz 182

CHAPTER 10   Outside of the Box: Constant Structure Progressions 203

CHAPTER 11   Jazz Voicings 210

APPENDIX A   The Standard Deceptive Resolutions of V7 233

APPENDIX B   Non-Resolving Dominant Seventh Chords 236

ABOUT THE AUTHORS 239

INDEX 241

AUDIO TRACKS

TRACK	DESCRIPTION
1	It Could Have Been the Summertime
2	It Could Have Been the Summertime, piano solo
3	Lucky (secondary dominants)
4	Lucky (substitute dominants)
5	To the Bitter Dregs
6	To the Bitter Dregs, piano solo
7	Bloo-Zee
8	The All–Nighter
9	Bopston Blues
10	Diminishing Returns
11	The Shadow of a Memory
12	Lithe and Lovely
13	The Slip-Up
14	Moonlight on Spot Pond
15	The Same Sky
16	Smooth Sailing, piano solo
17	Smooth Sailing

ACKNOWLEDGMENT

We would like to acknowledge all the members of the Boston jazz community, from whom we have learned so much while playing and discussing this music we love. Our colleagues at Berklee, both past and present, have set a high standard of inquiry and rigor that we have tried to honor in our presentation. In particular we would like to acknowledge Bob Share, Herb Pomeroy, Alex Ulanowski, Michael Rendish, Ted Pease, Ken Pullig, and Barrie Nettles (among many others) as originators and stewards of a groundbreaking approach to thinking about jazz harmony in a systematic way. Their conceptual organization and tireless striving for clarity inspired and challenged us as we worked.

INTRODUCTION

The harmony of jazz music is a syncretic blend of the harmonic practice of European extended tonality and the melodic inflection, rhythmic syncopation, and forward propulsion of the music of the West African diaspora—an indisputably American phenomenon. From field holler to free atonality, the music has traveled a long road, from its humble origin in the streets and dance halls of New Orleans to its present day status as a world-recognized art form. Largely an oral tradition, jazz in its hundred-plus year history has achieved a level of musical complexity that only a very few are capable of absorbing on a solely aural level. As the economics of the art form have changed and the venues for learning have moved from the clubs to the classrooms of colleges and conservatories, theorists have sought to assist aspiring practitioners of the music by attempting to demystify and define its intricacies. While many fine books have been written on the subject of jazz theory, they often adopt a pluralistic approach, seeking to give advice simultaneously about harmony, improvisation, arranging, and composition. This volume will focus more narrowly on the aspect of harmony.

Berklee College of Music has always placed the study of harmony at the center of its core music studies. The arranging, composition, improvisation, and performance curricula of the college all depend on the common language of the knowledge base and analytical techniques taught in harmony class. In this book, we seek to clearly communicate that body of knowledge so that the committed student may acquire the necessary foundation to achieve true personal artistic expression through further study in arranging, composition, and improvisation.

To make the best use of this text, you should already have a firm grasp of the fundamentals of music theory: the ability to read the grand staff, a knowledge of major and minor scales, intervals (both simple and compound), key signatures, and the standard 4-note chord qualities. The persistent study of the concepts and analytical techniques outlined in this book will enable you to:

- recognize recurring harmonic patterns and relationships to aid in the learning and memorization of repertoire,

- understand the patterns of expectation created by a series of harmonic events,

- define the harmonic envelope provided by the composer for clarity in improvisation and arrangement,

- conceptualize the chord scale as an expression of harmonic function,

- develop a hierarchical concept of chord-scale options,

- employ chord scales for personal artistic expression, and

- ponder the poetic ambiguity of the finest examples of the repertoire.

It is our hope that this book will empower the aspiring jazz musician with a comprehensive understanding of the role that harmony plays in the practice of the art. As one old-timer once said: "Rhythm is our business, but chords are what we love!"

DEFINING CHORD TYPES AND CHORD SYMBOL NOMENCLATURE

There has always been great variation in chord symbol practices among musicians. As a result, there is a vast array of different chord symbols in the published jazz literature. Learning to decipher them can be a daunting task. Although it is essential to be flexible when encountering unfamiliar chord symbols, there are good practices that inform chord symbol usage; clarity of meaning and ease of use in reading situations are foremost. The symbols used in this book are standard at the Harmony Department at Berklee College of Music. Although it differs in some respects, *The New Real Book, Volume 1* (Hal Leonard Corp., 1988) has a comprehensive chart that shows good versions of chord symbols.

In order to facilitate quick identification of the interval structure of a chord, the following numbers are used as generic shorthand for intervals within the octave:

- 1 = the root of the chord

- 2 = a major second above the root

- ♭3 = a minor third above the root

- 3 = a major third above the root

- 4 = a perfect fourth above the root

- ♭5 = a diminished fifth above the root

- 5 = a perfect fifth above the root

- ♯5 = an augmented fifth above the root

- 6 = a major sixth above the root

- °7 = a diminished seventh above the root

- ♭7 = a minor seventh above the root

- 7 = a major seventh above the root

In this context, the symbols ♭ (flat) and ♯ (sharp) are used freely, regardless of the spelling of the chord.

Triad Types (Four Basic Types and Two Common Accepted Variations)

- The letter name defines the root of the chord.

- A letter name by itself indicates a *major* triad in root position, C: 1 3 5.

- A letter name followed by sus4 or sus2 indicates a *major triad with a perfect fourth* (substituting for the major third), Csus4: 1 4 5; a *major triad with a major second* (substituting for the major third), Csus2: 1 2 5. Typically, suspensions resolve to a major 3. If the chord quality is listed as only sus, assume it is sus4.

- A letter name followed by a – sign indicates a *minor* triad, C–: 1 b3 5.

- A letter name followed by a ° sign indicates a *diminished* triad, C°: 1 b3 b5.

- A letter name followed by a + sign indicates an *augmented* triad, C+: 1 3 #5.

Seventh and Sixth Chord Types (Twelve Basic Types)

- The letter name indicates the root of the chord.

- A letter name followed by Maj7 indicates a *major seventh* chord, CMaj7: 1 3 5 7. Also written MA7.

- A letter name followed by 6 indicates a *major sixth* chord—a major triad with an additional note a major sixth above the root, C6: 1 3 5 6.

- A letter name followed by a 7 indicates a *dominant seventh chord*—a major triad with an additional note a minor seventh above the root, C7: 1 3 5 b7.

Note: The term "dominant 7" is used throughout this book to refer to a chord with the interval structure 1 3 5 b7. This chord type may or may not *function* as a resolving dominant (primary, secondary, or substitute). In common practice, it is referred to as a dominant seventh chord regardless of function. Despite its generality, we will follow that practice.

- A letter name followed by a 7sus4 indicates a *dominant 7sus4* chord—a major triad with a perfect fourth (substituting for the major third) and an additional note a minor seventh above the root, C7sus4: 1 4 5 b7.

- A letter name followed by –7 indicates a *minor 7* chord—a minor triad with an additional note a minor seventh above the root, C–7: 1 b3 5 b7.

- A letter name followed by –7b5 indicates a *minor 7b5* chord—a diminished triad with an additional note a minor seventh above the root, C–7b5: 1 b3 b5 b7. (Sometimes called C°7; this symbol is not preferred.)

- A letter name followed by +7 indicates an *augmented 7* chord—an augmented triad with an additional note a minor seventh above the root, C+7: 1 3 ♯5 ♭7.

- A letter name followed by 7♭5 indicates a *dominant 7♭5* chord—a major triad with a lowered 5 and an additional note a minor seventh above the root, C7♭5: 1 3 ♭5 ♭7.

- A letter name followed by –Maj7 indicates a *minor-major 7* chord—a minor triad with an additional note a major seventh above the root, C–Maj7: 1 ♭3 5 7.

- A letter name followed by °7 indicates a fully *diminished 7* chord—a diminished triad with an additional note a diminished seventh above the root, C°7: 1 ♭3 ♭5 °7.

- A letter name followed by –6 indicates a *minor 6* chord—a minor triad with an additional note a major sixth above the root, C–6: 1 ♭3 5 6.[1]

Defining Tensions

Tensions are tertian extensions—extensions by the interval of a third—of the basic seventh chord. Tensions are indicated in chord symbols by the numbers 9, 11, and 13, and their alterations. Tensions add color (i.e., a stylistically acceptable amount of dissonance) to the basic chord type.

Tensions are named for their distance from the root of the chord when the chord is in root position and closely spaced:

FIG. i.1. Chord Extension by Thirds. (Note: In actual practice, chords are not always voiced this way. See chapter 11, or a good jazz piano or jazz arranging book, for more detail on chord voicings.)

Numerical notation of tensions (e.g., ♭9 or ♯11) is shorthand for their interval above the root. The symbols ♭ and ♯ are used regardless of the actual spelling of the notes of the chord. For example: D is ♭13 on an F♯7 chord, F♯ is tension 9 on an E7 chord.

---

1   Minor 6 chords do *not* contain a minor sixth: ♭6!

The following numbers are used in naming the tensions added to the basic triad and seventh chord types. Optional tensions—tensions other than those suggested by the chord's function—are given in parentheses next to the basic chord type:

- ♭9 = a minor ninth above the root of a chord

- 9 = a major ninth above the root of a chord

- ♯9 = an augmented ninth above the root of a chord

- 11 = a perfect eleventh above the root of the chord

- ♯11 = an augmented eleventh above the root of a chord

- ♭13 = a minor thirteenth above the root of a chord

- 13 = a major thirteenth above the root of a chord

AN INTRODUCTION TO CHORD-SCALE THEORY

The names of the seven modal scales—Ionian, Dorian, Phrygian, Lydian, Mixolydian, Aeolian, and Locrian—have their origin in the music theory of late antiquity and have come to mean something quite different than originally intended. While most theory students are familiar with the modes as displacements of the major scale (the Ionian mode), we should make clear that modal names are used in two ways in this text. The first is to serve as descriptive names for chord scales. The second is to describe separate modal tonic systems. Modal jazz will be more fully explored in chapter 9.

Chord-scale theory is an indispensable aspect of Berklee harmony study. It is a practical approach for making sense of the dizzying variety of chord qualities and functions that characterize contemporary jazz and popular music. Chord-scale study can distill the set of relationships between harmonic ideas to a more manageable set and allow for clearer thinking about how to interpret progressions when arranging them or improvising.

A *chord scale* is a linear rendering of a complex chord—an extended chord structure, with tensions and non-chord tones arrayed within an octave.

Chord scales come in two broad categories:

1. The *diatonic* result of melodic/harmonic activity in a clearly defined key

2. *Chromatic* variations and alternate choices for the same situations

In tonal (key-related) music, chord scales are implied even if not all seven notes of the scale are sounded. Diatonic chord scales are inherent even in a two-part texture consisting of just melody and bass. Context, harmonic stress, melodic cadences, and more combine to create a context that allows our ears to fill in the "missing" notes.

At Berklee, the notes in a chord scale are labeled to clarify their role in the harmonic moment:

1. *Chord Tones:* they are a given, and reflect whether the chord is major, minor, diminished, etc. They are shown as open note heads labeled 1, 3, 5, and 7 (for a Maj7 chord) or 1, 4, 5, and ♭7 (7sus4), etc.

2. *Available Tensions:* extensions of the basic chord that sound acceptable in a voicing. They are also represented by open note heads and are labeled as compound intervals to reflect their status as acceptable extensions of the chord. Depending on the chord, they might be T9, T♭9, or T♯9; T11 or T♯11; T13 or T♭13.

3. *Harmonic Avoid Notes:* notes that are diatonic to the key and are necessary to complete the scale but do *not* sound stylistically acceptable when sustained against the basic chord. The note head is darkened, the label is "S" (for "scale degree"), and a number shows its relation to the root of the chord, for example S4, S♭2, or S♭6. The "scale degree" designation marks them as auxiliary members of the scalar unit but not acceptable extensions of the basic chord.

In C major, the full expression of the IMaj7 chord is the Ionian chord scale:

| 1 | T9 | 3 | S4 | 5 | T13 | 7 | 1 |

FIG. i.2. C Ionian Scale

The full expression of the III–7 chord is the Phrygian chord scale:

| 1 | S♭2 | ♭3 | T11 | 5 | S♭6 | ♭7 | 1 |

FIG. i.3. E Phrygian Scale

A V7 chord in C minor is fully expressed by a Mixolydian chord scale with diatonic tensions ♭9, ♯9, and ♭13:

| 1 | T♭9 | T♯9 | 3 | S4 | 5 | T♭13 | ♭7 | 1 |

FIG. i.4. G Mixolydian (♭9,♯9, ♭13)

This introduction is simply meant to provide initial definitions and a general overview of the way chord scales are derived. Don't worry if you do not yet understand all the terms; they will be fully explained in the chapters to come. Throughout the book, we will describe the most common chord scales for all the harmonic functions we explain, as well as creative substitutions and alterations.

CHAPTER 1

Major Key Harmony

Mainstream jazz harmony is both *tonal* and *functional*.

- *Tonal music* has one pitch as its primary focus: a *tonal center* that serves as a reference point for all the other chords and melody notes in the piece.

- *Harmonic function* describes the relationship of a chord to its tonal center. Chords function by creating and resolving motion around the tonic.

We will return to the concept of function repeatedly, in order to describe or explain the underlying forces that make progressions logical and compelling.

One thing that distinguishes mainstream jazz harmony from other tonal styles is the tremendous amount of harmonic color that arises due to the pervasive use of tertian extensions of the basic chord types. Jazz musicians refer to these notes as *tensions*.

Jazz harmony is also characterized by a strong progressive drive or forward propulsion analogous to the rhythmic character of the music. This arises from the frequent use of *chromatic voice leading*.

This chapter will lay out the foundations of a theory of chord progression by examining the melodic tendencies of scale tones in the major mode, harmonic functional groups, cycles of root motion, harmonic rhythm, and metrical stress patterns and their effect on phrase and cadence. Although we will start with just the seven notes of the major scale, subsequent chapters will show that jazz harmony is really about all twelve notes of the chromatic scale and the hierarchy that they occupy. As the number of available notes increases, so do harmonic freedom and expressivity. The challenge is to use the chromatic tones to aid and abet the basic diatonic functions in a way that is surprising, yet stylistically consistent.

THE MAJOR SCALE AND BASIC DIATONIC FUNCTIONS

The major scale and the chords that are derived from it are the reference point for our thinking about harmony in general. The melodic tendencies inherent in the major scale are the basis for harmonic motion. Anyone who has sung up and down a major scale has sensed these tendencies on a physical level:

- Scale degrees 1, 3, and 5 are quite stable; they have no tendency to move towards other notes.

- Scale degree 4 has a strong tendency to move *down* to 3 (*Fa–Mi*).[2]

- Scale degree 7 has a strong tendency to move *up* to 1 (*Ti–Do*).

- Scale degree 2 has a strong tendency to move *down* to 1 (*Re–Do*).

- Scale degree 6 has a strong tendency to move *down* to 5 (*La–Sol*).

Of these, the strongest tendencies are 4 to 3 (*Fa–Mi*) and 7 to 1 (*Ti–Do*).

The unstable tones also feel resolved moving to other adjacent stable tones:

- Scale degree 2 can move *up* to 3 (*Re–Mi*).

- Scale degree 4 can move *up* to 5 (*Fa–Sol*).

Scale degrees 6 and 7 often pass through each other on their way to a more stable resting place:

- 6 can move stepwise *up* through 7 to 1 (*La–Ti–Do*).

- 7 can move stepwise through 6 *down* to 5 (*Ti–La–Sol*).

Here is a more complete summary of scale-tone tendencies. The stable tones are represented by open note heads; unstable tones are represented by darkened note heads:

FIG. 1.1. Scale-Tone Tendencies

Scale degrees and their tendencies are like the letters of a language—the most basic unit. Next, we will look at the "words"—diatonic chords, the vocabulary of harmony. We will do this through the lens of *harmonic function*: the essential dynamic role each chord plays. After those basic identities are defined, we will combine them and explore the grammar of harmonic progression.

---

2   References to solfege employ the movable Do system in which Do is the tonic note.

Triads vs. Seventh Chords

In earlier tonal music, the interval of a seventh was considered a dissonance that needed to be resolved melodically. One characteristic that differentiates jazz from many other styles of tonal music (e.g., Classical music of the 16th through 19th centuries, rock, or folk) is that the seventh chord is the basic harmonic building block.[3] Seventh chords have a more complex sound than triads and support extensions of chords (e.g., 9, 11, and 13) that characterize jazz language. All of the progressions in this book will use seventh chords as the basis of the harmony.

Tonic, Dominant, and Subdominant

Harmonic function describes the relationship of a chord to its tonal center. Each chord has a role to play in a piece of music. In the same way that all the different parts in an engine help it to run smoothly—they each have a *function*—the chords in a progression also have a role in making the music move forward and come to a satisfactory conclusion.

Three basic functions define major key harmony: tonic, subdominant, and dominant.

Throughout this book we will use the word "function" to describe a chord's stability relative to other chords within a piece of music, as well as its potential to progress in a certain manner within a given phrase.

Tonic: Home Base

- The function of tonic is to provide a stable point of departure and return.

- IMaj7 or IMaj6 is the primary tonic chord.

The term *tonic* expresses the idea that one note or *tone* serves as the fundamental reference and central point of rest in a piece or section of a piece. The tonic chord serves as the ultimate point of stability in a progression. Most tunes start on the tonic I chord, and almost all end with it.

Subdominant: Moving Away from Tonic

- The function of subdominant chords is to contrast with tonic (I IV, IV I, I IV I), or to prepare the dominant (IV V).

- IVMaj7 or IV6 is the primary subdominant chord.

The *subdominant* chord is rooted a perfect fifth *below* tonic. Although connected to the tonic chord by a common tone, the IV chord is a separate and distinct harmonic

---

3   Sixth chords—root, 3, 5, and 6—are also included in this group.

area within the key; it is different in its essential sound and function from both the tonic and dominant triads.

By sounding and sustaining a I chord, we become oriented to it as tonic or home base; if it is followed by a IV chord, there is a certain tension created by the pull away from tonic. This is due to the fact that the root of the IV chord is the least stable note in the key; it tends strongly back to 3 (*Fa* to *Mi*). In addition, the 3 of the IV chord is also an unstable tone in the key; scale degree 6 tends to move back to 5 (*La* to *Sol*).

Together, the root and the 3 of IV can gravitate back toward tones of the I chord:

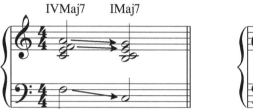 

FIG. 1.2. Subdominant to Tonic Motion

Subdominant to tonic motion is not so powerful as dominant resolution, for three reasons:

1. The IV chord lacks the *leading tone*, scale degree 7.

2. The IV chord is more closely related to the tonic triad by an important common tone, the tonic note itself.

3. The root motion of the subdominant chord back to tonic is a perfect fifth *ascending* (or perfect fourth descending) rather than a perfect fifth *descending* (or perfect fourth ascending):

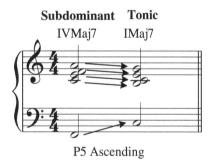 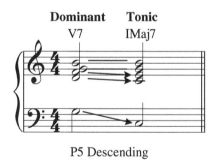

FIG. 1.3. Subdominant to Tonic vs. Dominant to Tonic

Nevertheless, there is still a release of harmonic tension. As we'll see in this and subsequent chapters, subdominant-to-tonic chord patterns and their chromatic variations have a very important functional relationship in jazz tunes.

Dominant: the Drive to Tonic

- The function of the dominant chord is to cause the listener to expect resolution to the tonic.

- V7 is the primary dominant chord.

This expectation is created by the vertical combination of unstable scale tones in the V7 chord—in particular, the interval of a *tritone* (augmented fourth or diminished fifth) created by the combination of scale degrees 4 and 7. The sound of the tritone is the defining characteristic of the dominant 7. In figure 1.4 there are three unstable tones that seek resolution: scale degrees 2 to 1, 7 to 1, and 4 to 3 (scale degree 5 is common to both chords). When they are combined in a chord, their effect is multiplied. The root of the V7 chord moves down by the interval of a perfect fifth to anchor the resolution. Bass motion by descending perfect fifth is a very satisfying, primal motion—so much so, that it can suggest resolution in and of itself.

FIG. 1.4. V7 to I: Dominant Resolution

Figure 1.4 depicts voice leading in which the leading tone resolves strictly to scale degree 1. Because the fundamental building block of jazz harmony is the seventh or sixth chord, it is more usual to see the following voice leading of the basic chord types:

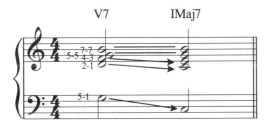

FIG. 1.5. Voice Leading V7 to IMaj7

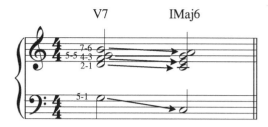

FIG. 1.6. Voice Leading V7 to IMaj6

In figure 1.5, the leading tone (B) is held over as a common tone becoming the major 7 of the tonic chord. No ascending melodic resolution of the leading tone is necessary. In figure 1.6, the leading tone descends to the 6 of the tonic chord, contrary to its strong melodic tendency.

Figure 1.7 is an alternate voice leading resolution to IMaj6. In this version, the strong upward melodic tendency of the lead voice (7 to 1) is realized. The downward melodic tendency of the scale tones in the middle voices is foregone in order to maintain efficient step-wise motion. The fact that jazz chord progressions usually employ chords in root position helps to support this freer resolution of scale tone tendencies in the inner voices.

FIG. 1.7. V7 to IMaj6 with Upward Motion

Dominant Variation: V7sus4

When V7sus4 precedes V7, it sounds subdominant: a suspension before the true dominant.

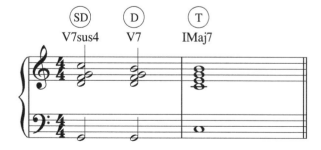

FIG. 1.8. V7sus4 Functioning as Subdominant

However, when V7sus4 directly precedes a tonic chord, we accept it as a substitute for the V7 chord even though it does not contain the interval of a tritone.

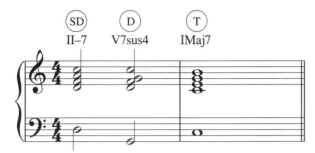

FIG. 1.9. V7sus4 Functioning as Dominant

The root motion by perfect fifth as well as the dissonant minor seventh interval between its root and seventh provide enough information in this context to create the expectation of resolution to tonic. Therefore, we classify it as a dominant function chord. In this instance, context helps to define the function.

FUNCTIONAL GROUPS

IMaj7 and IVMaj7 are the primary tonic and subdominant chords in a major key. What about the other chords: II–7, III–7, and VI–7? These chords can be thought of as alternate versions of the primary functions. Chords that share a function have similar sounds and similar effects in a progression. Using alternate tonic and subdominant chords adds variety of root motion and chord quality to a progression.

The Other Members of the Tonic Group

IMaj7 is the primary tonic: nothing can truly replace the chord built on the tonic of the key for its musical stability and finality. However, III–7 and VI–7 are considered to be functional substitutes for IMaj7 in jazz harmony. This is due to two factors: they each share three common tones with IMaj7 and neither chord includes the unstable fourth scale degree *Fa*.

FIG. 1.10. Common Tones between IMaj7 and VI–7 and between IMaj7 and III–7 (Tonics)

VI–7 is slightly more stable than III–7 because III–7 contains the unstable scale degree 7 as a chord tone and also lacks the tonic pitch.

The Other Member of the Subdominant Group

The fourth scale degree *Fa* is the defining tone for subdominant chords in a major key. It is an unstable tone that has a strong tendency to resolve to scale degree 3. Three common tones and the presence of scale degree 4 make II–7 a good functional substitute for IV:

FIG. 1.11. Common Tones between IVMaj7 and II–7 (Subdominants)

The II–7 V7 I chord pattern is one of the hallmarks of the jazz style. In this pattern, II–7 replaces IVMaj7 as the pre-dominant chord.

Is There Another Member of the Dominant Function Group?

The defining characteristic of the dominant seventh chord is the tritone interval that combines scale degrees 4 and 7. It would seem that the VII–7♭5 would fit the definition of dominant function, but in the last hundred years, it has been so rarely used in this way that it can be excluded from the dominant category. Jazz musicians have consistently preferred the stronger perfect fifth-to-root motion of V7 to I. In major key music, for all practical purposes, dominant function is embodied by V7 and its variant V7sus4.

Summary of Chord Functions

- *Tonic group:* IMaj7 (tonic), VI–7, and III–7 (alternate tonics)

- *Subdominant group:* IVMaj7 (subdominant) and II–7 (alternate subdominant)

- *Dominant:* V7 or V7sus4 (VII–7♭5 is not an alternate)

DIATONIC CHORD PROGRESSIONS

The harmonic functions that originate in the scale-tone tendencies of the major scale form a tight-knit family. When used in phrases, they create a basic expressive grammar that includes:

- *progression* (forward motion)

- *prolongation* (color variation within a functional group)

- *retrogression* (retreat from tension)

- *resolution* (release of tension)

Diatonic progressions are the bedrock set of harmonic statements that allow us to frame the basic structural elements of a tune. There are a large number of possible combinations of diatonic chords, but the number of common gambits is actually quite limited. It is very common to start with IMaj7, and the vast majority of tunes end with a subdominant-dominant-tonic cadence, almost always II–7 V7 IMaj7. Inside these bookends, the other possibilities play out: they can be categorized and understood as sets of chords organized by *root motion*. For clarity, we will start with two-chord patterns. At the end of the chapter, we will mix and match them to create harmonic phrases and progressions that are familiar from famous jazz compositions.

Root Motion by Step: "Cycle 2"

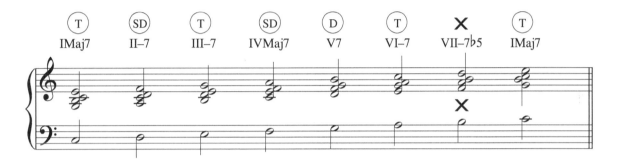

FIG. 1.12. Root Motion by Step

We'll use the term *cycle 2* to refer to root motion by major or minor second. Diatonic chord pairs that have roots a second apart have an interesting property: they have only one tone in common. For instance, in the key of C, the root of the IMaj7 chord is common only with the 7 of the II–7 chord (**C**EGB; DFA**C**). Depending on circumstances such as melody and range, it is equally acceptable to voice lead from one chord to the next maintaining the common tone in the same voice, or by using complete parallel motion in all voices:

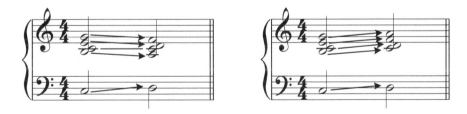

FIG. 1.13. Stepwise Root Motion: Contrary and Parallel Motion

Parallel motion from chord to chord provides efficient stepwise voice leading and also emphasizes the unique sonority of each vertical structure. It is also notable that in cycle-2 diatonic seventh-chord pairs, there is always a change from one functional group to another. As a result, the relative stability of the chord changes in relation to the tonal center.

Cycle 2 Pair	Change of Function	Musical Effect in Phrase
IMaj7 to II–	tonic to subdominant	most stable to less stable: *progression*
II–7 to III–7	subdominant to tonic	less stable to more stable: *partial resolution*
III–7 to IVMaj7	tonic to subdominant	stable to less stable: *progression*
IVMaj7 to V7	subdominant to dominant	unstable to very unstable: *progression*
V7 to VI–7	dominant to tonic	very unstable to relatively stable: *resolution*[4]
VI–7 to VII–7♭5	NA	weak
VII–7♭5 to IMaj7	NA	weak

Adjacent cycle-2 diatonic seventh-chord pairs can also descend: II–7 to IMaj7, etc. The functions are reversed, and so, of course, is the musical effect.

Cycle 2 Pair	Change of Function	Musical Effect in Phrase
II–7 to IMaj7	subdominant to tonic	less stable to most stable: *resolution*
III–7 to II–7	tonic to subdominant	more stable to less stable: *progression*
IVMaj7 to III–7	subdominant to tonic	less stable to more stable: *partial resolution*
V7 to IVMaj7	dominant to subdominant	very unstable to unstable: *retrogression*
VI–7 to V7	tonic to dominant	relatively stable to very unstable: *progression*
VII–7♭5 to VI–7	NA	weak
IMaj7 to VII–7♭5	NA	weak

Root Motion by Thirds: Cycle 3

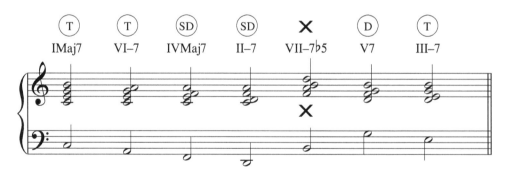

FIG. 1.14. Descending Cycle 3 Pairs

We use the term *cycle 3* to refer to chords that have roots a third (or its reciprocal interval, a sixth) apart. Cycle 3 diatonic chord pairs share three tones in common. Because of the common tones, some pairs belong to the same functional group, allowing for a prolongation of function with a variation of chord color within a phrase.

---

4   Because the expectation created by the V7 chord is to return to I, this pair is an example of a deceptive resolution of the V7 chord.

The other pairs provide continuity of chord tones in contrast with a change in harmonic stability. The *descending* cycle 3 pairs are most commonly used in the jazz repertoire.

Cycle 3 Pair	Change of Function	Musical Effect in Phrase
IMaj7 to VI–7	none	most stable to somewhat stable: *prolongation*
VI–7 to IVMaj7	tonic to subdominant	somewhat stable to somewhat unstable: *progression*
IVMaj7 to II–7	none	somewhat unstable: *prolongation*
II–7 to VII–7♭5	NA	weak
VII–7♭5 to V7	NA	weak
V7 to III–7	dominant to tonic	most unstable to somewhat stable: *resolution*
III–7 to IMaj7	tonic to tonic	retreat to tonic; rarely found

Of all the *ascending* cycle 3 pairs, only IMaj7 to III–7 is widely used.

FIG. 1.15. Ascending Cycle 3 Pairs

Cycle 3 Pair	Change of Function	Musical Effect in Phrase
IMaj7 to III–7	none	most stable to somewhat stable: *prolongation*
III–7 to V7	NA	weak
V7 to VII–7♭5	NA	weak; almost never found
VII–7♭5 to II–7	NA	weak; almost never found
II–7 to IVMaj7	none	weaker than IV to II: *prolongation*
IVMaj7 to VI–7	subdominant to tonic	weaker; can sound like a *prolongation* of IV

Once again, the VII–7♭5 chord is not part of the picture. It simply is not present in the repertoire as a cycle 3 pair. Movement between V7 and VII–7♭5 or VII–7♭5 and II–7 are theoretically possible, but do not appear in standard tunes.

Root Motion by Fifths: Cycle 5

Root motion by fifths is powerful and strongly progressive in character. A large proportion of the harmonic movement in jazz progressions involves descending fifths. We'll use the term *cycle 5* to refer to root motion by *descending* fifths as well as its reciprocal interval, the ascending fourth. Each of these adjacent pairs has two common tones. Functional relationships vary from pair to pair.

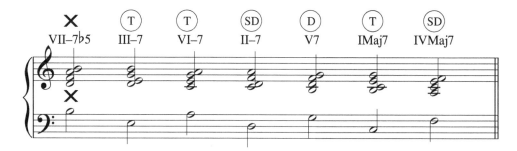

FIG. 1.16. Descending Cycle 5 Pairs

Cycle 5 Pair	Change of Function	Musical Effect in Phrase
VII–7♭5 to III–7	NA	weak, not used
III–7 to VI–7	none	somewhat stable to more stable: *prolongation*
VI–7 to II–7	tonic to subdominant	stable to unstable: *progression*
II–7 to V7	subdominant to dominant	unstable to most unstable: *progression*
V7 to IMaj7	dominant to tonic	most unstable to most stable: *resolution*
IMaj7 to IVMaj7	tonic to subdominant	most stable to unstable: *progression*

Ascending by fifths (descending by fourths) reverses the functional relationship between the chords. It is worth examining each of these pairs individually.

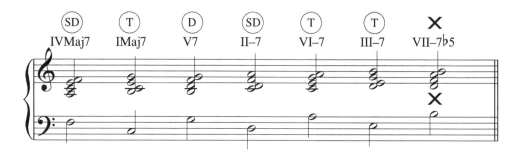

FIG. 1.17. Ascending Cycle 5 Pairs

Cycle 5 Pair	Change of Function	Musical Effect in Phrase
IVMaj7 to IMaj7	subdominant to tonic	unstable to most stable: *resolution*
IMaj7 to V7	tonic to dominant	most stable to most unstable: *progression*
V7 to II–7	dominant to subdominant	most unstable to unstable: *retrogression*
II–7 to VI–7	subdominant to tonic	unstable to more stable: *partial resolution*
VI–7 to III–7	tonic to tonic	stable to less stable: *prolongation*

Organizing chords by root relationship—that is, by "cycle"—is a helpful way to categorize the musical effects that they create. These combinations of chords are like amino acid groups in DNA. They create small units of harmonic motion that can be strung together to create larger units—harmonic phrases. These phrases eventually form a whole—the entire harmonic structure of a tune, which serves as the envelope for jazz improvisation.

HARMONIC RHYTHM, METRICAL STRESS PATTERNS, PHRASE, AND CADENCE

Before we can move from pairs of chords to longer harmonic phrases, we have to consider rhythm: specifically, harmonic rhythm.

The term *harmonic rhythm* refers to the rate at which the chords change in a piece of music. The term is also used with regard to the perceived emphasis that chords receive due to their placement in time relative to the meter, phrase, and overall form of the piece.

This is often expressed by note values: a harmonic rhythm of a whole note means the chords change every four beats, as in this example where the harmonic rhythm is one chord per measure:

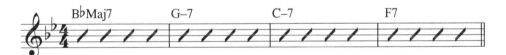

FIG. 1.18. Whole Note Harmonic Rhythm

In this progression, the harmonic rhythm is a half note, two chords per measure:

FIG. 1.19. Half Note Harmonic Rhythm

This phrase has quarter-note harmonic rhythm, four chords per measure:

FIG. 1.20. Quarter-Note Harmonic Rhythm

This phrase has a mixture of durations:

FIG. 1.21. Mixed-Duration Harmonic Rhythm

Change in the harmonic rhythm is an important, sometimes dramatic way of increasing excitement or tension in a progression. For example, in the A section of Thelonious Monk's "Well You Needn't," the chords change once per measure:

FIG. 1.22. Whote-Note Harmonic Rhythm in A section of "Well You Needn't"

The bridge starts with one chord every two measures:

FIG. 1.23. Two-Measure Harmonic Rhythm in Bridge of "Well You Needn't"

It then changes to two chords per measure—a dramatic increase in the harmonic rhythm.

FIG. 1.24. Half-Note Harmonic Rhythm in B Section of "Well You Needn't"

Metrical Stress Patterns and Their Effect on Chord Progression

Music that is organized with meter exhibits a regular hierarchy of rhythmic stress. In a measure of 4/4 meter, the first beat will have the strongest stress, the second will seem weak by comparison, the third will seem accented (but not so strong as the first), and finally the fourth beat will be the weakest of all.

FIG. 1.25. Metrical Stress Patterns: Strong (S) and Weak (W)

When the harmonic rhythm in a tune is four chords per measure, our perception of the progression coincides exactly with the metrical stress pattern. The first chord we hear will be most prominent, the second of lesser importance, the third will seem strong again, and the fourth chord will seem the weakest in the measure. This in turn causes us to anticipate a strong stress on the next downbeat and so on, as the pattern recurs. This Strong/Weak/less strong/weaker beat pattern conditions us to hear chord progressions in a certain way: The expectation is that relatively stable harmonies will coincide with the strong stresses in a pattern, while unstable harmonies usually coincide with the weak.

"The expectation is that relatively stable harmonies will coincide with the strong stresses in a pattern, while unstable harmonies usually coincide with the weak."

Stress Patterns and Slower Harmonic Rhythm

The same natural stress pattern we feel in a measure is also in operation at a larger rhythmic level: the phrase. As we have seen above, when the harmonic rhythm is the same as the meter, the stress pattern is obvious. However, when the harmonic rhythm is regular but slower than the beat, the listener will still sense an alternation of strong and weak stresses.

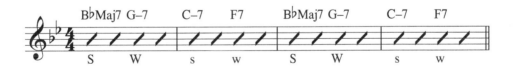

FIG. 1.26. Harmonic Rhythm Twice as Slow as the Meter

FIG. 1.27. Harmonic Rhythm Four Times Slower than the Meter

Understanding the expectation of the listener (stable chords on strong stresses, unstable on weak stresses) affords us the opportunity to play with that expectation. To illustrate the point, let's look at the effect of the metrical stress pattern on a series of four chords. Figure 1.28 shows stable and unstable functions aligned with the strong and weak stresses of the metrical pattern:

FIG. 1.28. Alternating Stable/Unstable Harmonic and Metric Functions

IMaj7 VI–7 II–7 V7 is a staple progression in the jazz repertoire. It's used in countless tunes to establish the parent tonality.[5] Positioning the most *stable* function in the strongest metrical position and the most *unstable* in the weakest creates a feeling of departure from the tonic, and thus, harmonic forward motion:

1.   IMaj7 is stable, on a strong stress.

2.   VI–7 is a less stable tonic-function chord.

3.   II–7, while less stable than the tonic chords that precede it, is more stable than the V7 chord on beat 4 of the measure.

4.   The V7, in turn, creates an expectation of resolution to the stable IMaj7 chord on the next strong downbeat.

This alternation of stable and unstable harmonies contributes strongly to a sense of harmonic *forward motion* that is analogous to the rhythmic propulsion of an improvised jazz melody.

Look what happens when we shift the sequence metrically. The progression in figure 1.29 is used as a variation in the bridge of a number of tunes:[6]

FIG. 1.29. IMaj7 in a Less Strong Position

The displacement puts II–7 in the strongest position; IMaj7 falls on a less strong stress. This diminishes the sense of consistent forward motion because the expectation created by the V7 chord is now resolved prematurely on the less strong third stress point. When repeated, this progression still has a forward moving quality, because the less stable harmonic functions occupy the weakest stresses. The cycle-5 root motion from G–7 back down to C–7 contributes to the sense of forward motion.

---

5   Examples include "Anthropology" by Charlie Parker (or any tune based on the changes of "I Got Rhythm" by George Gershwin), "I Can't Get Started" by Vernon Duke, and "Blue Room" by Rodgers & Hart.

6   Examples include the bridge of "At Last" by Harry Warren, the bridge of "Blue Moon" by Rodgers and Hart, and measures 9 to 12 of "I'll Remember April" by Raye, DePaul, and Johnstone.

Let's try another shift. In figure 1.30, the relationship of harmonic stability/ instability to metrical stresses is reversed. Even though we're employing the same chords, this example seems to stall and then restart with each repeat. The forward motion falters because the stable IMaj7 is now in the *weakest* metrical position:

FIG. 1.30. IMaj7 in a Weak Metrical Position

The final displacement, figure 1.31, is completely unsatisfactory. It's the musical equivalent of a capsized boat. Most of one's mental energy seems to go toward trying to will the downbeat to a different position. This is because the pattern of harmonic stability/instability is at odds with the expectation of strong and weak stresses created by the meter:

FIG. 1.31. Harmonic Functions in Inappropriate Metrical Positions

When the Harmonic Rhythm Changes

When the rate of change in the progression increases, chords that appear on beats 3 or 4 of a "strong" measure will be perceived as *weaker* than those on a following downbeat. Figure 1.32 has a prevailing harmonic rhythm of one chord per measure. But, in the third measure, the rate of the chord change increases to two chords per bar. The V7 on beat 3 of the measure creates an expectation of resolution to the IMaj7 chord on the "strongest" beat of measure 4. This effectively halts forward motion, bringing the harmonic phrase to a point of rest:

FIG. 1.32. Mixed Harmonic Rhythm, Unstable V7 Chord on a "Less Strong" Beat

Stress Patterns in 3/4 Time

Jazz waltzes usually have a harmonic rhythm of one chord per measure, so the metrical stress pattern will alternate strong and weak stresses with each bar line. If the harmonic rhythm speeds up, the chords that come on weaker beats of the bar will invariably be less strong than any chord that occurs on a downbeat.

Summary of Harmonic Rhythm

- The rhythmic position that a harmonic function occupies in a phrase has a great effect on a listener's perception.

- Harmonic forward motion is dependent on positioning the unstable harmonic functions on weak stresses and stable functions on strong stresses.

Harmonic Phrase

- A harmonic phrase is a musical idea the length of a breath.

- The length of the harmonic phrase depends on the tempo of the tune.

- The harmonic phrase is often separate from the melodic phrase.

Let's be clear: we're *not* talking about phrases in the melody. The harmonic phrase is a potentially independent *accompaniment* to the melodic statement.

Let's test our premise about phrase length. Count off a tune, take a deep breath, and sing the roots of the chords until you need to take a breath. What you'll find is that harmonic phrases in the standard jazz repertoire are generally two, four, or eight measures in length.[7] The length of the phrase depends on the tempo of the tune. Slow tempos (45 to 90 bpm) will divide into 2-measure phrases, medium tempos into 4-measure phrases, and in really "up" tempos, the phrases happen every eight measures.

One of the joys of jazz improvisation is to transcend the confines of the envelope created by the form of the tune. In fact, in some groups, it's a matter of duty and honor to stretch the boundaries as much as possible! But no matter how elaborate the musical surface becomes, unless deliberately playing "free," the musicians are referring mentally to the underlying structure of the harmonic phrase.

Harmonic Cadence

We have seen how harmonic functions interact with metrical stress patterns to define a tonal center through the alternation of stable and unstable musical materials. As we seek to understand motion to and away from tonic at the level of the harmonic phrase, let us consider the concept of the harmonic cadence. A harmonic cadence is a recognizable accumulation or release of harmonic tension at the end of a phrase.

---

[7]   Although phrases of asymmetrical length sometimes occur, our reaction to them is based on our expectation of symmetry, so we'll use symmetrical phrases as the basis of our discussion.

> ## *"A harmonic cadence is a recognizable accumulation or release of harmonic tension at the end of a phrase."*

A harmonic cadence defines whether a phrase will be open-ended (unfinished, seeking further resolution) or closed-ended (complete, coming to rest). It serves as punctuation, much as a comma or period does in verbal language. Just as punctuation marks will cue a speaker as to which tonal inflection to use in a spoken phrase, certain combinations of chords are used to create open-ended phrases that beg to continue or closed phrases that come to rest.

There are different kinds of cadences, each with its own distinctive character. Let's define the common cadences that stem from purely diatonic chords in a major key:

1. A harmonic phrase that ends with the chord combination V7 I is called a *full dominant* cadence. It will sound closed-ended, or finished. Subdominant function chords often precede the dominant in chord progressions. Over its history, jazz has shown a preference for the II–7 as the subdominant preparation. A phrase ending in II–7 V7 I is a *full jazz cadence.*

2. A harmonic phrase ending on the dominant seventh chord of the key is called a *half cadence.* The harmonic instability created by the dominant is left unresolved; we say the phrase feels open-ended. A phrase ending in II–7 V7 is called a *jazz half cadence.*

3. A phrase ending in IVMaj7 I or II–7 I is a *subdominant* or *plagal cadence.* While not as strong as the tonic/dominant relationship, motion from subdominant to tonic represents a move from instability to stability as well.

4. A phrase ending on IVMaj7 or II–7 can be termed an *incomplete subdominant cadence.* Phrases that end on a subdominant function chord will become especially important in later chapters, as we explore all the varieties of alternative subdominant function represented by modal interchange and special function dominant chords.

5. The chord combination V7 VI– occurring at the end of a harmonic phrase is called a *deceptive cadence.*

As our system of harmony grows with the inclusion of minor-key formulae and chromaticism, we will continue to define additional cadential patterns. (See "Appendix A. Standard Deceptive Resolutions of V7.") These distinctive chord formulas or patterns are one of the markers of jazz style. Watch for them, and be aware of their musical effect as you listen to or play tunes from the jazz repertoire.

TENSIONS: EXTENDING THE CHORD TO THE 13 FOR COLOR

Distinguishing jazz from other styles of music is its constant use of tertian extensions of the basic chord types: *tensions*. In jazz, tensions may be added freely to chords to increase the amount of harmonic color without the necessity to resolve the dissonance they create. A deep understanding of jazz harmony depends on investigating tensions thoroughly: they are an indispensable part of the language. This section begins with diatonic tensions. The use of diatonic tensions maintains the clear identity of the key. Understanding their use will lay the groundwork for more chromatic variety examined later in the chapter.

Tensions are named for their intervallic distance from the root of a chord in close position. Imagine a IMaj7 chord in C, extended by thirds and using only notes from the C major scale. Here is the result of this *tertian* extension:

FIG. 1.33. Diatonic Extensions of CMaj7

The chord symbol for a IMaj7 chord with all of the diatonic tensions from the C major scale would be:

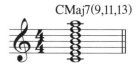

FIG. 1.34. Chord Symbol for CMaj7 with All Diatonic Tensions: CMaj7(9,11,13)

While almost every note in the scale can be applied to a chord voicing, there are some extensions that are either too dissonant to sound attractive musically or that obscure the chord's harmonic function. If we visualize the tertian chord voicing as a scale and examine the intervals between each chord tone and the tension to its immediate right, we can tell which notes will be too dissonant to be musically attractive if left unresolved.[8]

FIG. 1.35. CMaj7 with Tensions

---

8   In a chord scale, only the relationship of the tension to the chord tone immediately below it matters. When stacked vertically, available tensions are a major ninth above their respective chord tones.

Tensions 9 and 13 sound acceptable when added to the basic chord. Notice that they are a *whole step above* the previous note in the scale. Musical perceptions change over time, but since circa 1945,[9] tensions 9 and 13 have been standard additions to a IMaj7 chord.

On the other hand, the diatonic 11 is generally considered too dissonant to be used in a voicing of a IMaj7 chord. It sounds harsh and out of place, especially when voiced above the basic chord tones. The 11 is unstable scale degree 4 in the key—the note that defines subdominant function. Employing the diatonic 11 in a voicing of a IMaj7 chord will obscure its tonic function. Notice that S4 is only a *half-step above* its chord tone neighbor. Let's qualify our chord scale[10] for IMaj7 in the key of C:

FIG. 1.36. C Ionian: Chord Scale for IMaj7 in the Key of C Major

The diatonic 11 has now been reclassified as a *harmonic avoid* tone. While it is diatonic, it is too dissonant to be used as a non-resolving vertical sonority. Rather than T11, we identify it as scale tone 4 or "S4." This indicates that it is unavailable for vertical use, but appropriate as a melodic approach tone (i.e., passing tone, neighbor tone, etc.).

The *chord scale* we have identified is a theoretical device that allows us to keep track of all of the notes that *agree* with a chord in a given context. A chord scale contains the basic chord tones and available tensions appropriate to the function of the chord, and identifies other tones that are appropriate melodically but inappropriate for use in a vertical chord voicing. Practically speaking, you might see CMaj7 on a lead sheet, analyze it as the tonic chord of the tune, and then know in reference to the chord scale that tensions 9 and 13 are available for use in a voicing of that chord. You will also know that of all the tones of C major, the fourth scale degree needs to be handled with care in relation to this chord; it sounds best melodically, when resolved by step, as in figure 1.37:

FIG. 1.37. S4 as a Melodic Note

---

9   Major 7 chords are kind of rare and exotic sounds in early jazz. In Ira Gitler's "Swing to Bop," a guitarist tells how strange it was to "make" the first chord of "Solitude" with the major 7 on top. The 7–6 approach was used melodically, but not Maj7 as an unresolved chord tone.

10   The names of the church modes (Ionian, Dorian, Phrygian, etc.) have long been co-opted by jazz musicians as the names for the diatonic chord scales. In this capacity they do not apply to modal chord progressions. We'll get to that in chapter 9.

Let's lay out the chord scales for the rest of the chords in C major. As we go, we'll identify the available tensions and discuss the avoid tones. The following illustrations are all in the key of C, but the same relationships exist in all major keys. Throughout the rest of the text, descriptions of chord-scale relationships will be based in large part on the seven scales presented here.

II–7 and Dorian

In the chord scale for II–7, all of the tensions are a whole step above their respective chord tones; as a result, they all appear to agree aurally with the chord.

FIG. 1.38. D Dorian: Chord Scale for II–7 in the Key of C Major

S6 (the note B in D Dorian) in a voicing of D-7 creates a beautiful sonority, but its addition causes the II-7 chord to sound a lot like the second inversion of V7. Note the difference in the top voice in these two examples:

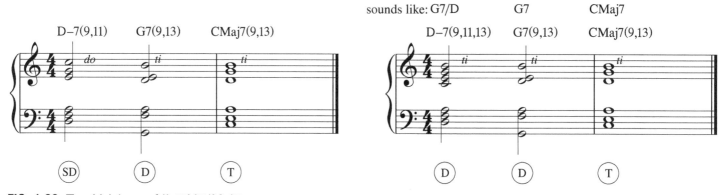

FIG. 1.39. Two Voicings of II–7 V7 IMaj7

Adding scale degree 6 (B of D Dorian) to the subdominant chord causes confusion about its subdominant function. This is of special concern in the progression II-7 V7 IMaj7, as its effect depends in large part on the clear change from subdominant to dominant to tonic sound.

III–7 and Phrygian

In the chord scale for III–7 (see figure 1.40), both the diatonic 9 and 13 are unavailable, as they are a half step above chord tones 1 and 5 respectively:

FIG. 1.40. E Phrygian: Chord Scale for III–7 in the Key of C Major

Only the 11 sounds pleasingly consonant; ♭2 and ♭6 are unacceptably dissonant in a voicing. The tonic function of III–7 would also be obscured by S♭2, which is *Fa*, the characteristic note of subdominant function. S♭6 is *Do*, the tonic note in the key. Its use in a voicing will cause the III–7 chord to sound like an inversion of IMaj7, compromising its identity as an *alternate* tonic sound.

IVMaj7 and Lydian

The chord scale for IVMaj7 shows three available diatonic tensions and no harmonic avoid tones. Any combination of 9, ♯11, and 13 will sound pleasing and appropriate.

FIG. 1.41. F Lydian: Chord Scale for IVMaj7 in the Key of C Major

V7 and G Mixolydian

Diatonic tensions 9 and 13 are available on the V7 chord. The diatonic 11 is a half step above chord tone 3 and therefore unavailable. Note also that it is *Do*, the tonic note in the key, and on that basis alone would clash with the tones of the V7 chord.

FIG. 1.42. G Mixolydian: Chord Scale for V7 in the Key of C Major

For V7sus4, the G Mixolydian chord scale is still appropriate; however, 4 is now the chord tone and 3 the avoid.

FIG. 1.43. G Mixolydian with G7sus4

There is one special case where S3 is used in conjunction with chord tone 4. This beautiful voicing is a V7sus4 chord in which 3 becomes a tension 10.

FIG. 1.44. G7sus4 with T10

This voicing is a special case; its effectiveness derives largely from its intervallic structure of fourths. Also note that T10 in this voicing is a major seventh above the chord tone C. Half steps and minor ninths above chord tones are much harsher; that is why S4 on a G7 chord is almost never an option.

Aeolian and VI–7

Diatonic tensions 9 and 11 are available on the VI-7 chord. The diatonic S♭6 is a half step above chord tone 5 and thus unavailable.

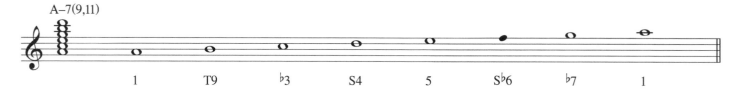

FIG. 1.45. A Aeolian: Chord Scale for VI–7 in the Key of C Major

Note that S♭6 is *Fa*, the subdominant characteristic note in the key. Using it in a voicing of VI-7 compromises the chord's tonic function, causing it to sound like the first inversion of IVMaj7.

Locrian and VII–7♭5

FIG. 1.46. B Locrian: Chord Scale for VII–7♭5 in the Key of C

While VII–7♭5 plays no role in a strictly major diatonic chord progression, it has an important role to play in relation to the secondary dominant chord V7/VI discussed in the next chapter. The chord scale in figure 1.46 shows VII–7♭5 with two available diatonic tensions: 11 and ♭13. S♭2 should not be used in a voicing.

The following tune demonstrates the principles we've discussed so far. There are questions following the lead sheet to test your understanding of what we have explored.

It Could Have Been the Summertime

By Tom Hojnacki

FIG. 1.47. "It Could Have Been the Summertime"

1. At the slow tempo of ♩ = 86, what length are the harmonic phrases?

2. What is the beginning harmonic rhythm?

3. Where and how does it vary?

4. How does this affect the position of the strong and weak metrical stresses?

5. What cycles of root motion are present?

6. Do you notice the shift from one to the next?

7. How do the harmonic phrases end?

8. What cadences are employed?

9. How does the choice of cadence affect the sense of restlessness or repose in the chord progression?

10. Can you find examples of prolongation, progression, resolution, and deceptive resolution?

Listen to the tune on the accompanying audio, do your own analysis, and then after you've had a chance to explore the piece thoroughly, check out our analysis on the following pages.

You'll notice that there are no Roman numerals in this analysis. Many of the things that are scrutinized here with regard to root motion, harmonic function, cadence, resolution, and the like, would be implied by Roman numeral analysis, but we felt it was important to make them explicit at first.

By Tom Hojnacki

Slow Ballad ♩ = 86

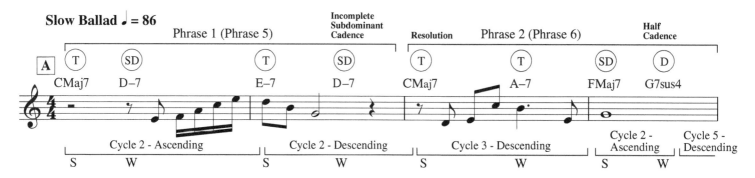

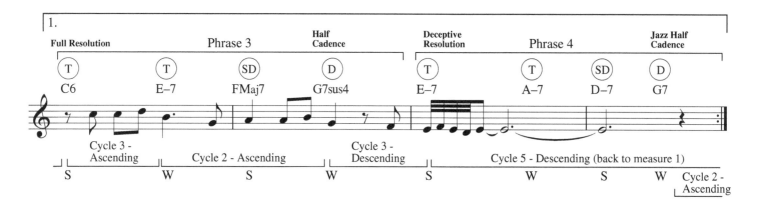

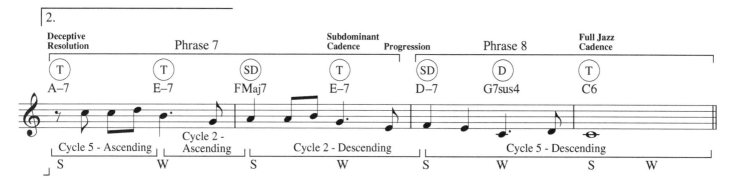

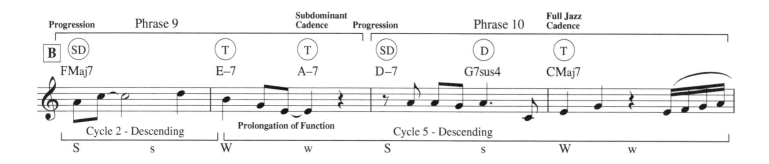

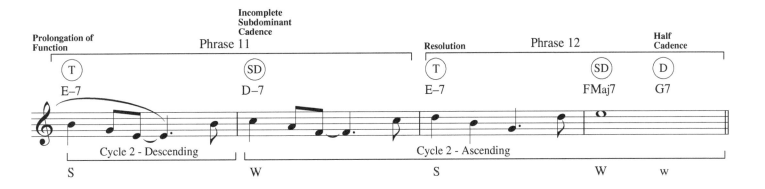

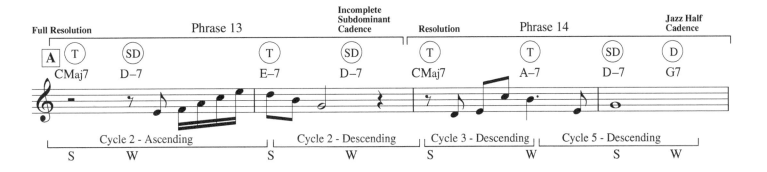

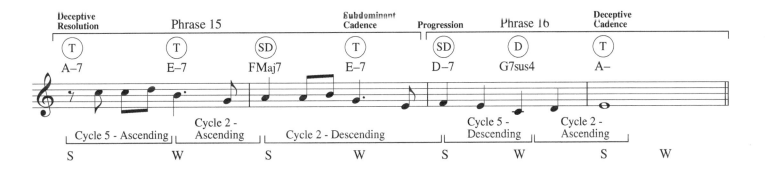

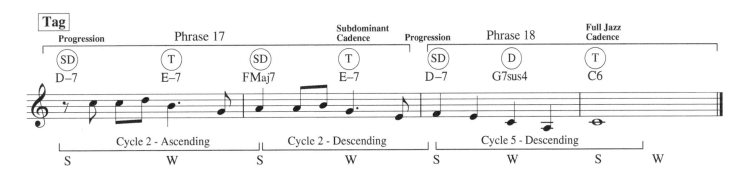

FIG. 1.48. Analysis of "It Could Have Been the Summertime"

Now let's take a look at a solo piano arrangement of "It Could Have Been the Summertime."

It Could Have Been the Summertime

TRACK 2

By Tom Hojnacki

FIG. 1.49. "It Could Have Been the Summertime" Piano Arrangement with Tensions

The chord symbols have been enhanced to reflect the tensions that are being added to the basic seventh chords. Every chord is voiced in root position. See if you can identify the individual chord tones and the extensions of 9s, 11s, and 13s. While you're at it, take the time to make note of the tensions that have been used (and not used) in each individual voicing and relate them to the chord scales defined for each harmonic function in the chapter.

You will notice that some of the tensions are *less* than an octave above the root and tensions are sometimes voiced *below* chord tones. These are simply arranging choices that are possible because of the spread nature of the voicings.

Increasing the Expectation of Resolution: Adding Chromatic Tensions to V7

Up until now, we have limited ourselves to diatonic pitches for extensions of the V7 chord. This allowed us to lay out clear principles about function and tonality. But jazz language ranges much wider than a pure diatonic pitch set: the colors introduced by chromatic alterations of chords are an integral part of that language. We will use the V7 chord as a platform to introduce chromatic alterations in diatonic harmony.

The dominant function of V7 is unstable, creating an expectation of resolution. Because of its unstable nature, our rule about available tensions can be relaxed somewhat: any tension is possible on a dominant chord, except 11.

Any tension is possible on a dominant chord, except 11.

Adding chromatic tones as tensions to the V7 chord increases the instability of the harmony, making the ensuing resolution more musically satisfying. Compare these full jazz cadences:

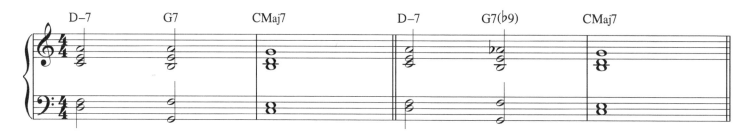

FIG. 1.50. II–7 V7 IMaj7 Cadence with ♭9

The first II–7 V7 IMaj7 employs only diatonic tensions: 9 on II–7, 9 and 13 on V7, and 9 on IMaj7. In the second, the ♭9 interval adds considerable dissonance to the G7 voicing. Notice the increased sense of release you feel when G7 resolves to CMaj7 in the second progression.

Adding a ♭13 is also possible. While not as dissonant, the chromatic note does increase the amount of restless tension we feel in the V7 chord.

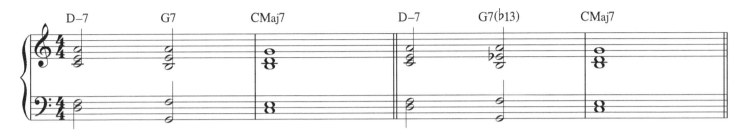

FIG. 1.51. II–7 V7 Cadence with ♭13

The two tensions combined increase the effect:

FIG. 1.52. II–7 V7 Cadence with ♭9 and ♭13

This suggests a number of further harmonic options. Each will increase the level of tension that can be applied to the V7 chord.

Optional Chord Scales for V7

We can express these options as chord scales. Organizing tension options in this way allows us to think of them hierarchically, when approaching different arranging situations. Here are the scales containing ♭9 and ♭13, in order of increasing harmonic tension:

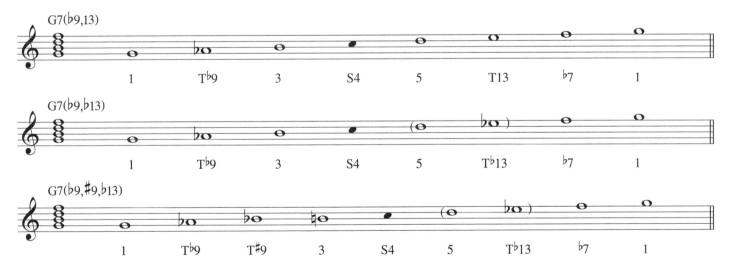

FIG. 1.53. Optional Chord Scales for V7

Each is a form of Mixolydian with "optional" chromatic tensions. The parentheses in the chord scales above indicate that either 5 or ♭13 can be used in a voicing, but not both at the same time.

In the second scale in figure 1.53 (Mixolydian ♭9, ♭13), the augmented second between A♭ and B creates a space for another chromatic tension: ♯9. T♯9 can be used alone in a V7 voicing.

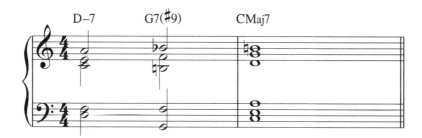

FIG. 1.54. V7 with T♯9

It could also be used sequentially with ♭9.

FIG. 1.55. V7 with ♭9, ♯9, and ♭13

Or all three tensions can be combined vertically for shock effect, as in figure 1.56.

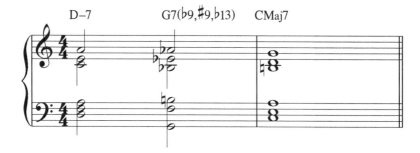

FIG. 1.56. V7 with ♭9, ♯9, and ♭13

The third scale in figure 1.53 expresses this sound: Mixolydian (♭9, ♯9, ♭13).

The Altered Dominant Scale

As you can hear in the examples above, the addition of each successive tension causes the expectation of resolution of V7 to become that much more urgent.

There is one more possible chromatic addition to the V7 chord. While the root, 3, and 7 are necessary in order to maintain the chord's essential identity, the perfect 5 is harmonically neutral. This gives us the option to alter it.

FIG. 1.57. G Altered Dominant

Known aptly as an *altered dominant* scale, this is the darkest possible set of chromatic tensions that can be applied to the V7 chord; it represents a dominant chord with everything altered except for the essential chord tones 1, 3, and ♭7.

The altered dominant chord scale provides a wide array of options for expressing dominant function. In figure 1.58, different combinations of chromatic tensions from the altered scale have been organized into *upper-structure triads* above the chord tones.

FIG. 1.58. G7 Altered Voiced With Upper-Structure Triads

The altered scale with its T♭13 projects an expectation of resolution to a minor chord.

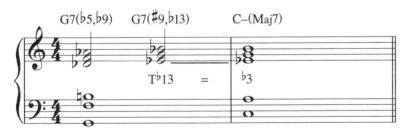

FIG. 1.59. T♭13 Resolving to I–(Maj7)

When V7(alt) resolves to IMaj7, a distinct brightening occurs.

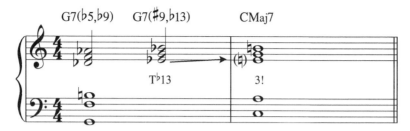

FIG. 1.60. V7(alt) to IMaj7

The Symmetric Dominant Scale

A chord scale that combines chromatic options with the diatonic T13 is useful in directing the listener's ear toward resolution to a major chord. This is called the *symmetric dominant scale*. It has an unusual regular interval structure of half steps and whole steps.

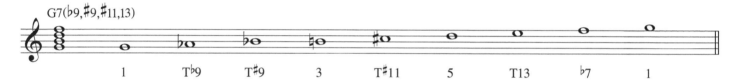

FIG. 1.61. G Symmetric Dominant Scale

The diatonic T13 creates an aural bridge to the major 3 of the CMaj7 chord.

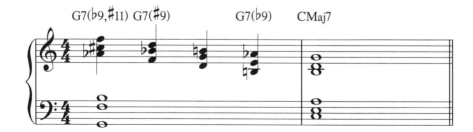

FIG. 1.62. T13 Mixed with Altered Tensions

Like the altered scale, the symmetric dominant scale is rich with upper structure possibilities. Here are some to explore.

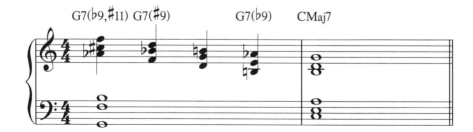

FIG. 1.63. Upper-Structure Triad Voicings from the Symmetric Dominant Scale

Now that we've visited all of the chromatic tension options for V7, let's revisit familiar territory. Listen to the sonic color and sense of urgency that chromatic tensions can lend to the cadences of the ballad "It Must Have Been the Summertime" (figure 1.47), explored earlier in the chapter.

FIG. 1.64. "It Must Have Been the Summertime" with Chromatic Tensions on V7

Summary of Chromatic Alterations to Dominant Chords

- Dominant chords can accommodate non-diatonic tensions.

- Adding chromatic tensions to a V7 chord increases its expectation of resolution.

- The only avoid note on a dominant chord is 11(S4).

- If 5 is present in the voicing, ♭13 is generally not used.

- Dominants with 13 create an expectation (but not necessity) of resolution to a major chord.

- Dominants with ♭13 create an expectation (but not necessity) of resolution to a minor chord.

- All dominant chord scales will be some form of Mixolydian scale: 1, 3, and ♭7, plus the chosen tensions.

CHAPTER 2

Secondary Dominants, Extended Dominants, and the "II V" Progression

One exciting aspect of jazz harmony is its liberal use of *chromaticism*: non-diatonic tones added to music in the prevailing key. They are aural "outsiders," not members of the diatonic pitch set. Besides adding strong colors to the music, chromatics exhibit a powerful tendency to resolve to diatonic neighbor tones. In the following section, we will begin to explore ways in which chromatic notes can be employed to create harmonic forward motion.

First, consider each of these three phrases:

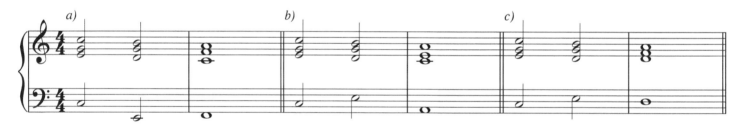

FIG. 2.1. Three Diatonic Patterns

After hearing the first measure of each example, our ears are open to any of the three possibilities. All are equally likely, and the outcomes in measure 2 of each pattern all sound acceptable. However, if we change a single note in the second chord, our expectations change dramatically.

FIG. 2.2. Same Three Patterns Adding G♯ to Chord 2

They all still sound familiar and musically acceptable, but to a careful listener example 2.2b has a strong sense of resolution. So what's happening? By changing the G to a G♯, we've changed the interval structure of the E–7 chord. The interval between D and G♯ is now an augmented fourth (a *tritone*), so E7 has an interval structure identical to the primary dominant of the key, G7:

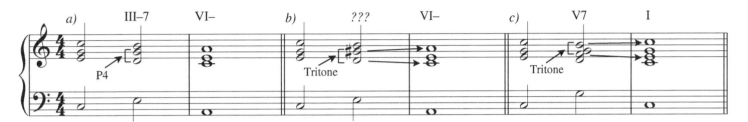

FIG. 2.3. E7 as a Secondary Dominant

That dominant quality, with G♯ as a leading tone, creates not merely progression, but an *expectation of resolution* to A–7. E7 functions as a secondary dominant, the V7 chord of the VI–7 chord. It is referred to as the V7/VI. Secondary dominants are an important harmonic function in jazz language. Secondary dominants are dominant chords that create an expectation of resolution down a fifth to a diatonic target other than the tonic.

> ## *"Secondary dominants are dominant chords that create an expectation of resolution down a fifth to a diatonic target."*

The momentary focus that secondary dominants bring to their diatonic target chords gives those chords a heightened priority in a progression.

Secondary dominants are strongly key-related. Their function is to draw the listener's attention to a diatonic chord by advertising its arrival. Their use does *not* mean we have left the key, even temporarily. If anything, the sense of relief associated with the normal resolution of a secondary dominant only reaffirms the original key identity.

For this reason, it is helpful to think of secondary dominants as chromatically altered diatonic chords. This focuses the attention on how the temporary leading tone resolves to the target chord. Consider this progression:

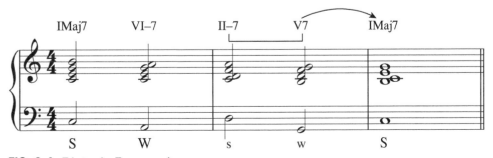

FIG. 2.4. Diatonic Progression

The tonic-function VI–7 chord can be altered by changing its minor 3 into a major 3, creating a dominant seventh chord.

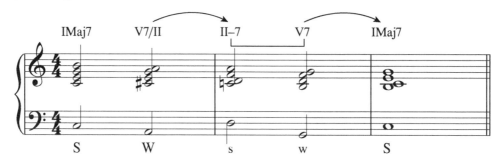

FIG. 2.5. VI–7 Altered to become the V7/II: A–7 becomes A7

The new chord functions as V7/II ("V7 of II"): the V chord of the II–7 chord. Changing the tonic function VI–7 chord into a dominant-quality chord destabilizes the harmony. The A7 chord creates a stronger sense of forward motion to II–7 on the downbeat of measure 2. As you play figure 2.5 above, notice how the secondary and primary dominant chords on the weak metrical stresses create a strong sense of forward motion to the goal chords on the strong stresses.

MAJOR KEY SECONDARY DOMINANTS

In this section, we will describe the ways in which each of the five major-key secondary dominants are constructed, their uses in progressions, and the chord scales for each.

V7/II

The VI–7 chord is altered by raising the minor third.

FIG. 2.6. VI–7 Altered to Become the V7/II: A–7 Becomes A7

V7/III

The VII–7♭5 chord is altered by raising the minor 3 and diminished 5.

FIG. 2.7. VII–7♭5 Altered to Become the V7/III: B–7♭5 Becomes B7

V7/IV

The IMaj7 chord is altered by lowering its 7.

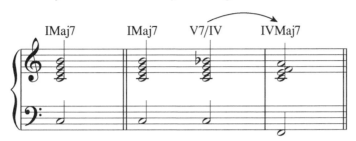

FIG. 2.8. IMaj7 Altered to Become the V7/IV: CMaj7 Becomes C7

V7/V

The II–7 chord is altered by raising its minor 3.

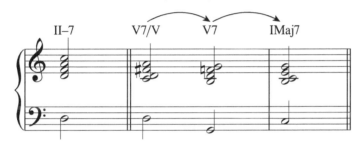

FIG. 2.9. II–7 Altered to Become the V7/V: D–7 Becomes D7

V7/VI

The III–7 chord is altered by raising its minor 3.

FIG. 2.10. III–7 Altered to Become the V7/VI: E–7 Becomes E7

V7/♭VII?

If we lower degree 7 of IVMaj7 to create a dominant seventh chord, the resulting resolution would take us to the key of B♭.

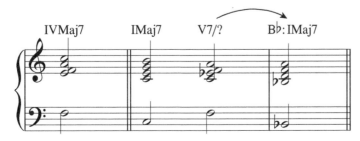

FIG. 2.11. IVMaj7 Altered: V7/?

So despite its diatonic root, the alteration does not result in a secondary dominant. In fact, this chord really just sounds like the subdominant with a lowered 7. We identify it as IV7, and it sounds best when it progresses back to IMaj or III-7.[11]

We will explore IV7 and similar chords in the chapters on substitute dominants, modal interchange, and non-functional dominant chords.

What, No V7/VII?!

In order to create a V7/VII (F♯7), we would have to build the dominant chord on a chromatic root: ♯4. It doesn't fit our definition: diatonic roots and diatonic targets.

In addition, VII-7♭5 is so unstable (as well as non-existent in basic progressions), it is meaningless as a target chord. Some progressions contain chords that might initially appear to be V7/VII, but they always resolve in other ways. See the section on substitute dominants and extended dominant series later in this chapter.

Let's say it one more time: Secondary dominants have diatonic roots and diatonic targets.

CHORD SCALES FOR SECONDARY DOMINANTS

Just as with the diatonic chords from which they are derived, chord scales for secondary dominants consist of chord tones and diatonic tensions—notes from the key.

"Chord scales for secondary dominants consist of chord tones and tensions diatonic to the key."

V7/IV and V7/V

Like the Mixolydian V7, V7/IV and V7/V each have a major chord as their target. If we extend the chord tones of V7/IV upward through the key of C, the result is a chord scale consisting of the notes of C major with a lowered 7—a Mixolydian scale.

FIG. 2.12. C Mixolydian Chord Scale

---

11   See Anne Ronnell's "Willow Weep for Me," Walter Gross's "Tenderly," Kent/Mason's "Don't Go to Strangers," or any of the myriad standard tunes with blues influence.

As we learned in chapter 1, diatonic tensions 9 and 13 are available in this chord scale. The diatonic 11 is a half step above chord tone 3, and therefore unavailable for use in chord voicings. As in V7, the vertical use of the 11 represents a premature arrival of the target chord's root, and it sounds unpleasantly dissonant.

Again, note the common-tone relationship between T13 in the chord scale of V7/IV and the 3 of the target chord IVMaj7. The 13 of a dominant-function chord scale creates an expectation of the 3 of the target chord.

FIG. 2.13. T13 in V7/IV and 3 in IVMaj7

The same principles hold true for the chord scale of the V7/V. It consists of chord tones plus diatonic tensions, scale degree 4 is a harmonic avoid note, and T13 is a common tone with the major 3 of the target chord.

FIG. 2.14. D Mixolydian Chord Scale

All well and good, these sounds are consistent with what we found for the primary dominant, V7. Now let's look at the other secondary dominants.

V7/VI

Here is E7 extended through the key of C, then arranged in scalar form.

FIG. 2.15. Chord Scale for E7 with Diatonic Tensions

This is the full expression of V7/VI in the key of C. The first aspect of this scale to notice is the different tensions: ♭9 and ♭13. Also, the augmented second between F and G♯ makes it possible to include an additional diatonic tension in the scale. The G natural is an enharmonically spelled T♯9.[12]

The 11 is once again a harmonic avoid note (S4), but the other tensions break the pattern we observed in major-key diatonic harmony. This apparent inconsistency—T♭9 is all right, but S4 is not—introduces a new principle: dominant function chords are unique in their capacity to carry greater levels of dissonance.

> ### *"Dominant function chords are unique in their capacity to carry greater levels of dissonance."*

In fact, the added dissonance increases the dominant chord's expectation of resolution. The tensions are instrumental in preparing the listener's ear for the resolution to follow. In figure 2.16, the augmented 9 and minor 13 above the root of E7 are common tones with ♭3, and ♭7 in the chord scale for A-7 to which it resolves.

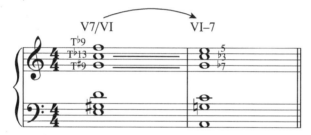

FIG. 2.16. V7/VI to VI–7. T♭13 anticipates ♭3, and T♯9 Anticipates ♭7

So, although we can't create a neat, one-size-fits-all chord scale for secondary dominants, we can divide them into two general categories:

- Mixolydian when resolving to a target with a major 3
- Mixolydian with ♭13 when resolving to a target with a minor 3

V7/III

This scale is a transposition of the V7/VI chord scale, Mixolydian ♭9, ♯9, ♭13:

FIG. 2.17. B Mixolydian (♭9, ♯9, ♭13)

---

12   It is essentially the Phrygian chord scale of III-7 with the addition of the temporary leading tone G♯. It is sometimes called "Phrygian dominant" with regard to dominant function chords. As a tonic function chord scale, it is also referred to as "Spanish Phrygian" (see the chapter on Modal Jazz).

The fact that V/III has its diatonic basis in VII-7♭5 presents us with another chord scale option for this secondary dominant. If we add only the temporary leading tone (D♯) to the Locrian chord scale of VII-7♭5, the result is the *altered dominant scale* that we saw at the end of chapter 1.

FIG. 2.18. B Altered. An alternate chord scale for V7/III in the key of C.

The altered dominant chord scale offers many colorful voicing options. Give these a try:

FIG. 2.19. Voicing Options for Altered Dominant

V/II

This chord has a new combination of tensions, 9 and ♭13:

FIG. 2.20. A Mixolydian (9, ♭13). The chord scale for V7/II in the key of C.

In this form, V7/II has issues:

1. The mixture of major and minor tensions (major 9 vs. minor 13) sends confusing signals about the quality of the target chord.

2. The diatonic 9 is major, but it is also the leading tone in the key. The leading tone has a strong upward melodic tendency that begs resolution.

3. In combination with T♭13, the diatonic major 9 produces a second tritone in the chord. The upper-structure tritone can sound harsh and possibly create some aural confusion about the direction of the progression, as in figure 2.21.

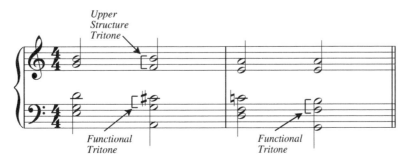

FIG. 2.21. Additional Tritone in V7/II

The use of 9 on V7/II was more common in swing era music. Since the advent of the bebop style (post 1945), it has been more common to choose the diatonic ♯9 as the partner for ♭13:

1. Since T♯9 is the tonic note in the key, it doesn't have the same urgent upward linear tendency as T9.

2. It makes a common tone connection with ♭7 of the target chord.

3. It leaves space in the scale for including an optional tension ♭9. This gives it a structure consistent with V7/III and V7/VI, as we can see in figure 2.22.

FIG. 2.22. A Mixolydian (♭9, ♯9, ♭13). An optional chord scale for V7/II in the key of C major.

Here are the three tensions arrayed in perfect fourths above A7. This voicing has a rich sound, and three tensions resolve smoothly by half-step or common tone:

FIG. 2.23. V7/II with Tensions Arranged as Perfect Fourths

SUMMARY OF SECONDARY DOMINANT CHORD SCALES

•   Chord tones + diatonic tensions = secondary dominant chord scale (see exception for V/II above).

•   The result is either the Mixolydian scale or a Mixolydian scale with specified altered tensions.

•   Scale tone 4 is an avoid note.

•   Major tensions (9 and 13) suggest a major quality target chord.

•   Minor and augmented tensions (♭9, ♯9, ♭13) suggest a minor quality target chord.

•   Substituting or altering tensions is a common creative option.

Secondary Dominants in Progressions

The diatonic progression in figure 2.24 consists of two phrases. The first phrase states the tonic and prolongs it by moving to VI-7. The second moves to the subdominant IV chord, is prolonged by the II-7 chord, and ends in a jazz half cadence on V7. The harmonic rhythm doubles at the end of the second phrase.

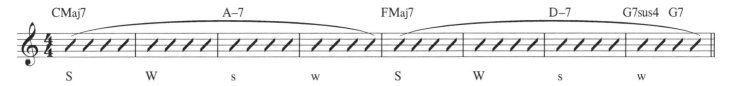

FIG. 2.24. Two Diatonic Phrases

If we speed up the harmonic rhythm of the entire phrase by inserting secondary dominants in the empty bars, the feeling of harmonic forward motion increases dramatically. With secondary dominant chords on the weak stresses in the phrase, the diatonic chords that follow become *targets*, as well as structural members. In a harmonic analysis of the new progression, the arrows show not simply progression, but *resolution* to the expected target:

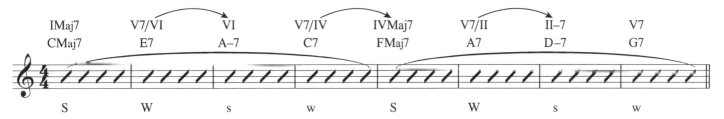

FIG. 2.25. Increasing Forward Momentum with Secondary Dominants

Deceptive Resolution of Secondary Dominants

Secondary dominant chords generally resolve directly to their target chords, but deceptive resolution is also possible. In the following progression, the E7 chord sounding on the weak metrical stress creates an expectation of resolution to an A-7 chord on the downbeat of the third measure. But E7 progresses instead to FMaj7. This is a deceptive gesture, analogous to V7 resolving up to VI- rather than down to IMaj.

FIG. 2.26. V7/VI to IVMaj7: Deceptive Resolution

In figure 2.27 the V7/II projects a resolution to the II–7 chord, but the chord of resolution does not fulfill that expectation. Our analysis does include the graphic arrow that indicates the resolution to the expected root a perfect fifth below. We also add parentheses around V7/II to indicate that the function and/or the quality of the chord of resolution will be *something other* than expected. In this case, it is secondary dominant rather than subdominant, dominant 7 quality instead of minor 7.

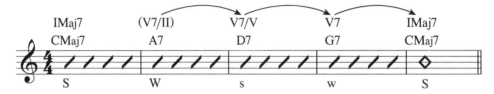

FIG. 2.27. Functional Resolution to an Unexpected Chord

Secondary Dominants on Strong Metrical Stresses

Although secondary dominants typically occur on weak stresses, they do not always do so. For example, because the V7 chord most often appears at the end of a phrase or section—on the weakest possible stress point—its secondary dominant, V7/V, will usually appear on a relatively stronger stress, as in measure 7 in this example:

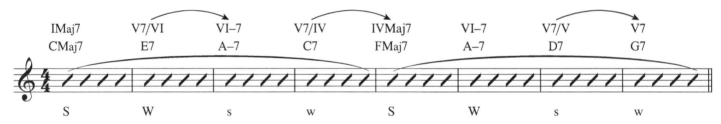

FIG. 2.28. Secondary Dominant on a Strong Stress

This relationship can be transferred to other points in the phrase or form. In tunes such as "In a Mellow Tone," "Our Love Is Here to Stay," and "But Not for Me," V7/V is in the strongest position possible: the very first chord of the song. In these songs, the secondary dominant/primary dominant pair serves as a very bright and powerful way of drawing our attention to the tonic chord and thereby establishing the key.

FIG. 2.29. Secondary Dominant V7/V as the First Chord

The notion of metric stress can be elusive and abstract, but the intersection of form and harmonic function deeply affects our perception of music. Awareness of that interaction can help explain everything from comfortable and predictable phrases to surprising and ambiguous progressions.

SUMMARY

- Secondary dominants, with the exception of the V7/V, typically appear on weak harmonic stresses. This promotes harmonic forward motion as the dominants resolve to their targets on strong stresses.

- Secondary dominants generally resolve as expected, but deceptive resolutions are possible (e.g., V7/VI to IV, V7/II to V/V).

- If a secondary dominant other than the V7/V appears on a strong harmonic stress, it resolves to its target chord. It may also progress to another dominant seventh chord (see next section).

Extended Dominants

Positioning a secondary dominant on the primary stress point in a progression can set the stage for even longer patterns of dominant resolution. Tunes such as "Nice Work If You Can Get It," "Prelude to a Kiss," and "I Got Rhythm" contain *extended dominant series*:

Extended Dominant: A string of three or more dominant chords that start on a strong harmonic stress point, and progress, one to the next, by descending perfect-fifth root motion.

The parallel chromatic scales in the essential voice leading create a very strong progressive pattern that continually delays resolution and a sense of rest. As a result, our sense of normal diatonic function is temporarily suspended while we are carried along by the progressive imperative.

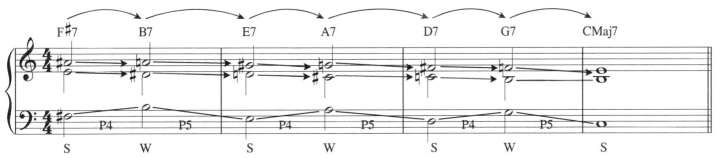

FIG. 2.30. Extended Dominant Series

Beginning as it does on a strong harmonic stress, the extended dominant string is, in effect, a backward extension of the sound of V7/V to V7 to I. Each chord that precedes the secondary dominant is another level removed from the key:

FIG. 2.31. Extended Dominant String from I

Since the ever-towering stack of Roman numerals quickly reaches the point of absurdity, our analytical convention is to dispense with them when we encounter an extended dominant series. The arrow suffices to convey the dominant pattern progression. The root that starts the series is labeled for convenient reference to the ultimate tonal center. This is the iconic extended dominant string found in the bridge of Gershwin's "I Got Rhythm."

FIG. 2.32. Extended Dominant String in "I Got Rhythm"

An extended dominant string can lead to diatonic goal chords other than IMaj, as in measures 2 and 4 of figure 2.21. Duke Ellington used this technique effectively in "Prelude to a Kiss."

FIG. 2.33. Extended Dominant String in "Prelude to a Kiss"

Or they can behave like a "stairway leading nowhere," as in the first four measures of Gershwin's "Nice Work If You Can Get It."

FIG. 2.34. Extended Dominant String: Indefinite Ending

For more extended dominant strings, see the bridge of Duke Jordan's "Jordu."

Related II–7 Chords

The II–7 V7 unit is a subdominant-dominant pair with cycle 5 root motion that triggers a strong expectation of resolution. The II V, as we will call it from here on, is one of the most important defining features of jazz harmony. The diatonic II–7 V7 plays a vital role in defining the overall tonality of a piece of music. This important progressive pattern can be extracted from its functional role in cadences, and applied to more localized situations. In our next outward push away from purely diatonic harmony, we will examine the patterns created when secondary dominants are preceded by their subdominant partners: *related II–7 chords.*

Related II of V7/IV: Ti Becomes Te

In figure 2.35, G–7 and C7 form a II V pair in measures 3 and 4. The G–7 in measure 3 introduces the chromatic tone B♭, preparing the ear for the secondary dominant C7 that follows. The introduction of "*Te,*" the lowered seventh degree of the key in the G–7 chord, starts a chromatic process of downward movement in the top voice; the tendency to resolve is intensified by the diminished fifth in V7/IV itself, and resolution occurs at the arrival of the IV chord.

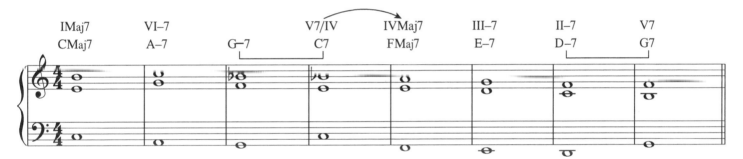

FIG. 2.35. G–7 in Measure 3 Introduces Te

In figure 2.35, the related II, G–7, is non-diatonic, and as such receives no Roman numeral analysis. Instead, we will use a *bracket* as a graphic symbol to indicate the II V. The bracket symbolizes two things:

1. The subdominant/dominant functional connection between the two chords

2. The descending perfect fifth/root relationship

The bracket identifies the chords as a functional pair, just as it does with the actual diatonic II–7 and V7. The arrow shows resolution to the expected target, IVMaj7.

If the duration of the IMaj7 chord were extended and the II V compressed into a single measure, the changes in harmonic rhythm would intensify the forward motion.

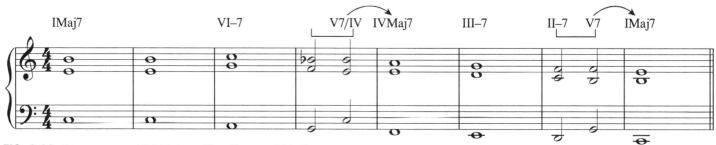

FIG. 2.36. Compressed II V Intensifies Forward Motion

II V pairs in this accelerated harmonic rhythm are typical in jazz progressions. The main structural chords are often given a longer duration in order to emphasize their function; the II V acts like a kind of switching mechanism to the next target.

If you examine the progression from a slightly higher structural perspective, you can perceive movement from tonic to subdominant and back, then through the dominant to the tonic again:

1. Measures 1 to 3 establish the tonic and prolong it with an alternate tonic VI-7 chord.

2. Measure 4 is a jazz half cadence that catapults us to the IV chord in the first measure of the second phrase (measure 5).

3. A measure of subdominant (FMaj7), one of alternate tonic (III-7), and the the primary II-7 V7 brings us back to the tonic in a full jazz cadence.

Related II of V7/VI: the Diatonic Function of VII–7♭5

Let's take the previous progression and add a II V between IMaj7 and VI-7:

FIG. 2.37. VII–7♭5 As the Related II of V7/VI

In this example, the related "II" chord in measure 2 has a different quality than we saw above: it is not -7, but -7♭5. This is a darker sound that effectively prepares the ear for the minor chord that is the ultimate target.[13] Because it is a diatonic chord, VII-7♭5 helps maintain the tonality while suggesting that a minor chord will follow.

---

13   We will see in chapter 4 that II-7♭5 is in fact the most common subdominant chord in minor key progressions.

In practice, musicians have come to freely substitute –7 and –7♭5 when employing related "II" chords. Compare the sound of figures 2.37 and 2.38: the B–7 chord in measure 2 of 2.38 is significantly brighter in sound than the analogous chord in 2.37. The F♯ creates a momentary distortion of the tonality of C major. But the strength of the root motion and essential voice leading still allow us to accept the chord as a brighter variation of VII–7♭5.

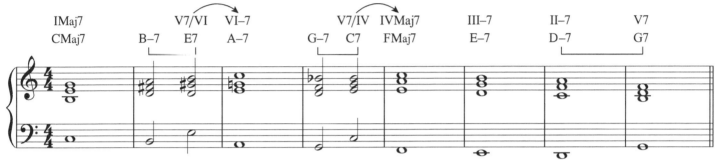

FIG. 2.38. Non-Diatonic Related II of V7/VI: A Brighter Variation of VII–7♭5

For an example of the non-diatonic related II of V7/VI, see Lennon/McCartney's "Yesterday."

Related II of V7/II: Dual Function

To continue elaborating the progression we started, we will put a II V in measure 6, targeting the actual diatonic II 7 chord.

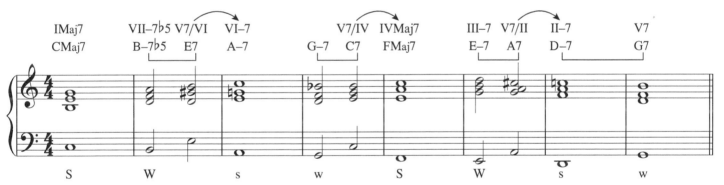

FIG. 2.39. II V in Measure 6

Now there is a regular pattern of harmonic rhythm: whole note-half note-half note, whole-half-half, etc. The secondary dominant A7 is on a very weak stress point, at the end of measure 6, typical of the V7/II.

As it happens, E–7, the related II of A7, is diatonic to the key. We say that this chord has *dual function*: it has nominal tonic function, but at the same time it is paired with a secondary dominant, giving it a secondary-subdominant relationship to its target chord. The relationship is emphasized by the compressed harmonic rhythm that causes the chords to be perceived as a functional pair.

Dual function can be a tricky concept. How can a single chord be two things at once? In fact, this kind of harmonic ambiguity is essential to diatonic music. Music exists in time: we do not hear it in tiny, disconnected slices, but rather as an evolving experience, based on an ever-widening context created by the flow of sound. We can hear and feel a chord operating one way when it first arrives, but our interpretation of it can also adjust *retrospectively*. The energy of a dominant chord coming after III–7 *overtakes* our initial experience of that chord's tonic function; it takes on secondary-subdominant character in hindsight.

As we mentioned a moment ago, the rhythmically compressed II V unit is very common in jazz. It ensures that the chords occupy the harmonic stress points that are congruent with their functions. Compare the progression in figure 2.39 with a phrase that gives the E–7 and A7 equal time:

FIG. 2.40. E–7 A7. Weak-Strong Stress in Measures 6–7. Not a II V.

- The displacement of V7/II throws the typical secondary dominant harmonic stress pattern askew and nudges the V chord out of the phrase. Instead of being on a very weak stress point (the last half of measure 6), it now occupies a relatively stronger stress, all of measure 7.

- The E–7 also occupies a full bar, giving it equal time with the other structural diatonic chords in the progression, strengthening our perception of it as a tonic function.

- If you listen carefully, the harmonic energy at the end of the phrase seems off kilter. The A7 draws attention to itself, rather than to the D–7 it is supposed to target.

- The connecting graphic bracket is absent in the analysis, because the III–7 chord is perceived as having only its own more conventional function.

Of course, this doesn't mean that you will never encounter a progression such as this. But its functional effect is quite different from that of the progression in figure 2.27. In jazz, related II– secondary dominant units typically take place within a single bar, in a faster harmonic rhythm than the rest of the progression.

Related II of V7/III: –7♭5 or –7?

The related II of V7/III is different than its counterparts in an important respect: it has a non-diatonic root (♯4). It adds a dramatic degree of tension when it is used in a progression. Because a minor 7 chord is the target, it is typical to employ a –7♭5 chord as the related II. The ♭5 of the chord, being the tonic note of the key, reinforces the diatonic resolution that is coming.

Here is our progression with V7/III and its related II. In order to avoid forcing the II V into just two beats, the III–7 chord is displaced to measure 6. There is now a pleasing sequential pattern due to the cycle 5 root motion in the last three bars. The II V's create a rolling forward motion through the half cadence:

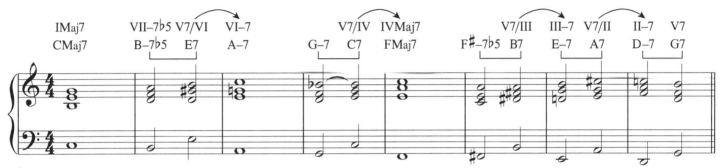

FIG. 2.41. V7/III and Its Related II

As a creative choice, a minor 7 chord could be used in place of the –7♭5 in measure 6. The use of minor 7 as a related II is distinctive:

* It has a brighter sound because its 5 is now one half step higher than the tonic note.

* The increased chromaticism adds an element of surprise and tonal ambiguity to tho progression.

* It suggests resolution to a major chord.

In certain progressions, it can also create increased parallelism. Here is our progression with F♯–7 replacing F♯–7♭5. Now, each II V is an exact transposition of the other, creating an exact sequence in the last three bars.

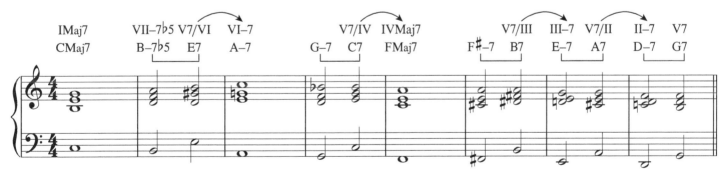

FIG. 2.42. F♯–7 Replacing F♯–7♭5

Once again, in the analysis of all II V's, the bracket is sufficient to represent the chord's intervallic relationship to the secondary dominant (perfect fifth above) and its function: secondary subdominant. Only related II's that are diatonic (the so-called dual function chords) receive Roman numeral designations.

Related II of V7/V

The related II of V7/V is the diatonic VI–7. When used in this way, it is a dual function chord, similar to III–7: tonic function is perceived first, and then retrospectively the secondary-subdominant function emerges. In figure 2.43 it is in measure 7.

FIG. 2.43. VI–7 as the Related II of V7/V

Compared to the progression that began this section (figure 2.35), this final version is a lot more colorful and dynamic. Although in this example the roots are all diatonic, the increased cycle 5 activity in the bass adds to the forward momentum of the progression. The additional chromatic notes in the upper voices create a complex ebb and flow of common tones and moving voices that engages the ear.

You probably noticed that the pattern of dominant resolution changed at the end of figure 2.43. Instead of resolving immediately over the bar line, like all the other secondary dominants, the resolution of V7/V is delayed by two beats because II-7 is *interpolated* between the two dominant seventh chords. The resolution occurs, just slightly delayed by the suspension created by the related II-7.

An extended dominant string such as the one we encountered in the bridge of "Rhythm Changes" may be elaborated with related II chords as well:

Original changes:

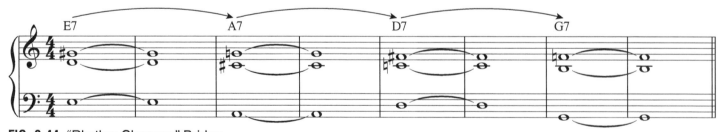

FIG. 2.44. "Rhythm Changes" Bridge

With interpolated II's:

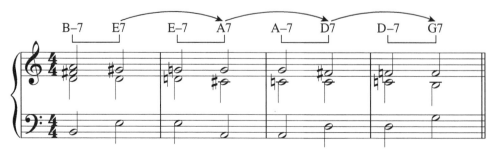

FIG. 2.45. "Rhythm Changes" Bridge with Interpolated II's

In figure 2.45, delayed resolution is the norm. A related II begins the progression and then a related II is interpolated between each dominant seventh chord in the extended series. When optional tensions are included, there can be a large number of variations on this theme.

Chord Scales for Related II Chords

The default chord scales for related II's reflect their function in a progression. For example, III–7 has tonic function; its diatonic Phrygian chord scale reinforces that perception.

FIG. 2.46. E Phrygian. The chord scale for III–7 in the key of C major.

In measure 2 of figure 2.47, the III–7 voicing avoids S♭2 but takes advantage of the available T11. The C natural (S♭6) acting as a neighbor tone in the melody reaffirms the tonic function of E–7.

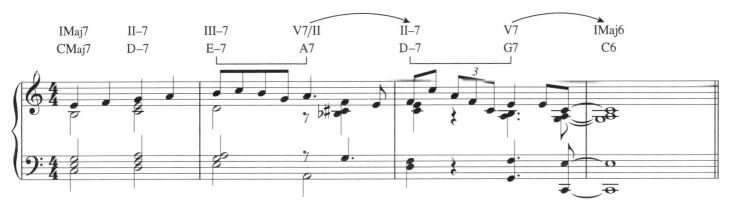

FIG. 2.47. III–7 as the related II of V7/II

Another possibility is to treat E–7 as a related II by employing an Aeolian chord scale.

FIG. 2.48. E Aeolian. Another chord scale for the related II of V7/II in the key of C major.

The E–7 in measure 2 is now voiced with T9. The introduction of the non-diatonic
F♯ creates a momentary brightening of the C tonality. It also creates a subsidiary
chromatic line as T9 (F♯) moves to T♭13 (F) on A7 to T9 (E) on D–7.

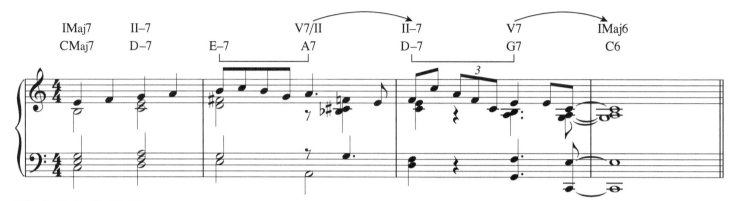

FIG. 2.49. E–7 with T9

Tunes that use the diatonic chord scale for dual function chords such as III-7 and
VI-7 sound more "inside." Introducing chromatic tensions as in figure 2.49 opens up
further chromatic possibilities for II V's. For example, the related II's of V7/IV and
V7/V are often expressed with a Dorian chord scale, reflecting a typical major key
II–7 sound: T9 and T13 prepare the listener for a resolution to a major quality chord.
Explore and experiment!

Related II's of minor chords are typically –7♭5 in quality. VII-7♭5 is the basic
reference for that sound, with its diatonic Locrian chord scale.

FIG. 2.50. B–7♭5. The chord scale for VII–7♭5 in the key of C major.

In figure 2.51, the Locrian scale is in evidence, with S♭2 used as a passing tone and
T♭13 as an expressive target tone in the melody:

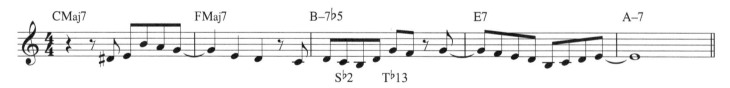

FIG. 2.51. Locrian Scale in Melody

Related II-7 Summary and Practical Considerations

- Any dominant function chord can be preceded by its related II-7 or II-7♭5 .

- VII-7♭5, III-7, and VI-7 are potential dual function chords: they are diatonic to the key and can also function as related II's.

- -7 and -7♭5 qualities are interchangeable, with these factors to consider:

  1. Diatonic related II's sound more "inside," conservative; they imply a predictable diatonic result.

  2. Alternate versions of related II's sound more adventurous and colorful, whether brighter or darker. They call the expected resolution into question.

  3. The related II always sounds on the relatively stronger harmonic stress point than the secondary dominant.

E-7 III-7 or E-7♭5	V7/II A7	II-7 D-7
F#-7 or F#-7♭5	V7/III B7	III-7 E-7
G-7 or G-7♭5	V7/IV C7	IVMaj7 FMaj7
A-7 VI-7 or A-7♭5	V7/V D7	V7 G7
B-7♭5 VII-7♭5 or B-7	V7/VI E7	VI-7 A-7

FIG. 2.52. Secondary Dominants and Their Related II's in the Key of C Major

For Further Study

Analyze the chord progression of the tune that follows with special attention to the functions that we discussed in this chapter. "Lucky" employs all of the secondary dominants. You will also see related II's in the harmony as well, both dual function and non-diatonic. Please note that the chord symbols are situated above the staff in the positions that they would occupy in a lead sheet. The arrangement, however, makes use of two rhythmic components of jazz syncopation: *delayed attack* and *anticipation*. In measure 1, the CMaj7 chord sounds late—*a delayed attack*. The E-7 chord indicated on beat 1 of measure 2 sounds earlier on the second half of beat 4 of measure 1—*an anticipation*. The A7, CMaj7, and E7 chords that follow in measures 2–4 are treated similarly as anticipations. The chords are voiced based upon the options presented by the chord scales discussed in the chapter. Take time to examine the way the chord tones and tensions are distributed in the voicings. The tune concludes with a variation on the famous Basie ending, a requirement for all pianists!

Lucky

By Tom Hojnacki

FIG. 2.53. "Lucky"

Substitute Dominants: "SubV's"

A characteristic harmonic device in jazz is *tritone substitution*: replacing one dominant chord with another dominant chord that shares the same tritone. The chord that replaces the original is called a *substitute dominant*, or simply a *subV*.

The substitute dominant has its historical antecedents in the augmented sixth chords of classical music. The augmented sixth chord is *not* a 6 chord in the modern sense (like CMaj6); rather, it is named for the interval created by a dual chromatic approach from the subdominant to the V chord. There are three different types of augmented sixth chords: Italian, French, and German. Each is identified by its own specific voice leading process. The sound of the French sixth is the closest to the jazz substitute dominant. In its original sense, it is a double chromatic alteration of II–7/5, the lowest and highest voices move chromatically outward. This leaves us with an inverted dominant 7♭5 chord: D7♭5/A♭. The relationship to secondary dominant function is obvious.

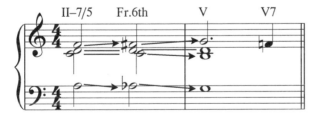

FIG. 3.1. French Sixth Chord

- The tritone (Do–Fi) targets the root and 3 of the V7 .

- The bass (Le) slips downward by a half step to the root.

- The interval between the bass and soprano of the French sixth is an augmented sixth: A♭ to F♯.

- The root (Re) is a common tone with the 5 of the V chord.

In music rooted firmly in the diatonic scale, the chromaticism of augmented sixth chords created an exotic sounding link to the V chord. Eventually, composers in the early 19th century began to use them as a colorful alternative to secondary dominants targeting functions other than V.

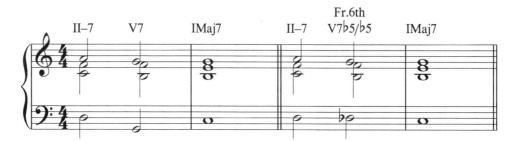

FIG. 3.2. French Sixth Chord as Secondary Dominant

In the example above, compare the II–7 V7 IMaj7 progression to the II–7 French sixth IMaj7. The French sixth chord is used as a substitute for the primary dominant in the key of C. Over time, the sound of the augmented sixth chord became commonplace. As parallelism was accepted stylistically in the music of composers such as Debussy and Ravel, our theoretical understanding of this phenomenon has become more object-based (vertical harmony) rather than process-based (linear counterpoint). In other words, in jazz, we think of these functions not as a linear process but as *root position chords in their own right*. The sound of the augmented sixth chord, popular in the late Romantic period, eventually filtered into the work of the Tin Pan Alley songwriters in the decades around the turn of the 20th century. Eventually, the dominant seventh chord that resolves downward by a half step came to full flower in jazz performance and composition.

PRINCIPLES OF JAZZ TRITONE SUBSTITUTION: THE CONTEMPORARY VIEW

The gradual development of the French sixth into a more widely applied harmonic function brings us to today's practice: every dominant chord has a potential mirror image that shares the same tritone but has a different root.

Tritone equivalence allows us to freely replace one root with the other, as long as the tritone remains constant. The distance between the root notes of each of these pairs is also a tritone. This has major implications for introducing a new level of chromatic freedom and color into a progression: Any dominant function chord—primary, secondary, or extended—can be *replaced* by a substitute dominant.

"Any dominant function chord—primary, secondary, or extended—can be replaced by a substitute dominant."

In the key of C, D♭7 is the substitute V7 chord, or "subV."

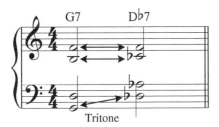

FIG. 3.3. D♭7 as the SubV of G7

CHORD SCALES FOR SUBSTITUTE DOMINANTS

Up until now, we have created chord scales using a diatonic model: chord tones + diatonic tensions = the chord scale. But substitute dominants represent a chromatic *departure* from the diatonic scale, even more so than secondary dominants. An attempt to flesh out these chords with diatonic tensions yields inconsistent and sometimes painful results. For an example, here is a diatonic version of a chord scale for D♭7, subV7 in the key of C:

FIG. 3.4. Diatonic Chord Scale for D♭7, SubV7

The resulting scale is problematic, although T♯11 works just fine. It is a whole step above the 3 of the chord, so it sounds consonant. The ♯9, either alone or combined with ♯11, is also acceptable, although not as widely used.

On the other hand, C natural conflicts with the chord quality, so it cannot be used. The non-diatonic root and 5 beg for tensions that agree with the chord and clarify its function. The dissonances produced by the diatonic ♭9 and ♭13 (so effective on primary and secondary dominants) in this instance lead the ear toward resolution outside of the key and do not work at all as an enhancement of subV. This is a problem, but there is an elegant theoretical solution.

Lydian ♭7 as a Displacement of the Altered Dominant Scale

At the end of chapter 1, we explored the use of altered tensions on the V7 chord as a way to increase its expectation of resolution. The most extreme example of this alteration resulted in a dominant structure with a lowered 5 as well as tensions ♭9, ♯9, and ♭13.

Compare the sound of the two II–7 V7 IMaj7 progressions in figure 3.5. The V7 chord in the second example seems almost to sink under the weight of the dissonant altered tensions imposed upon it.

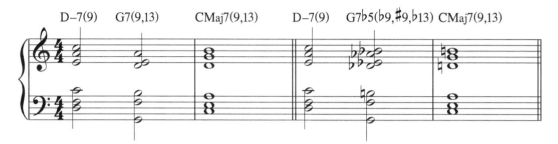

FIG. 3.5. Two Progressions: With and Without Altered Tensions

Let's use the principle of tritone substitution to invert the V7(alt) chord in measure 3, putting the ♭5 in the bass and respelling the 3. The result is subV/I, now with tensions 9, ♯11, and 13:

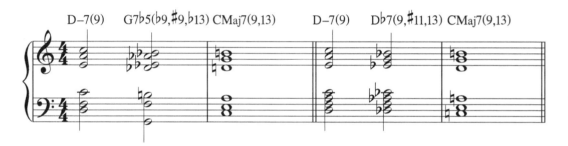

FIG. 3.6. SubV/I

This chord is expressed as the *Lydian ♭7* or *Lydian dominant* scale:

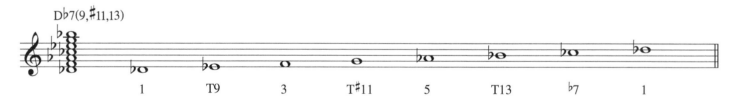

FIG. 3.7. Lydian ♭7 Chord Scale

As the substitution above implies, the Lydian ♭7 scale can be thought of as a displacement, or mode, of the altered dominant scale:

FIG. 3.8. Lydian ♭7 as Mode of Altered Dominant

The full expression of the subV is an inversion of V7♭5 and its altered tensions. The chord scale of subV7 maps onto that of V7(alt), thus:

FIG. 3.9. G Altered Dominant and D♭ Lydian ♭7 Equivalence

So, the very notes that serve as tensions to increase the expectation of the resolution of V7(alt) are the same as those that define the function of the subV.

The tensions are each a whole step above a chord tone, hence there are no avoid notes. Lydian ♭7 is the default chord scale for any substitute dominant chord, no matter what its target. It is a reliable source for solo lines or voicings, and is far and away the most widely used expression of this function.

THE TENSION CONNECTION, PART 1

Although the Lydian ♭7 chord scale contains many chromatic tones, it is easy to integrate this harmony into the diatonic context. The most important connection is tension #11. It is the root of the original primary or secondary dominant chord and diatonic to the key:

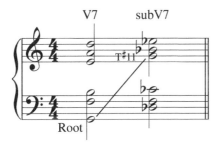

FIG. 3.10. Lydian ♭7 with T♯11

The sections that follow will have voicing illustrations using other tension connections that help to show the connection of subV's to the diatonic fabric.

SUBSTITUTE SECONDARY DOMINANTS AND THEIR RELATED II'S

Each major key has six subV's: one for the primary dominant and each of the five secondary dominants. This section will illustrate and describe them in more detail. All the examples will be in the key of C major.

Since related II's have been introduced in the previous chapter, we will include them as partners to each subV. Just as the subV resolves down a half step to the target, it is preceded by a related II a half step higher. This creates a descending chromatic root motion from inside the key—out of the key—back into the key. For analysis purposes, the dashed bracket shows the relationship between related II and subV. The dashed arrow indicates resolution to the expected target chord.

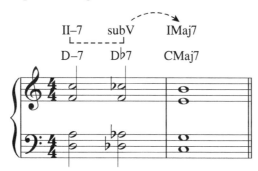

FIG. 3.11. D♭7 as SubV

SubV/II

E♭7 is the substitute secondary dominant of A7, the V7/II in the key of C.

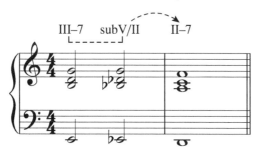

FIG. 3.12. E♭7 as SubV/II

E♭7 introduces not just one, but three chromatic tones into the phrase, dramatically increasing the amount of color and harmonic tension. As a diatonic function, III–7 would be expressed as a Phrygian chord scale. Another possibility is to treat E–7 as a related II and not as a tonic function chord in the key.

Figure 3.13 shows one possible voicing for the II V pattern using tensions from Aeolian on E–7 and from the Lydian ♭7 chord scale on E♭7.

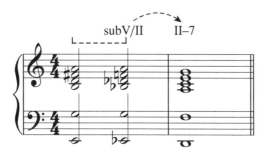

FIG. 3.13. III–7 SubV/II II–7 with Tensions

All three chords are now extended through 9 and 11/♯11. The Aeolian chord scale for the E–7 chord provides an F♯ in the voicing, not the F natural diatonic to C major. The F♯ alerts the listener to the coming chromaticism and brightens the color of the E–7. Notice how the non-diatonic pitches have been voice-led to diatonic pitches.

SubV/IV

Here is subV/IV with its most common related II chord, G–7.

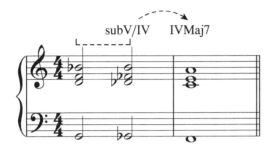

FIG. 3.14. G♭7 as SubV/IV

G♭7 is replacing C7, the original V7/IV. The related II is not analyzed with a Roman numeral because it is not a diatonic chord, but the dashed bracket shows its relationship to the subV. The Dorian chord scale is appropriate for this non-diatonic related II.

This time, let's extend each chord out to the 13.

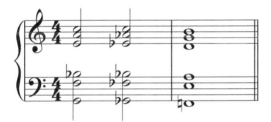

FIG. 3.15. Related II, SubV/IV, IVMaj7 with Tensions

In this voicing, the basic chord sounds in the bass clef; the tensions are isolated and stacked 13, 9, 11/♯11. Notice that the E natural (13 in the G–7 voicing) creates a tritone with the B♭. Full Dorian voicings for related II's have to take this tritone into account. In simpler, more exposed situations, the interval can be confusing to the ear, since it suggests dominant quality on a subdominant functioning chord. Here, its effect is softened by being buried in the middle of the voicing. Tensions 9 and 11 also compete for our aural attention, mitigating the influence of the tritone.

SubV/V

SubV/V has a diatonic—and therefore, dual function—related II chord.

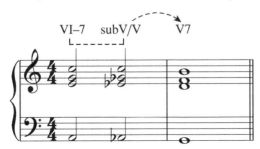

FIG. 3.16. A♭7 as SubV/V

Here is a voicing using parallel fifths in both registers.

FIG. 3.17. VI–7, SubV/V, V7sus4, V7 with Tensions

The minor and major seconds in the middle range add a pleasing dissonance that roughens up the overly "clean" open fifths. The common tones C and D in the treble emphasize the connectedness of the chords and contrast with the pure parallel motion in the lower three voices. Don't try this in your 18th century counterpoint class: we count four instances of motion by parallel fifths!

SubV/III

In the key of C, B7 (V7/III) can be replaced by F7: subV/III.

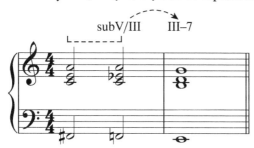

FIG. 3.18. F7 as SubV/III

The substitute secondary dominant for V7/III is potentially confusing because:

- It is the only major key substitute dominant that has a diatonic root. (Secondary dominants all have diatonic roots; based on that characteristic, subV/III might appear to belong to that functional group.)

- It is superficially identical to the IV7 chord found in the blues.

- In its triadic form, it is the subdominant chord of the key.

These factors create a strong prejudice toward hearing subdominant function for dominant chords built on scale degree 4. Nevertheless, it *is* a half step above III-7, and can resolve there. There are several ways to create the conditions for it to clearly function as subV/III:

- Precede the chord with its related II.

- Position it on a very weak harmonic stress.

- Use quick harmonic rhythm.

- Interpolate it between V7/III and its target chord, III-7.

These factors will all clearly support the function of subV/III, especially when more than one of them is in play. Consider the progression in figure 3.19, in which F7 functions as a blues subdominant chord. It is on a relatively strong harmonic stress, and it lasts for two full bars, putting it on an equal footing with the tonic IMaj7. It has subdominant function in this context.

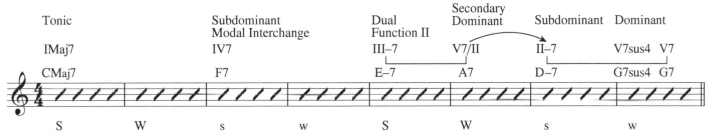

FIG. 3.19. Progression in C with F7 Functioning as IV7

Next is an F7 chord in very different surroundings. It is now preceded by the V7/III and its related II–7♭5. It is also on the weakest possible point in the phrase and has a short duration of only two beats. All these factors contribute to a strong sense that III–7 is inevitable; it has a clear subV function.

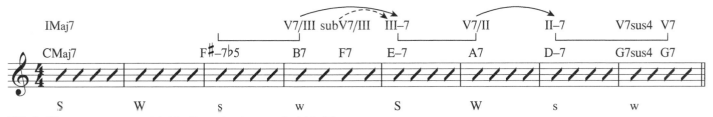

FIG. 3.20. Progression with F7 Functioning as SubV7/III

The chord quality for its related II of subV/III is usually minor 7♭5, as in the example at the beginning of this section. This helps to foreshadow the resolution to a minor chord. A minor-seventh chord is the other option. It adds a dramatically brighter color to a diatonic progression, because the 5 of the chord is a half step above the tonic note of the key. Voicings with the 5 "in the lead" (as the topmost voice) emphasize that brightness, as in figure 3.21.

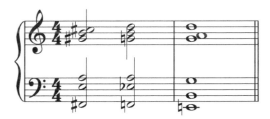

FIG. 3.21. Related II of SubV7/III with 5 in the Lead

SubV/VI

In the key of C, B♭7 is generally used as a modal interchange chord from the parallel minor key. Like IV7 in the preceding section, it performs a subdominant function that most often leads back to IMaj7 in the majority of chord progressions. Although subV/VI has a non-diatonic root, it is similar to subV/III in that it functions most clearly when it is:

1. prepared by a diatonic related II chord,

2. has a shorter duration compared to that of the prevailing progression,

3. and is interpolated between a secondary dominant and the target chord.

So when this chord is preceded by VII–7♭5, the descending chromatic root motion causes us to expect VI–7.

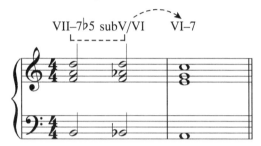

FIG. 3.22. B♭7 as SubV7/VI

This voicing adds diatonic tensions, including 11/♯11 exposed in the lead.

FIG. 3.23. Sub V7/VI and Related II with Tensions

Harmonic rhythm and stress patterns can also be exploited to clarify the subV/VI function. On the one hand, this progression has a very regular harmonic rhythm, giving all the chords fairly equal weight, and the B♭7 is on a relatively strong stress in the phrase. [14]

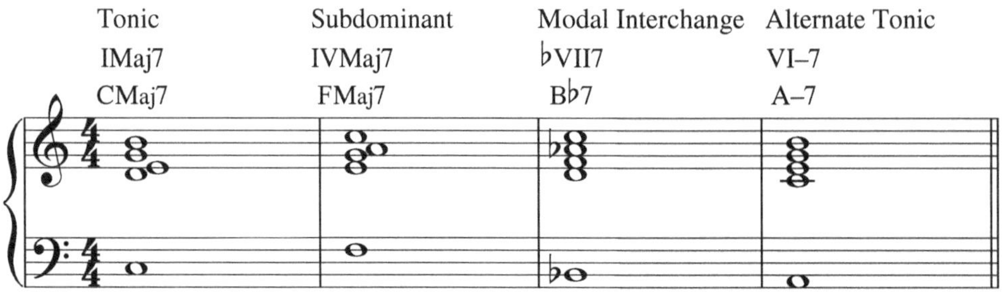

Tonic	Subdominant	Modal Interchange	Alternate Tonic
IMaj7	IVMaj7	♭VII7	VI–7
CMaj7	FMaj7	B♭7	A–7

FIG. 3.24. B♭7 as ♭VII7

---

14   In this progression, it functions as a modal interchange chord. For a full explanation of modal interchange, see chapter 5.

In figure 3.25, the B♭7 is moved to a much weaker stress point and is preceded by a diatonic related II and a conventional secondary dominant. The B♭7 also has ♯11 in the voicing from the Lydian ♭7 chord scale. All of this further reinforces the subV sound and function.

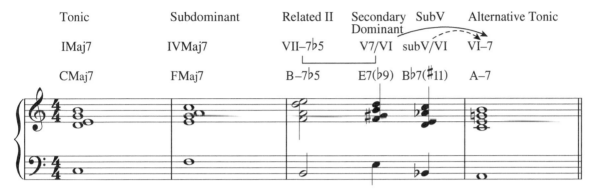

FIG. 3.25. B♭7 as SubV7/VI

THE TENSION CONNECTION, PART 2

There are six subV's associated with each major key: subV of the primary dominant and one for each secondary dominant as well. Applying a Lydian ♭7 chord scale to each creates two sub-categories for these chords: those with *only* diatonic tensions and those with only *one* diatonic tension. Conveniently, the categories are also consistent in another way:

• SubV's with diatonic tensions have a minor target.

• SubV's with only one diatonic tension (e.g., ♯11) have a major target.

Diatonic tensions make for a more natural-sounding connection with the home key.

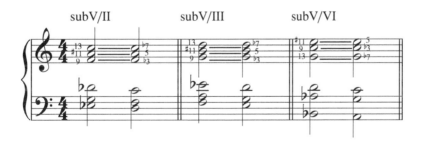

FIG. 3.26. Diatonic Tensions on SubV's, Common Tones with Chords of Resolution

SubV/I and subV/IV have non-diatonic T9 and T13. In order to better integrate these chords into a diatonic passage, the diatonic tension ♯9 can substitute for 9. This creates a common tone connection with the 3 of the major target chord and often serves to support an important melody note.

FIG. 3.27. #9 as an Optional Tension on SubV/I and SubV/IV

Voicing subV's to create contrary motion between the top voice and the bass can also be an effective way to de-emphasize the subV's "out" nature.

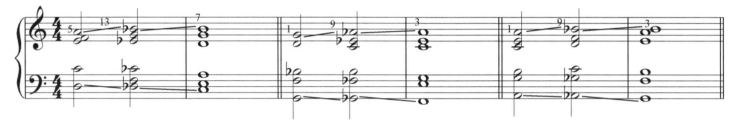

FIG. 3.28. Contrary Motion in the Outer Voices

In practice, musicians use a variety of strategies for voicing progressions. The full range of possibilities is beyond the scope of this book, but some of the issues to consider are the melodic pitches being supported, range, and relative density of tension across a phrase.

Alternate Related II's for SubV's

The cycle 5 root motion that characterizes II V's can potentially be applied to subV's, but it is not commonly used for three reasons:

1. The related II is no longer actually "II" of the target chord.

2. The extended chromaticism introduced by the related II suggests modulation to a new tonal center, rather than back to a diatonic target.

3. The disparity between the perfect fifth leap and the chromatic resolution destroys the smooth bass line and can be disturbing to the listener.

In this example, subV is preceded by Ab−7. If the intention is to resolve to CMaj7, this configuration will obscure that target. The II V pair in this harmonic rhythm and stress placement strongly signals a resolution to Gb.

FIG. 3.29. Related II of SubV pointing to Gb Resolution

Never say never, of course. Harmonic rhythm and the presence of other secondary II V patterns can prepare the ear for this ambiguous combination, so that a resolution to a diatonic chord is not as unexpected. In this version of the progression, all those elements are in place, leading to a much clearer expectation of resolution to D–7.

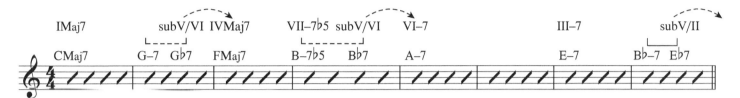

FIG. 3.30. Related II of SubV/II Prepared by Earlier II V Pairs

This configuration is occasionally found in compositions when there is a sequence of chromatically resolving dominants. It is often occasioned by a melodic sequence, as in Thelonious Monk's "'Round Midnight" at measure 4...

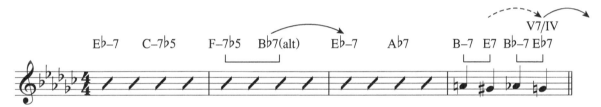

FIG. 3.31. Cycle 5 Motion in Related II of a SubV

...or in this harmonization of the first bar of Benny Golson's "Stablemates."

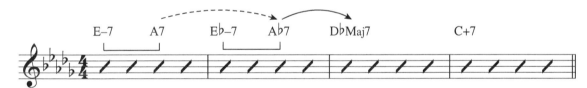

FIG. 3.32. Cycle 5 Motion in Related II of SubV/V

In the flow of a performance, bass players and pianists will sometimes conspire to elaborate less complex progressions with II V's that have a mix of cycle 5 and chromatic root motion; Art Tatum was a consummate master of this tactic. Nevertheless, mixtures of chromatic and conventional II V's are predominantly found in transitional modulations and arrangements of tunes that contain a number of sequential dominants. The number of possible combinations is dizzying, as this chart illustrates. It shows a dozen possible progressions in the key of C, with IVMaj7 as the target.

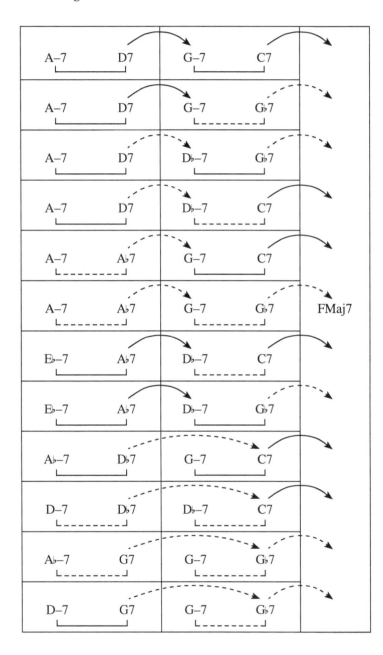

Just to make it even deeper, remember that any or all of the minor seventh chords could be replaced by a minor 7♭5, but we would need a 3-D chart for that!

If we add extended dominants to the mix, it gets even better:

A7	D7	G7	C7	
A7	D7	G7	G♭7	
A7	A♭7	G7	C7	
A7	A♭7	D♭7	C7	
A7	A♭7	G7	G♭7	
E♭7	A♭7	D♭7	C7	FMaj7
E♭7	A♭7	G7	C7	
E♭7	D7	G7	C7	
E♭7	D7	D♭7	C7	
E♭7	A♭7	D♭7	G♭7	

...and keep in mind that each of these dominants could be preceded by a related II (either flavor) or a sus4 chord! There are an enormous number of possibilities in any situation. The ultimate choice is determined by the relationship of the chord to the melody and the degree of desired chromaticism between the interpolated progression and the target key.

SubV Summary

- SubV's have dominant function; all the observations about harmonic stress patterns and related II's that were discussed in the secondary dominant chapter still apply.

- The chord scale for a subV is Lydian ♭7.

- SubV's with a Maj7 quality target have only one diatonic tension: ♯11.

- SubV's with a minor quality target have diatonic tensions that are common tones with the target chord.

- T♯11 is the root of the original dominant chord that has been replaced.

- The most commonly used chord scale for related II's is Dorian (for –7), or Locrian for –7♭5.

Summary of Chord Scales for SubV's

subV: Replaces the primary dominant of the key. #11 is the root of the primary V7 chord. It is a common tone with the 5 of the chord of resolution.

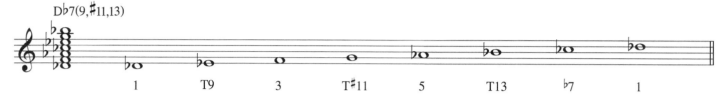

FIG. 3.33. Chord Scale for SubV/I

Substituting diatonic T#9 for T9 creates another diatonic connection. T#9 on subV/I is a distinctive sound and creates an aural expectation of the major 3 of the I chord. Tensions #9 and 9 are not used in combination.

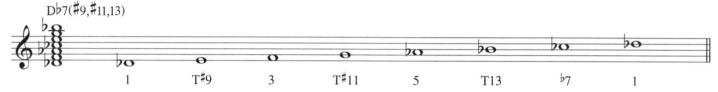

FIG. 3.34. Optional Chord Scale for SubV/I

subV/II: Diatonic tensions are consistent with the Lydian ♭7 chord scale. Tensions 9, #11, and 13 are common tones in the chord of resolution:

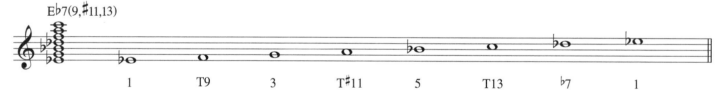

FIG. 3.35. E♭ Lydian ♭7: Chord Scale for SubV/II

subV/III: As with subV/II, diatonic tensions create a Lydian ♭7 chord scale. Tensions 9, #11, and 13 are common tones in the chord of resolution:

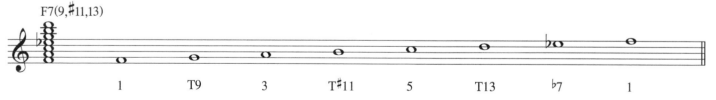

FIG. 3.36. F Lydian ♭7: Chord Scale for SubV/III

subV/IV: Chord tone 7 and T♯11 are common tones with the chord of resolution:

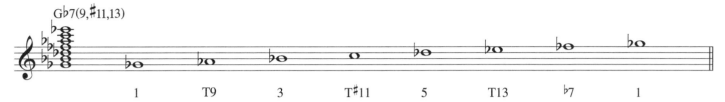

FIG. 3.37. G♭ Lydian ♭7: Chord Scale for SubV/IV

Substituting T♯9 for T9 creates another diatonic connection. T♯9 on subV/IV is a distinctive sound and creates an aural expectation of the major 3 of the IV chord.

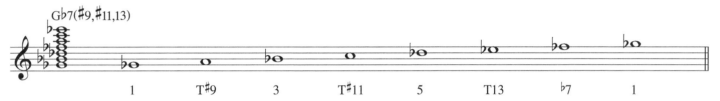

FIG. 3.38. Optional Chord Scale for SubV/IV

subV/V: A mix of diatonic and non-diatonic tensions. T♯11 and T13 are common tones with the chord of resolution:

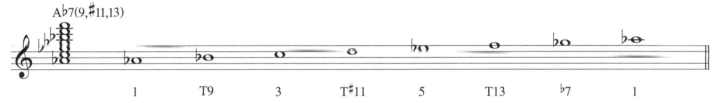

FIG. 3.39. A♭ Lydian ♭7: Chord Scale for SubV/V

subV/VI: Diatonic tensions. Tensions 9, ♯11, and 13 are common tones in the chord of resolution.

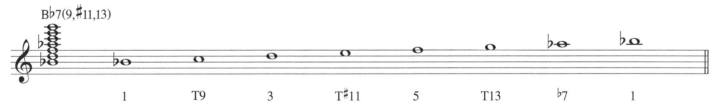

FIG. 3.40. B♭ Lydian ♭7: Chord Scale for SubV/VI

For Further Study

Here's "Lucky" once again, this time reharmonized with subV's. Do a complete analysis of the harmony with a special emphasis on what was discussed in this chapter. Notice how the use of interpolated subV's can speed up the harmonic rhythm. Look for instances of voicings that use the Lydian ♭7 scale and the Lydian ♭7(♯9) scale.

Lucky

By Tom Hojnacki

TRACK 4

FIG. 3.41. "Lucky," Reharmonized with SubV's

CHAPTER 4

Minor Key Harmony: A Sea of Options

The minor key repertoire presents substantially greater harmonic variety than that of the major key. A Roman numeral analysis of tunes such as Gigi Gryce's "Minority," John Lewis's "Django," Matt Dennis and Earl Brent's "Angel Eyes," and Charlie Haden's "First Song" reveals a larger number of chords that can be considered diatonic. The melodic material for these tunes is similarly diverse; it transcends the seven-note major key model.

Some attempts to explain this richness start by referring to multiple scales. Most musicians are familiar with the natural, harmonic, and melodic minor scales as well as two additional tonic minor modes: Dorian and Phrygian.

FIG. 4.1. Familiar Minor Scales

Minor key jazz tunes are rarely diatonic to just one of these scales. Typically, chords from several of these sources are used interchangeably in minor key compositions. A large collection of chords can be derived this way, but constantly flipping between separate scales does not accurately reflect how we hear or play minor key music. In addition, this model does nothing to explain *why* one particular chord is used rather than another.

As another approach to explaining the large number of diatonic possibilities, theorists have put forward the notion of a "composite" or "blended" minor scale to serve as the conceptual basis for minor key harmony:

FIG. 4.2. Composite Minor Scale

However, presenting all of the theoretical options from the composite-minor scale as equally important is not an accurate reflection of the reality of the music either. In truth, there are certain chords (or combinations of chords) from each of the source scales that are the predominant colors in the minor key repertoire.

This chapter will help untangle some of this apparent complexity. We will discuss harmonic function in minor key tunes, present the most common chords from the separate minor source scales, discuss the chord scales for those options, and then show them in the context of a tune.

TONIC FUNCTION

The tonic function chord in the lead sheet of a minor key tune is often given simply as a triad. As you might imagine, this does not fully reflect what musicians actually play and can lead to confusion: should the chord be minor 7, minor 6, or min(Maj7)? For the answer, we can look to the principal *source scale* options for tonic function: a *source scale* is the scale from which a chord is derived.

"A source scale is the scale from which a chord is derived."

In minor key music, the tonic chords usually come from melodic minor or Dorian, although Aeolian and Phrygian are possibilities as well. Let's examine each in turn.

Tonic Source 1: Melodic Minor

FIG. 4.3. Melodic Minor Source

The melodic minor scale gives us two tonic chords: I-6 and I-(Maj7). Both of these chords arc bold and assertive in character. The tritone between the ♭3 and 6 of I-6 and the major 7 cast against the root of the I-(Maj7) account for this quality.

Since these chords are rooted on the tonic, the source scale (sometimes called the "modal source") and chord scale are the same. When expressed as chord scales, we can see that they contain no harmonic avoid tones, as each of the tensions is a whole step above its respective chord tone. This allows a great deal of freedom in voicing chords and improvising, since there are no "wrong" notes.

FIG. 4.4. C Melodic Minor. The chord scale for I–(Maj7).

Although there are no true avoid notes in melodic minor scales, minor sixth chords are not regular tertian structures. In order to help preserve the integrity of the I-6 sound, it is preferred to conceive of scale degree 7 as a tension. It is best to leave tension 7 out of a voicing of I-6, restricting its use to melodic embellishment.

FIG. 4.5. C Melodic Minor. The chord scale for I–6.

Another member of the minor key tonic group is VI-7♭5. VI-7♭5 usually serves as a prolongation of tonic, as in the progression I- VI-7♭5 II-7♭5 V7♭9, the minor key counterpart of IMaj7 VI-7 II-7 V7. The chord scale for VI-7♭5 is Locrian natural 9, a displacement of the melodic minor source scale. All tensions are available.

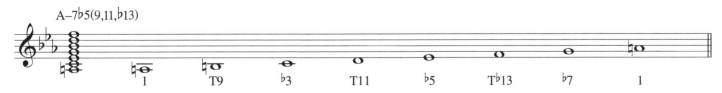

FIG. 4.6. A Locrian Natural 9, the Chord Scale for VI–7♭5

Although it appears infrequently, ♭III+ (Maj7) is another member of the tonic group from the melodic minor source.

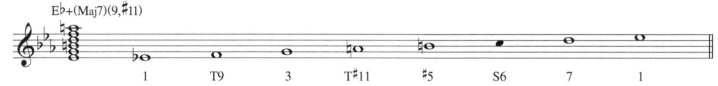

FIG. 4.7. E♭ Lydian Augmented, the Chord Scale for ♭IIII+(Maj7)

Avoiding the tonic note ensures that this chord maintains its own identity distinct from an inversion of I-(Maj7). It also eliminates the harsh dissonant minor ninth interval it would create if exposed in a voicing.

FIG. 4.8. S6 Is an Avoid Note on ♭III+(Maj7).

Tonic Source 2: Dorian

Another frequently used source scale for tonic function chords in minor key is the Dorian scale.

FIG. 4.9. C Dorian Tonic Source

This serves as the source scale for I-7 and as an alternate source for I-6. As tonic I- chords, their chord scales are identical to their source. (On I-6, ♭7 is an avoid note, a half step above the chord tone 6.) All three tensions are available for use in voicings.

FIG. 4.10. C Dorian, the Chord Scale for I–6 and I–7

Music using the tonic Dorian source scale is often expressed with *quartal* chord voicings:[15] chords voiced in fourths rather than in thirds.

FIG. 4.11. Voicings in Fourths on a C Dorian Scale

Some of these voicings involve only perfect fourths, while some introduce augmented fourths. The "modern" sound of the constant quartal structures mitigates the dissonance of the major seventh interval between ♭7 and T13 (B♭ to A). In figure 4.11, some chords can be parsed as C–6(9), C–6(9, 11), or C–7(11), while the chord that anticipates the downbeat of measure 3 really doesn't have a clear identity because it contains no 3. The entire passage, however, creates a C Dorian macro-harmony. Wayne Shorter's "Footprints" is a clear example of a tune in a minor key that employs a tonic Dorian source scale.

Tonic Source 3: Aeolian

FIG. 4.12. Natural Minor Source

I–7 can be derived from an Aeolian source when a darker sound is desired. Voicing possibilities are limited slightly by the avoid note S♭6. Nevertheless, the Aeolian tonic sound is fundamental to our experience of minor key.

♭IIIMaj7 is also part of the tonic group in a minor key. Its Ionian chord scale is a displacement of the Aeolian or natural minor source.

FIG. 4.13. E♭ Ionian, the Chord Scale for ♭IIIMaj7

---

15   A fuller treatment of quartal voicings can be found in chapter 11.

Because the ♭IIIMaj7 chord is directly related by common tones to I-, and of our innate tendency to hear stable major chords as tonic, any use of the ♭IIIMaj7 chord in a primary metric position (or any tonicization of the ♭IIIMaj7 chord, for that matter) can cause a tonal shift to the relative major key. Consider figure 4.14.

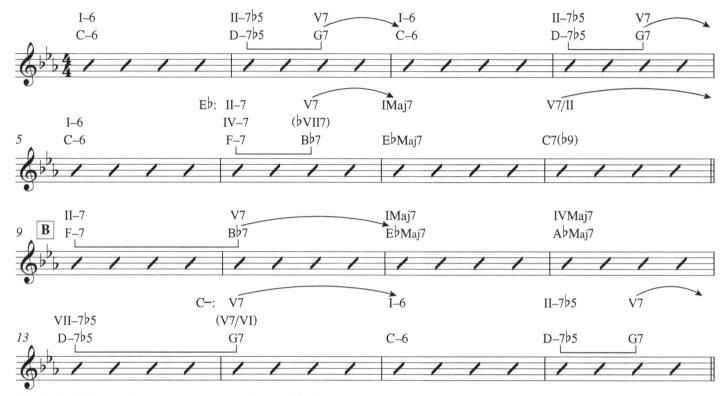

FIG. 4.14. C Minor Progression with an Area of E♭ Major

- The first 4-measure phrase section with the II V pattern and the leading tone in the V7 chord establish C minor unequivocally as tonic.

- The second 4-measure phrase begins again with a I-6 chord moving on through subdominant IV-7 followed by ♭VII7.

- Because IV-7 ♭VII7 sounds identical to II-7 V7 in the key of E♭, it is in effect a diatonic sequence of the root motion in measures 2 and 4.

- When E♭Maj7 appears on the downbeat of measure 7 (a strong metrical stress in both the phrase and the section), voila! We have a shift of key center so that the relative major now sounds like tonic.

- The first phrase of the B section confirms the new tonality with a II V I progression in E♭.

- As the diatonic cycle 5 motion continues, we have a retonicization of C minor via V7/VI.

- Because C minor was established as the parent tonality of the tune in the first phrase, our ear now slips back to this assumption effortlessly.

- The final minor II V in measure 16 reconfirms C minor as tonic.

Many minor key tunes make use of a shift from tonic minor to relative major in order to create contrast. "Black Orpheus" by Luis Bonfa and "Autumn Leaves" by Joseph Kosma and Jacques Preévert are classic examples of this ambiguous minor/relative major relationship. Tunes like Richard Rodgers & Lorenz Hart's "My Funny Valentine" and Don Raye & Gene DePaul's "You Don't Know What Love Is" are in minor keys but have bridges that begin in the relative major.

Tonic Source 4: Phrygian

In a handful of tunes, the Phrygian scale is used as the tonic source/chord scale.

FIG. 4.15. Phrygian Source

In figure 4.16, the I– is expressed by quartal voicings that make use of the entire Phrygian scale.

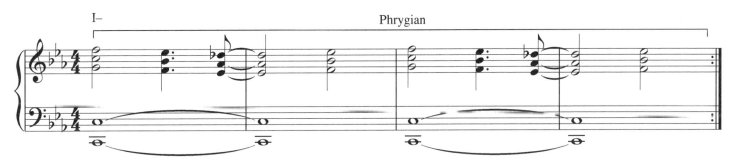

FIG. 4.16. C Minor Phrygian Tonic Voiced in Fourths

As in the Dorian figure 4.11, some vertical voicings are clearly minor, some are vague, and others pungently dissonant. Overall, the passage communicates the sound and character of the Phrygian scale. Chick Corea's tune "Captain Marvel" expresses the tonic minor function in a similar manner.

Subdominant Function: Scale Degree ♭6

In major key harmony, the fourth scale degree defines subdominant function. The half step dissonance above the 3 of the tonic triad creates the sonic contrast necessary to define the subdominant sound as distinct from tonic and dominant. However, in minor keys, the interval between scale degree ♭3 and 4 is a whole step. Instead, the ♭6 scale degree in the Aeolian scale (a half step above the 5 of the tonic triad) provides the necessary contrast to define the subdominant. In minor key harmony, the natural minor scale is the primary source for subdominant chords.

"In minor key harmony, the natural minor scale is the primary source for subdominant chords."

FIG. 4.17. Aeolian Source Scale

Chords that contain scale degree ♭6 as a *primary chord tone* and do not include the leading tone are mostly responsible for the subdominant minor sound. This results in more subdominant options in minor key harmony than in major key.

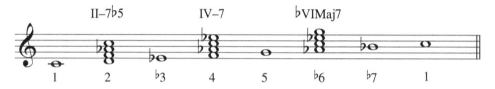

FIG. 4.18. Subdominant Chords from an Aeolian Source

The chord scales for each of the chords of the subdominant group are displacements, or modes, of the natural-minor source scale.

FIG. 4.19. D Locrian, Chord Scale for II–7♭5

FIG. 4.20. F Dorian, Chord Scale for IV–7

FIG. 4.21. A♭ Lydian, Chord Scale for ♭VIMaj7

All three chords can be used interchangeably in the pre-dominant position. In these examples, the available diatonic tensions from each chord scale have been used in each voicing.

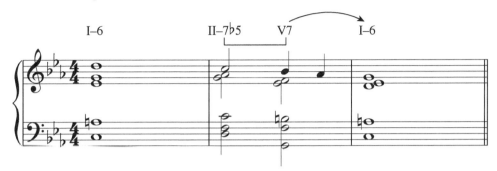

FIG. 4.22. II–7♭5 V7 I–6

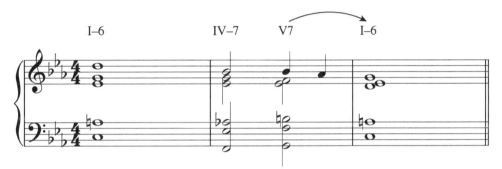

FIG. 4.23. IV–7 V7 I–6

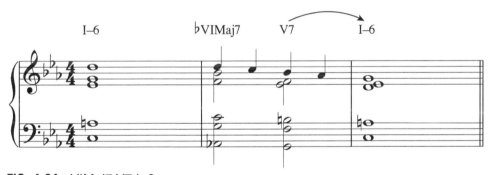

FIG. 4.24. ♭VIMaj7 V7 I–6

The Phrygian Source: A Darker Subdominant Chord

The Phrygian mode is the source of another subdominant function chord: ♭IIMaj7.

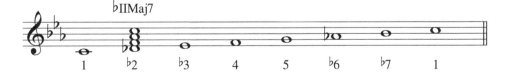

FIG. 4.25. ♭IIMaj7 from Phrygian Source

♭IIMaj7 is similar to II–7♭5: both chords share three notes with the most common minor key subdominant chord, the IV– triad.

FIG. 4.26. The IV– Triad Shared between IV–7, II–7♭5, ♭IIMaj7

If we displace the C Phrygian source scale to the root of ♭IIMaj7, the result is a Lydian chord scale.

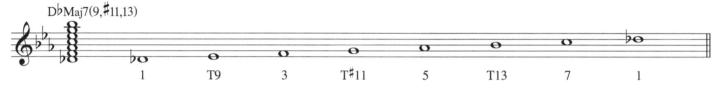

FIG. 4.27. D♭ Lydian, Chord Scale for ♭IIMaj7

The ♭IIMaj7 is a more exotic-sounding subdominant chord that evokes the sound of Spanish flamenco music. Miles Davis and Wayne Shorter used it to evoke a dark mood in some of their most famous compositions of the 1960s, "Nardis" and "Deluge."

Wayne Shorter is fond of ♭IIMaj7 as a subdominant cadence chord in his tunes. In "Deluge," he establishes the tonality in the first 4-bar phrase by alternating I– on the strong metrical stresses with the subdominant chord ♭IIMaj7 on the weak stresses in the phrase.

FIG. 4.28. Tonic-Subdominant Pattern in Wayne Shorter's "Deluge"

Dorian Source: A Brighter Minor Subdominant

While the Dorian scale does not contain the ♭6 scale degree, subdominant chords derived from it are still viable in minor key harmony because our responses to function are conditioned largely by our experiences of major key repertoire. The Dorian mode is the source of two colorful minor-key subdominant chords: II–7 and IV7.

FIG. 4.29. Minor Key Subdominant Chords from Dorian Source

II–7 almost never appears as the pre-dominant in a minor key II V. Because of the lack of scale degree ♭6, it does not function clearly as a minor-key subdominant.[16] It is more common in tonic-area patterns, like this elaboration of C–7.

FIG. 4.30. Dorian Tonic-Subdominant Pattern

The chord scale for II–7 is Phrygian, a displacement of its Dorian source scale.

FIG. 4.31. D Phrygian, Chord Scale for II–7 from a Dorian Source

Like II–7, the IV7 chord can also be alternated with tonic in order to create a Dorian tonic sound. I–7 IV7 is often used as a vamp introduction or ending or as an interlude between choruses.

FIG. 4.32. I–7 IV7 Vamp

While the chord pair here might look like a II V, within the context of a tune in C minor, the chords will function as tonic and a bright subdominant. This *dual* identity allows jazz composers to play a little musical sleight of hand. More about that later, when we discuss modulation in chapter 7.

The basic chord scale for IV7 is Mixolydian, a displacement of the Dorian source scale.

FIG. 4.33. F Mixolydian, Chord Scale for IV7 from a Dorian Source

---

16   "Minority" by Gigi Gryce is the exception that proves the rule; the II–7 in measure 3 supports scale degree 3 rather than ♭3 in the melody. It is really an "import" from the parallel major. See also "The Shadow of Your Smile" by Johnny Mandel. Much more on that topic in chapter 5, "Modal Interchange."

Lydian ♭7 is another, brighter option, derived from the melodic minor scale:

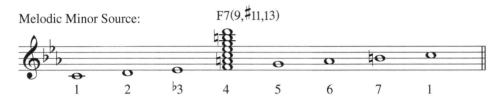

FIG. 4.34. IV7 from Melodic Minor

FIG. 4.35. F Lydian ♭7, Chord Scale for IV7 from a Melodic Minor Source

MINOR KEY DOMINANT FUNCTIONS: V7 AND VII°7

The need for dominant resolution in progressions brings us to the next source of harmony in minor key music: the so-called harmonic minor scale.

FIG. 4.36. C Harmonic Minor Scale

In reality, this is an oversimplification. Rather than a discrete scale, it is more accurate to think of the source of minor-key dominant function as a combination of both the natural minor and harmonic minor scales. Instead of an artificially limited seven-note construction, this *composite minor scale* is a more accurate reflection of musical reality:

FIG. 4.37. Natural Minor Scale with Leading Tone

It supplies the half-step leading tone, and therefore the tritone necessary for dominant function. We now have a scale that neatly accounts for tonic, subdominant, and dominant chords in minor. The inclusion of Aeolian scale tone ♭7 smooths out the augmented second in the harmonic minor scale, and it accounts for one of the most idiomatic sounds in jazz harmony: V7(♯9).

FIG. 4.38. G7(♯9) from Composite Minor Source Scale

Reordering the source scale from the fifth degree produces the chord scale for V7 in a minor key: G Mixolydian (♭9, ♯9, ♭13).

FIG. 4.39. G7(♭9,♯9,♭13) from Composite Minor Source

- The ♯9 tension is spelled enharmonically, reflecting its status as a diatonic note in the key.

- The parentheses around 5 and T♭13 indicate that these two notes are *provisional avoid tones*: if ♭13 appears in a voicing, the 5 of the chord is usually omitted and vice versa.

- Tensions ♭9, ♯9, and ♭13 all heighten the instability of the V7 chord creating an even stronger expectation of resolution.

- T♭13 foreshadows the minor quality of its target, since it is a common tone with the ♭3 of the I- chord.

An alternative chord scale choice for the V7 chord is the altered dominant scale. The ♭5 chord tone adds yet another pull toward the tonic.

FIG. 4.40. G7(alt), Optional Chord Scale for V7

VII°7 is the other dominant function harmony that is derived from this source.

FIG. 4.41. Chord Scale for VII°7

While VII°7 is clearly a dominant function chord, it is not used commonly as an alternative to V7 in the minor key. When it does appear in chord progressions in the standard repertoire, it is generally used as a pivot chord to slip gracefully into another key area.

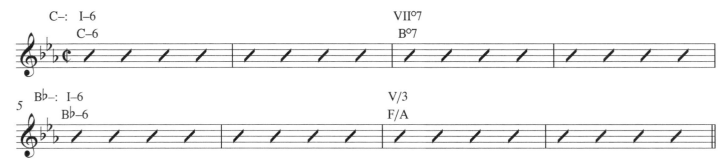

FIG. 4.42. VII°7 as a Pivot Chord

"How Insensitive" by Antonio Carlos Jobim uses this device effectively. We'll investigate this more thoroughly in our discussion of diminished seventh chords in chapter 6.

"Dominant" Function V–7 and ♭VII7: Alternative Cadential Options from the Natural Minor Source Scale

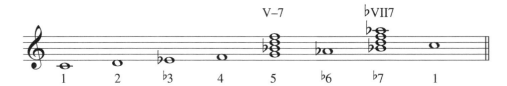

FIG. 4.43. V–7 and ♭VII7 from Aeolian Source

V–7 is clearly a part of the minor key chord vocabulary, but its function is ambiguous. By definition, V–7 can't be said to have dominant function, because it lacks the interval of a tritone. The absence of a half-step leading tone from scale degree ♭7 to 1 renders the progression I– V–7 I– weaker than its corollary in the parallel major mode. (It has a much more prominent role in modal progressions, which we will explore in chapter 9.)

But even though V–7 lacks the leading tone, it can stand in *syntactically* for a true V7 chord: it is often used effectively mid-phrase or at a cadence because of the strength of the cycle 5 root motion. An example from the repertoire can be found in the coda of Luis Bonfa's "Manha De Carnaval," a.k.a. "Black Orpheus."

The attenuated dominant potential of an Aeolian V7 chord appears in other ways as well. Here is the chord scale for V–7:

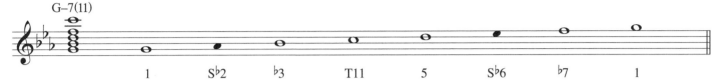

FIG. 4.44. G Phrygian, Chord Scale for V–7 from Natural Minor Source

This chord scale is the basis for the chords in figure 4.45.

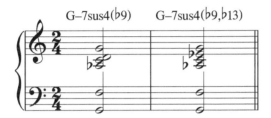

FIG. 4.45. V7sus4(♭9) Voicings

Sometimes called Phrygian voicings, these chords have the increased dissonance of tensions ♭9 and ♭13, which imbue the V–7 chord with a greater expectation of resolution.

The ♭VII7 chord in the minor key repertoire is also fraught: it is dominant in quality, but it lacks the leading tone of the V7 chord. As a dominant *function* chord, it is neither fish nor fowl: its tritone actually points *away* from the minor tonic, toward the relative major. In the standard repertoire, it is far more common to find ♭VII7 as part of a cycle 5 progression passing through the relative major, as in "Autumn Leaves."

Nevertheless, it can be found in conjunction with IV–7 in this pattern:

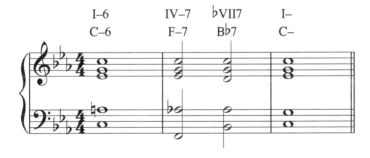

FIG. 4.46. IV–7 ♭VII7 I– Cadential Pattern

The effect is more that of an elaborated subdominant minor cadence than a dominant one. Along with V–7, we will turn our attention back to ♭VII7 in chapter 8.

Summary of Diatonic Functions in Minor Key

Tonic	Source Scale	Chord Scale
I-6 I-(Maj7)	Melodic Minor	Melodic Minor
VI-7♭5	Melodic Minor	Locrian Natural 9
♭III+(Maj7)	Melodic Minor	Lydian Augmented
I-7 I-6	Dorian	Dorian
I-7	Phrygian	Phrygian
I-7	Aeolian	Aeolian
♭IIIMaj7	Aeolian	Ionian
Subdominant	*Source Scale*	*Chord Scale*
IV-7	Aeolian	Dorian
II-7♭5	Aeolian	Locrian
♭VIMaj7	Aeolian	Lydian
♭IIMaj7	Phrygian	Lydian
II-7	Dorian	Phrygian
IV7	Dorian	Mixolydian
Dominant	*Source Scale*	*Chord Scale*
V7	Aeolian + Leading Tone	Mixolydian (♭9, ♯9,♭13)
VII°7	Aeolian + Leading Tone	Mixolydian (♭9, ♯9, ♭13) from the Third Degree
Aeolian Cadence	*Source Scale*	*Chord Scale*
V-7 (not a true dominant)	Aeolian	Phrygian
♭VII7 (not a true dominant function)	Aeolian	Mixolydian

SECONDARY DOMINANTS IN MINOR KEYS

Secondary dominants in minor key tunes operate on the same premise as in the major key: they create the expectation of resolution down a perfect fifth to a diatonic target.

> *"In minor keys, just as in major, secondary dominants create the expectation of resolution down a perfect fifth to a diatonic target."*

Naturally, the target chord qualities are often different than in major, e.g., IV– instead of IVMaj7. The relative stability of the target functions often differs as well.

The natural minor (Aeolian) scale is the default source for determining the appropriate tensions. It is the scale of the key signature and broadly defines the minor tonality. The wide range of diatonic target chords does allow for more flexibility in tension choices. Still, the most direct approach is to start with diatonic tensions and then consider variations based on the quality of the target chord.

V7/IV and V7/V in Minor Keys

We will start by looking at the most common minor-key secondary dominants: V7/V and V7/IV.

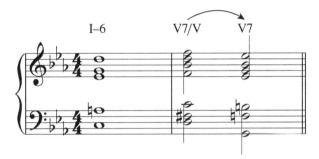

FIG. 4.47. V7/V in Minor Key

V7/V is generally expressed as Mixolydian (♯9, ♭9, ♭13), since all tensions are diatonic to the natural minor scale—the scale of the key signature.

FIG. 4.48. Mixolydian (♭9, ♯9, ♭13), Chord Scale for V7/V in Minor

Its related II is VI–7♭5, a member of the large minor key diatonic family. Because of its similarity to I–6, it requires a root position voicing to function clearly.

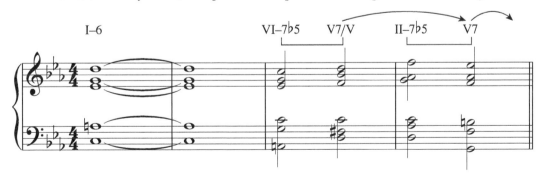

FIG. 4.49. V7/V with VI–7♭5 as Related II

V7/V is also often used as a brighter sounding alternative to II–7♭5. This progression begins the solo changes for John Lewis' "Django."

FIG. 4.50. V7/V with VI–7♭5 as Prolongation of Minor Tonic

V7/IV is also widely found in minor key tunes. It targets the primary subdominant function chord and adds urgency to the departure from the tonic area. It also transforms the tonic I-7 chord into a major-quality chord. Any alteration of the tonic chord's quality constitutes a dramatic change, especially a change from minor to major. (Just ask Cole Porter!) Using the notes of the natural minor scale as the default diatonic tensions, the chord scale for V/IV would be Mixolydian (♭13). However, the target of V7/IV is a minor chord. In common practice, it shares the same set of tensions as V7 and V7/V: Mixolydian (♯9, ♭9, ♭13).

FIG. 4.51. Mixolydian (♭9, ♯9, ♭13), Chord Scale for V7/IV in Minor

Using a natural minor source would give us a diatonic related II chord that is minor 7 in quality: G-7, in this case. In practice, the related II is usually –7♭5, in keeping with the minor-quality target chord.

The tensions in the voicing of V7/IV are either related by common tone or move by half step to a chord tone or tension of the IV–7 chord.

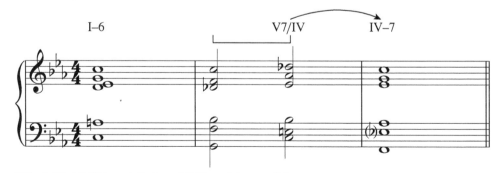

FIG. 4.52. V7/IV and Related II Resolving to IV–7

OTHER MINOR KEY SECONDARY DOMINANTS

V7/II

The diatonic chord scale for V7/II is again Mixolydian (♯9, ♭9, ♭13).

FIG. 4.53. Mixolydian (♭9, ♯9, ♭13), Chord Scale for V7/II in Minor

V7/II is not nearly as common as V/IV and V/V in standards and mainstream jazz tunes in the minor key, for three reasons:

1. It has a root that is not diatonic to the key signature.

2. The 5 of the chord is the major 3 of the key.

3. Minor 7♭5 chords are unsatisfactory target chords.

Still, V7/II is a viable function; it can be used as a brighter variant of VI–7♭5 to further alter a minor I VI II V pattern.

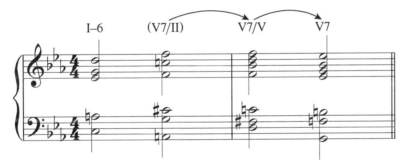

FIG. 4.54. Deceptive Resolution of V7/II in Minor. I VI II V root pattern harmonized with dominants.

V7/♭VI

The diatonic tensions for the V7/♭VI produce a Mixolydian chord scale. The diatonic root and major tensions agree perfectly with the definition of a secondary dominant with a major target.

FIG. 4.55. Mixolydian, Chord Scale for V7/♭VI in Minor

The non-diatonic related II is minor 7 in quality.

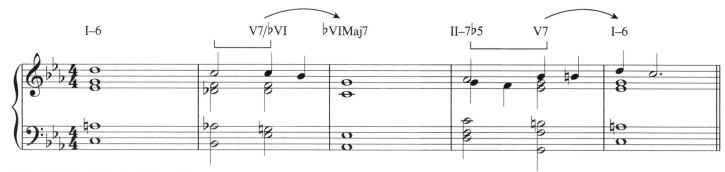

FIG. 4.56. V7/♭VI with Related II

V7/♭III

The diatonic chord scale for V7/ ♭III is Mixolydian.

FIG. 4.57. Mixolydian, Chord Scale for V7/♭III

Because of the issues around tonicizing ♭III in minor keys, musicians generally spend a lot of time trying to *avoid* doing just that. The slippery behavior of this chord—will it step back to I–, or will it resolve definitively to ♭III?—makes it a candidate for a more nuanced look. Please review the discussion around figure 4.14.

V7/♭III is complicated because it is identical to the diatonic chord ♭VII7. As a pure diatonic chord, it lacks one of the key descriptors of secondary dominants: an altered pitch. The related II of V7/♭III is also diatonic: IV–7. Pairing these two purely diatonic chords creates merely the appearance of a secondary dominant pattern, with none of the chromatic surprise or drive. Progressions containing IV–7 ♭VII7 ♭IIIMaj7 are heard as *diatonic* minor key activity, with no *secondary* dominant effect. The tendency toward the relative major is purely coincidental, an artifact of the "displaced" dominant quality ♭VII7.

If the intention is to dramatize the arrival of ♭IIIMaj7, adding T♭9 to the chord scale will help to clarify its role as a dominant function chord. This creates a stronger resolving potential that differentiates it from a simple diatonic chord that could just as easily return to I–.

FIG. 4.58. Mixolydian ♭9, Optional Chord Scale for V7/♭III

A further way to tonicize ♭IIIMaj7 is to precede V7/♭III with its related II–7♭5. This is an effective aural signal that a tonicization of ♭III is specifically intended. Richard Rodgers uses this to fine effect in "My Funny Valentine" in the last two measures before the bridge.

A SUMMARY OF SECONDARY DOMINANT DIATONIC CHORD SCALES IN MINOR KEYS

Secondary Dominant	Chord Scale
V7/IV	Mixolydian (♭13) but *better* the optional Mixolydian (♭9, #9, ♭13)
V7/V	Mixolydian (♭9, #9, ♭13)
V7/II	Mixolydian (♭9, #9, ♭13)
V7/♭VI	Mixolydian or optional Mixolydian (♭9)
V7/♭III	Mixolydian but *better* the optional Mixolydian (♭9)

Substitute Dominants in Minor Keys

The subV also plays a role in the minor key repertoire, although not every diatonic chord has a clearly functioning subV associated with it. The larger number of potential diatonic targets can create uncertainty about which resolution is "expected." Make peace with this ambiguity! It will help you ask the right questions about context and expectation.

We will start with the same definition of substitute dominants that applies in major keys. Substitute dominants have:

- Non-diatonic roots

- The expectation of resolution down a half step

- A diatonic target chord

- Lydian ♭7 chord scales

"Diatonic" in this context means the natural minor scale of the key signature. That will allow us to deal with exceptions by comparing them to more clear-cut examples. The illustrations that follow are all set in the key of C minor.

SubV7

SubV7 is one of the clearest examples of substitute dominant function in minor. It has a non-diatonic root and each of the available tensions is diatonic to the key; taken together, they form a major triad, ♭III of the key.

FIG. 4.59. Lydian ♭7, the Chord Scale for SubV7 in Minor

SubV/IV

The non-diatonic root of subV/IV marks it as another clear example of subV function. The available tensions are diatonic and form a major triad, ♭VI of the key.

FIG. 4.60. Lydian ♭7, the Chord Scale for SubV/IV in Minor

SubV/V or ♭VI7?

The primary tonic and the primary subdominant both have subV's associated with them. It would seem natural that the primary dominant should also have this potential, but the diatonic root of this chord puts it outside the strict definition of a substitute dominant. Built on diatonic scale degree ♭6, subV/V could be thought of as an altered version of the subdominant ♭VIMaj7. The chord's 7 is also the ♭5 of the blues scale. The pervasive nature of bluesy vamps and chord patterns further condition us to hear this chord simply as an altered subdominant chord, ♭VI7. Matt Dennis' "Angel Eyes" uses ♭VI7 in a repeating pattern with I–7 in just this way.

When it does function as subV/V, it will immediately precede the V7 chord in a progression. Since V7 most often comes in a weak metrical position, the subV/V generally appears on a strong metrical stress in the phrase where II–7♭5 or the V/V would usually occur.

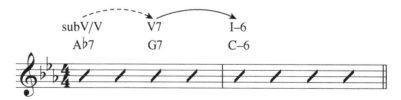

FIG. 4.61. SubV/V in a Typical Harmonic Stress Pattern

The last two bars of Nat Adderley's "Work Song" and Sonny Rollins' "Strode Rode" are typical of this pattern.

SubV/V may also be preceded by its diatonic related II: VI–7♭5. The compressed harmonic rhythm and descending chromatic root motion (A, A♭, G) increases the expectation of resolution to V7.

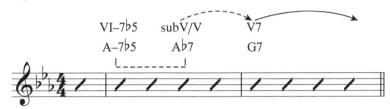

FIG. 4.62. SubV/V with Related II

See measure 7 of Thelonious Monk's "'Round Midnight" for an example from the repertoire.

SubV/V is sometimes preceded by a non-diatonic related II, to create a bass pattern consistent with a II V that follows:

FIG. 4.63. SubV/V with Alternate Related II, Creating a Chromatic II V

SubV/♭VI, SubV/♭III, and SubV/II

SubV's of other stable tonic and subdominant functions are also possible in minor key chord progressions. The progression in figure 4.64 uses subV's to tonicize I–, ♭VI, and IV–.

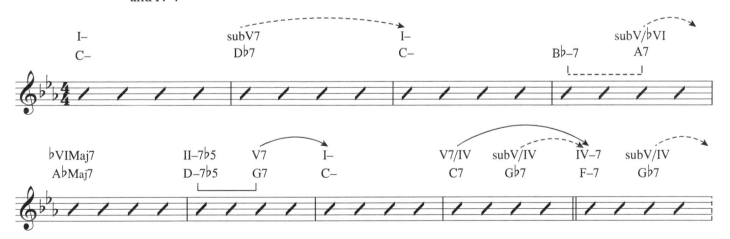

FIG. 4.64. SubV Tonicizing a Minor Key Progression

See Wayne Shorter's "Black Nile" for instances of subV7, subV/♭VI, and subV/IV in a minor key context.

The interlude in Dizzy Gillespie's "A Night in Tunisia" makes use of subV7 and then sets up the infamous solo break with the subV/♭III. Diatonic scale degree 5 changes its relationship with each of the chords in the progression. As the harmonies change, we hear it first as 11, then #11, then 5, then 9, and finally as a dramatic #9 on the G♭7 chord (subV/♭III) where it anticipates the arrival of the major 3 of ♭IIIMaj7.

SubV/II is rather rare in the minor key literature, but there's an example in the last four bars of the chorus of Bronislaw Kaper's "Invitation," a perennial film-noir favorite.

A Summary of Substitute Dominant Chord Scales in Minor Keys

Substitute Dominant	Chord Scale
subV7	Lydian ♭7
subV/V	Lydian ♭7
subV/IV	Lydian ♭7
subV/II	Lydian ♭7
subV/♭VI	Lydian ♭7 or optional Lydian ♭7(#9)
subV/♭III	Lydian ♭7 or optional Lydian ♭7(#9)

LINE CLICHÉS

A *line cliché* is a device that imparts a sense of forward motion to a static prolongation of a given harmonic function. It is a single-note chromatic line that embellishes a single triad with an evolving spectrum of harmonic color. Line clichés are certainly used in major key progressions, but they are even more common in minor where the chromatic territory between scale degree 5 and the octave is fully available.

While the basic chord tones sound in the same register or elsewhere in the texture, a chromatic line descends from the root or ascends from the 5. The moving line results in small variations on the original chord without changing its essential function. Figure 4.65 shows a C minor chord with a line cliché in the tenor voice.

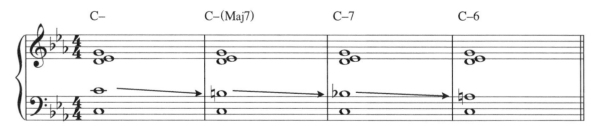

FIG. 4.65. Line Cliché

"A line cliché is a device that imparts a sense of forward motion to a static prolongation of a given harmonic function."

A line cliché like the one in figure 4.65 can cause our perception of the tonic C– chord to change over time. The chromatic pitches that are introduced subtly suggest the following harmonic progression:

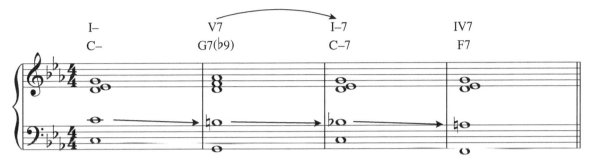

FIG. 4.66. Line Cliché with Implied Harmonic Change

A line cliché may appear in any voice: lead, alto, tenor, or bass, as in Richard Rodgers' "My Funny Valentine."

The line cliché launched from the 5 of the chord (I– I–(♭6) I-6 I–(♭6)) has been familiar to James Bond audiences for years.

FIG. 4.67. Line Cliché from 5 of C– Triad

It can also be found in the bridge of Jimmy Van Heusen's "Witchcraft." The min♭6 chord quality is not a standard tonic tertian structure. It is tempting to interpret it as ♭VIMaj7 in first inversion, but in context the min♭6 chord symbol communicates the musical device: a familiar moving line.

In summary, a line cliché:

- is a moving line through static harmony,

- creates changes in chord quality that leave the basic triad intact,

- creates a moving melodic line between the 5 and octave of the chord, and

- can imply a change of harmonic function even though the basic triad remains unchanged.

For Further Study

Here's a tune written in the mainstream hard-bop style that embodies a number of the concepts that we've explored so far in this chapter. Listen to track 5 of the accompanying audio, as you follow the lead sheet in figure 4.68. Try your hand at analyzing the harmony of the tune. Remember to note the following:

- The length of the harmonic phrases based on the tempo and their harmonic rhythm

- The metrical stress patterns and the way each phrase cadences

- The function of each chord in the tune and its likely chord scale

To the Bitter Dregs

By Tom Hojnacki

FIG. 4.68. "To the Bitter Dregs"

Here's the written piano arrangement of "To the Bitter Dregs." You can learn a lot by carefully examining the voicing of each of the chords with particular attention to the choice of tensions. How do these agree with the chord scale choices you made in your analysis?

To the Bitter Dregs

TRACK 6

By Tom Hojnacki

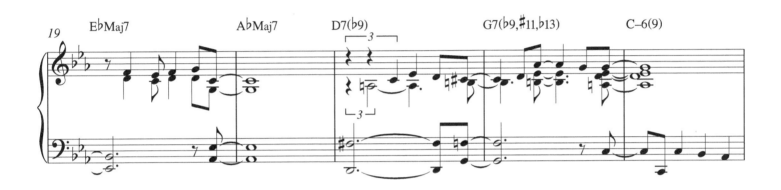

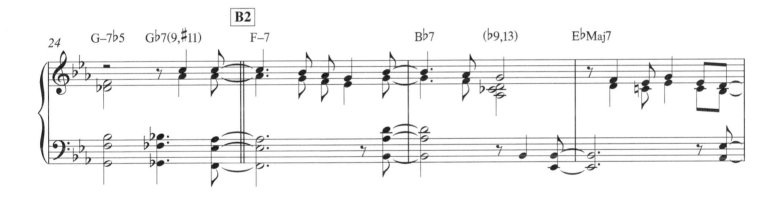

FIG. 4.69. Full Arrangement of "To the Bitter Dregs"

Here is a complete analysis of the harmony of "To the Bitter Dregs." At the fast tempo ♩ = 169, the harmonic phrases coalesce into 4-measure lengths. The first eight measures of the intro establish the tonality of C minor. The alternating I-7 IV7 Dorian vamp evokes a brighter mood than an Aeolian I-7 IV-7. Measure 8 ends in a half cadence; the dominant chord appearing on the weakest metrical stress of the phrase creates a sense of propulsive forward motion to the beginning of the A section.

To the Bitter Dregs

By Tom Hojnacki

Fast Swing ♩ = 169

Harmonic phrases are 4 measures long.

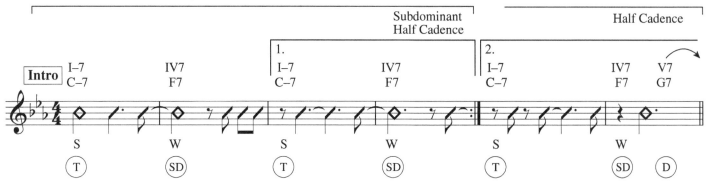

FIG. 4.70. Analysis of Introduction

The first phrase of the A section consists of two modified repetitions of the minor I VI II V pattern. The first replaces the V7 with a subV7, resulting in a more colorful melody/harmony relationship of ♯11. The second reharmonizes the II-7♭5 with the subV/V. Its Lydian ♭7 chord scale accommodates the E♭ in the melody. Notice the distribution of tonic function group chords versus subdominant and dominant. The half cadence propels us onward to the second phrase.

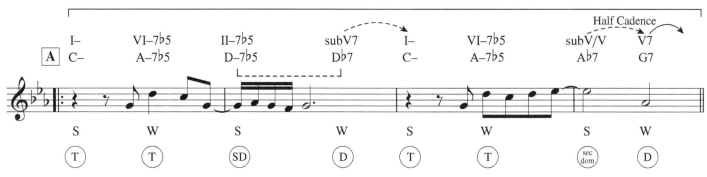

FIG. 4.71. Analysis of First Phrase

The second phrase of the A section progresses with strong cycle 5 motion to the subdominant function ♭VI on the strong downbeat of measure 13. The harmonic rhythm slows to highlight the contrast created by the prolongation of the subdominant sound, which serves as an important structural feature of the formal architecture of the tune.

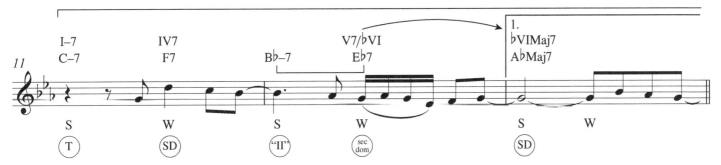

FIG. 4.72. Analysis of Second Phrase

In measure 14, the D♭Maj7 chord introduces the darker subdominant sound of the Phrygian source scale. Its root, a half step above tonic, intensifies the subdominant half cadence. We return for a repetition of the A section. In the second ending, the G–7♭5 in combination with the V7/IV creates a strong expectation of forward movement to IV–.

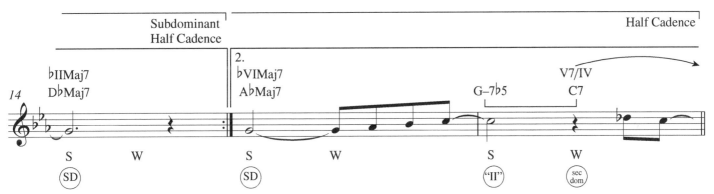

FIG. 4.73. Comparison of the 1st and 2nd Endings

In the first phrase of the B section, F–7 plays a dual role. It is the first time we hear the primary subdominant chord of the key. Then, in combination with the subsequent B♭7, it is responsible for a temporary tonicization of ♭IIIMaj7, a return to the tonic function group. At this tempo, the tonicization is so brief that it does not suggest a change to the relative major key. An immediate move to ♭VI creates a subdominant half cadence again.

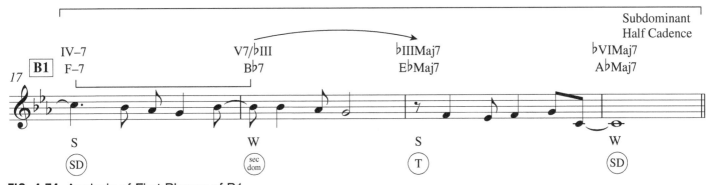

FIG. 4.74. Analysis of First Phrase of B1

The second phrase of B1 employs a modified full jazz cadence (V7/V substituting for II–7♭5), which strongly re-tonicizes I–. Note how the melody emphasizes T♭9 on each of the dominant chords increasing the drive home toward tonic. The phrase ends in a half cadence to IV–, similar to that in measure 16. This time, the subV/IV rather than V/IV creates the forward motion. T♯11 (C), in the melody, helps to connect the chord with its non-diatonic root, to the key.

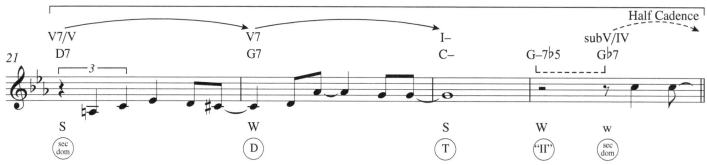

FIG. 4.75. Analysis of Second Phrase of B1

The first phrase of B2 is identical to that of B1. The optional ♭9 added to the B♭7 chord, nudges us just a little more to expect a resolution to E♭Maj7.

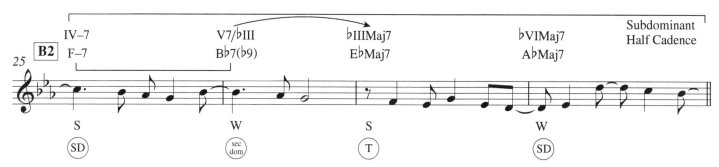

FIG. 4.76. Analysis of First Phrase of B2

In the final phrase of the tune, the modified full jazz cadence appears again, this time with a subV interpolated between V7 and I– for a *super* push toward home base. The optional turnaround will take us back to the head for solos.

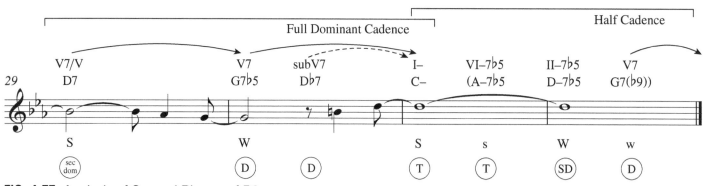

FIG. 4.77. Analysis of Second Phrase of B2

Further Exercises

Analyze the tune "Django" by John Lewis.

* What is the form?

* Which chords are secondary dominants?

* What is the function of each chord?

* Transpose the melody up a diatonic third, keeping the chord progression the same. What new tensions are created on the chords?

* Transpose the melody up another diatonic third. Write a chord scale for each chord based on your results.

CHAPTER 5

Modal Interchange

As you listen to these three short phrases, be aware of the harmonic function of each chord and how the mood changes:

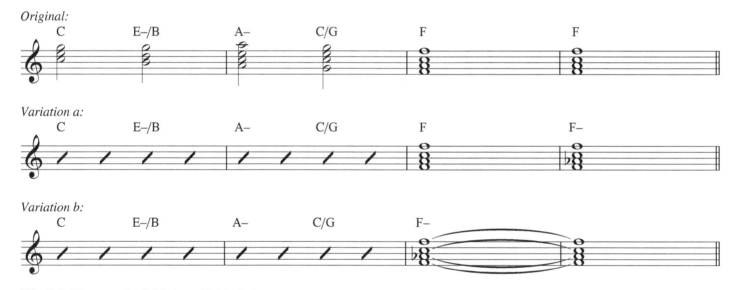

FIG. 5.1. Phrases in C Major with Variations

The original is a standard diatonic progression used in a wide range of musical styles. In variations *a* and *b* that follow it, the IV chord is chromatically altered by lowering its third degree, creating a **IV–** chord. The descending bass motion, tonic to subdominant functional progression, and harmonic rhythm are unaffected, but there is a dramatic difference in color and emotional effect. This difference is heightened in variation b, where the darker IV– chord replaces IV major completely. The lowered sixth degree of the key of C that is present in the F– chord creates a more somber atmosphere that contrasts with the brighter C major color.

Altering the IVMaj7 chord to create IV–7, or using IV–7 as a *substitute* for IVMaj7 are among the most common ways of creating variety in a progression. This substitution and others like it are grouped under a new functional category. Using scale degrees from a parallel source to alter diatonic chords is called *modal interchange.* It is most commonly used in major key music, but minor key music occasionally has instances of modal interchange as well.

"Using scale degrees from a parallel source to alter diatonic chords is called modal interchange."

Modal interchange (sometimes called *modal mixture*) is an important part of the expressive language of jazz. Its use provides a much wider variety of emotional shading than is possible within the confines of the seven major key diatonic chords. Since the prevailing modality of a composition is one of the most important factors in creating its mood, chords from a contrasting mode create moments of emotion where the basic mood is altered. These emotional moments are bumps in the road on a musical journey. They may excite, distract, or cause a detour, but they don't change the overall landscape. Like secondary dominants, they do not automatically cause key change—although they can be used as a device to accomplish that. Rather, they are effective because they contrast with the clearly established home key.

This chapter will explain the concept of modal interchange in detail. In the process, we will raise issues of function, bass motion, and relationship to the melody. We will drill down to the chord scale level and show how modal source can subtly affect the procession of colors in a harmonic progression.

PARALLEL LINES SOMETIMES MEET

Modal interchange is a more focused technique than simply changing chord qualities randomly. In order to have meaning as a concept, and utility as an analytic or compositional tool, there has to be a unifying subtext at work. That subtext is *parallelism.*

There are several kinds of parallel relationships in music; for this discussion, parallel means *sharing the same tonic.* For example, the C major and C Aeolian scales are parallel, because the tonic is the same, C. Scale degrees 2, 4, and 5 are also identical; the important differences lie in the third, which defines the major or minor modality, as well as the sixth and seventh.

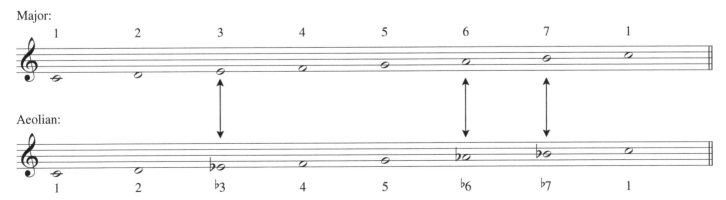

FIG. 5.2. Differences between Parallel Scales

We start with Aeolian as the parallel mode for the simple reason that the overwhelming majority of modal interchange examples are related to this source. Later in the chapter, we will look at chords from other sources.

Modal interchange preserves the essential tonality of the composition; it does *not* cause a change of key.[17] This is because the *source* of the chords is still related to a single tonic pitch. The listener perceives that the expressive range is widened, but the overall major sound is preserved; subdominant minor chords simply provide contrast to the predominant major modality.

DON'T MESS WITH TONIC

If major key music is generally perceived as being "happy," "bright," or "positive," the emotional effect of using a chord from the parallel minor can be described as "somber," "dark," or "sad." The obvious candidate for pitch alteration in major key progressions would seem to be scale degree 3; after all, it defines the very difference between major and minor. But a search of the literature shows that this kind of exchange is actually less common than other choices.

The dramatic effect of modal interchange (we will call it *MI* in analysis of tunes) is achieved by injecting material from a parallel minor scale into a major key passage. But without a stable sense of the prevailing major modality, modal interchange is meaningless. There are two overarching principles that set the stage for its effective use:

1. Altering the primary tonic, the I chord, can confuse the listener's perception of the modality of the music.

2. Changing the quality of V7 eliminates the resolving tendencies provided by scale degrees *Fa* and *Ti* (4 and 7): if we change the V7 chord, we lose the dominant cadence that defines major key harmony.

These considerations make chords with *subdominant function* uniquely suited for creating variety. For now, we will stay away from using anything that would alter the I or the V chord in the major key. We will touch on tonic modal interchange later in the chapter.

---

17   Extended modal interchange passages can in fact create the feeling of a shift to the parallel minor; that is not the focus here. See chapter 8, "Modulation."

SUBDOMINANT MINOR: SDM

The sixth degree of the parallel Aeolian scale (♭6, *Le*) is pivotal in modal interchange.

- It is the *defining pitch* of subdominant function in minor key.

- It has a *darker, more somber* sound than a major 6.

- It is an *unstable pitch*, with a strong tendency to resolve by half-step to scale degree 5.

With this in mind, consider the difference between chords that are diatonic to C major when scale degree 6 appears as the root, 3, or 5.

FIG. 5.3. Major Key Chords That Contain Scale Degree 6

Now compare the chords that contain scale degree ♭6 of C Aeolian as the root, 3, or 5:

FIG. 5.4. Minor Key Chords That Contain ♭6

...and listen to the pairs side by side.

FIG. 5.5. Comparison of Chords with 6 and ♭6

If we include these Aeolian-derived chords as harmonic resources, we now have a bigger library of chords for harmonizing melodies and creating progressions, while still retaining the bedrock harmonic functions of major key. Here is what our ever-expanding harmonic universe looks like.

FIG. 5.6. Major Key Diatonic Sevenths and Chords That Contain Scale Degree ♭6

The C major tonal resources have multiplied: instead of six usable chords,[18] we now have ten. (And there are more on the way....)

Since ♭6 is the defining pitch of subdominant function in minor, these chords are grouped together as *subdominant minor* chords. These three chords, especially IV–7 and ♭VIMaj7, are by far the most common modal interchange chords. We will refer to them as **SDM MI** chords when we analyze them.

Recall that in major, II– and IV are subdominant functions; VI– is a tonic substitute. Something important happens when SDM chords elaborate or substitute for their major key counterparts: a tonic substitute (VI-7) is lost, but a subdominant chord (♭VIMaj7) is gained. The subdominant functional area is thereby enriched, throwing tonic and dominant into even sharper contrast.

MODAL INTERCHANGE CHORDS IN PROGRESSIONS

In practical terms, subdominant minor chords replace major key subdominant chords or serve as variations of them. The most basic form of this occurs when the chords share a common root, either scale degree 2 or 4. In figure 5.7, IVMaj7 yields to IV-7 and finally IV-6. Both have an Aeolian source; sixth chords and seventh chords can be freely substituted for one another:

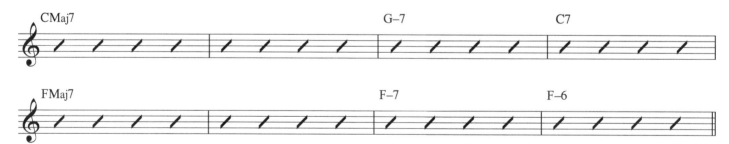

FIG. 5.7. C Major Progression with IV–7 and IV–6

The ever-present potential for line cliché on minor chords was explained at the end of chapter 4. Use of line cliché does not imply rapidly changing modal sources; it is just a momentary process that employs chromatic motion to elaborate on the basic chord quality. In example 5.8, there is a line cliché in measure 4 on the modal interchange IV– chord:

---

18   Remember that VII-7♭5 is not part of the essential major key vocabulary.

FIG. 5.8. Line Cliché on IV−

- In measure 2, V7/IV has ♭9 in the lead, foreshadowing the upcoming subdominant minor incursion.

- In measure 4, all the garden variety IV minor chords are sounded: IV−, IV− (Maj7), IV−7, and IV−6: a line cliché.

- Measure 4 represents a *subdominant minor half cadence*; it will be partially fulfilled in measure 5.

- The progression continues in measure 5 with a tonic substitute (III−7) that serves double duty as the related II of V7/II, A7.

- The A7 resolves deceptively to ♭VIMaj7 in measure 7; II−7 and ♭VIMaj7 both have subdominant function.

- A♭Maj7 becomes F−7 through stepwise motion in measure 7, beat 3.

- In measure 8, F−7 gives way to the least stable subdominant chord of all, D−7♭5.

- The subdominant D−7♭5 is followed by the dominant V7.

- V7 has ♯9 and ♭9 in the melody. This carries on the Aeolian shading introduced by the subdominant minor modal interchange chords.

- The final chord, C6 firmly restates the overall major key modality.

As the example above shows, once subdominant minor has intruded on a progression, it can act as a wedge: because of multiple common tones, IV−7 can morph into ♭VIMaj7. The reverse is just as likely. Evolution from IV−7 to II−7♭5 is a powerful way of further darkening a progression. II−7♭5 is almost always a precursor to V7, often with altered tensions. The next section will explore these combinations in more detail.

A PARTNER FOR THE V7 CHORD

A subdominant minor (SDM) chord will inject a darker color into a subdominant-dominant cadence. Any of the SDM chords from Aeolian can be paired with V7 to create a cadential pattern. Play this diatonic phrase:

FIG. 5.9. Diatonic Phrase in C Major

Either IVMaj7 or II–7 will work as subdominant preparation for V7.

We can take that choice between subdominant chords a step farther and replace them with SDM chords:

FIG. 5.10. Same Phrase with Subdominant Minor Options

Any of these three choices works well with the given melody, and there is a wider variety of possible root motion:

1. Symmetric cycle of thirds with a half-step movement to V7:

FIG. 5.11. Half-Step Approach to V7

2. Ascending third and seconds:

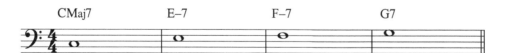

FIG. 5.12. Mixed-Cycle Ascending Root Motion

3. Mixed intervals and direction:

FIG. 5.13. Diverse Root Motion

The last example uses II–7♭5. This is a stylistic option used almost exclusively in combination with the V7 chord (usually expressed as V7♭9). Together they form a II–7♭5 V7 subdominant-dominant pair. It is very rare to see II–7♭5 as part of a stepwise or cycle-3 pattern of root motion, or as a functional substitute for II–7 outside of this specific combination.

♭VII7: SUBDOMINANT, DOMINANT, OR ?

We first encountered ♭VII7 in the discussion of subV's, and made the point that it only rarely functions as subV/VI. Its most common role is as a modal interchange chord. Like IV–7, it is diatonic to Aeolian and contains the characteristic ♭6 scale degree. It would seem to belong to the SDM function category. Here is the tricky part: unlike II–7♭5 and IV–7, it has *dominant quality*. However, it does not have true dominant *function* because it lacks the leading tone *Ti*. Yet any chord with dominant quality has a powerful effect on a progression, no matter how it is used. How can we characterize it clearly?

Although its function is ambiguous, ♭VII7 often acts as a *cadence* chord: it adds harmonic tension to a phrase. When it is followed by a more stable chord (especially one on a stronger harmonic stress point) there is a release of tension. For example, it can be paired with IV–7 to progress back to IMaj7, as in Tadd Dameron's "Ladybird":

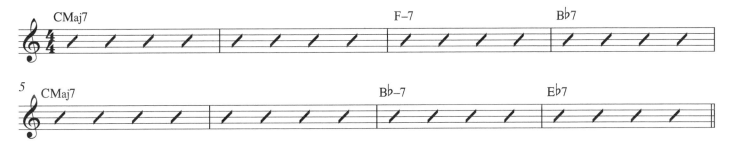

FIG. 5.14. Harmony for First Eight Bars of "Ladybird"

...or in Charlie Parker's "Yardbird Suite."

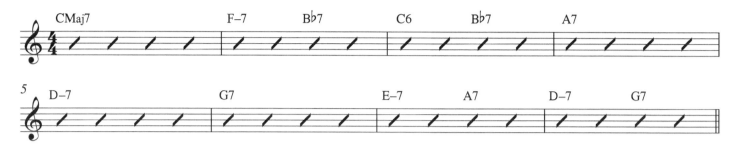

FIG. 5.15. Harmony for First Eight Bars of "Yardbird Suite"

This is the most common deployment of ♭VII7 in jazz. It is sometimes referred to as a "back door cadence" because of its strong tendency to return to the tonic. The ♭VII7 also sounds like IV–6, because of their shared tritone. For this reason, it can be inserted as a stand-alone substitute for IV–6. When it is, it brings with it its weight as a cadence chord.

Referring to figure 5.16, we can see why ♭VII7 would not function well as a subdominant preparation for V7:

- It has a parallel quality to the V chord, weakening its dramatic effect.

- It has neither chromatic, nor IV V, nor II V root relationship to the V chord:

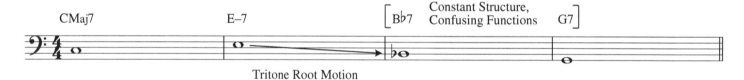

FIG. 5.16. ♭VII7 Is a Poor Choice for Pre-Dominant Chord.

OTHER SUBDOMINANT POSSIBILITIES: IV7, ♭IIMAJ7

We have seen that context is crucial to understanding how chords work in a progression: is B♭7 ♭VII7 or subV/VI? Is E♭7 V7/♭VI in C minor or subV7/II in C major? It depends on harmonic stress, the presence of a related II chord, and other factors that condition our expectations.

IV7 is another slippery customer: because of its dominant quality it *can* act as subV/III, given the right surroundings (see chapter 3, subV's), but more often, it will be found supplanting the typical IVMaj7, adding a bluesy color to a progression. In this capacity, it is a subdominant function chord with dominant quality! Not so strange as it might seem; the language of blues suffuses jazz composition and improvisation. These examples use IV7 in much the same way as it appears in Tadd Dameron's "If You Could See Me Now":

FIG. 5.17. IV7 in Measure 2

...or the Arthur Kent/Dave Mann/Red Evans ballad "Don't Go to Strangers."

FIG. 5.18. IV7 in Measure 2

They both have IV7 functioning as a typical IV chord often does: providing moderate movement away from and back to the tonic.

Since IV7 does not contain the characteristic ♭6 of Aeolian chords, it could be understood simply as a unique syntactical replacement from blues vocabulary. However, it can be brought into the theoretical fold of modal interchange if it is framed as the IV chord of a tonic Dorian or melodic minor source scale:

FIG. 5.19. IV7 Derived from Dorian and Melodic Minor Sources

This allows us to think more consistently about its relationship to the surrounding harmony. It also allows for a second set of options in voicing and style:

- The Mixolydian chord scale that expresses the first option is "harder," more purely bluesy.

- The Lydian ♭7 option on the second version has more common tones with the home key and no avoid notes.

The Dark Lord: ♭IIMaj7

The ♭IIMaj7 is the darkest of all the common modal interchange chords. Its modal source is Phrygian, lowering degrees 2, 3, 6, and 7 of the parallel major scale. Scale degrees ♭2 and ♭6 are especially dissonant and crave resolution back to *Do* and *Sol* of the major key. T9 on ♭IIMaj7 (♭3 of the key) obviously cannot continue to sound in a major environment, and will usually relax in parallel motion down to *Re* of the key, or move up to *Mi*.

FIG. 5.20. Typical Voice Leading from ♭IIMaj7 to IMaj7

In progressions, ♭IIMaj7 appears in several guises:

- A further darkening of II–7♭5 by lowering the root

FIG. 5.21. ♭IIMaj7 Following II–7♭5

- A deceptive resolution of V7/V, as in Kaper and Washington's "On Green Dolphin Street"

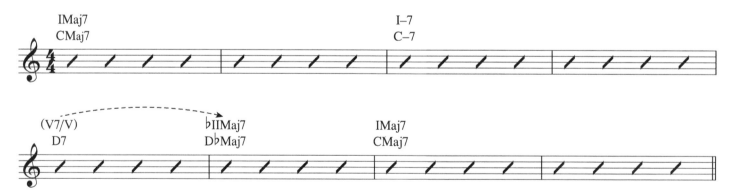

FIG. 5.22. ♭IIMaj7 as a Deceptive Resolution of V7/V

- As part of a cyclical pattern, often at the end of a tune

FIG. 5.23. ♭IIMaj7 in a Cycle 5 Pattern

- ...or as a gentler replacement for a subV7. In this example, ♭IIMaj7 stands in for an interpolated D♭7 in measure 4

FIG. 5.24. ♭IIMaj7 Replacing SubV/I

In any case, ♭IIMaj7 always has cadential function related to its Phrygian modal source. Its instability relative to the prevailing key virtually guarantees that it will be the last chord prior to tonic in a phrase.

V–7

V–7 is another MI resource from Aeolian. It is obviously different from V7 because it lacks the leading tone and tritone necessary to set up resolution. As we saw in our study of secondary dominants, it can function as the related II of V7/IV. In that capacity, it is merely an auxiliary chord to the more important secondary dominant.

Nonetheless, it can be found in major and minor key progressions as a chord with its own distinctive color. Although it is not truly dominant, it can stand in as a rhetorical commentary on the V7 chord. (In fact, traditional analysis refers to it as a "minor dominant.") Its root so strongly suggests the dominant area that it will often fill in for V7 in tonic-dominant vamps, providing an oscillation from dark to light, as in this example:

FIG. 5.25. V–7 Is a Darker Replacement for V7.

It is found on a weak harmonic stress point, and although it lacks dominant function, we can say it functions as a *cadence chord*. The chromatic♭7 scale degree adds tension to the phrase; the tension is released with the return to tonic. The melodic resolution is *Te–Do* instead of *Ti–Do*, but what's a half step among friends?

TONIC MODAL INTERCHANGE

Subdominant minor modal interchange is certainly the most prevalent use of the device, but there are instances of tonic modal interchange in the repertoire. Neal Hefti's "Girl Talk" has a short parallel minor episode, starting on I–7 in measures 5 and 6, that is a darker echo of the clearly established major key statement that begins the tune. Measures 3 and 4 of "On Green Dolphin Street" also clearly sound this duality.

The Dorian scale serves as the most common tonic modal source, giving us two chords to add to the expanding list of possibilities: I– and ♭III. They can appear as clearly tertian seventh chords or as sixth chords. In the case of I–Maj7 and I-6, this implies a melodic minor source, but in any case, the minor triad is the salient feature; it creates an unexpected emotional shift. The last phrase of Tom Harrell's "Sail Away" is a powerful example. It is a long composition that modulates a number of times, but the home tonality is C major. And yet, listen to what happens in the coda:

FIG. 5.26. Final Harmonic Phrase of "Sail Away"

The final C– chord casts a shadow over everything that has come before. The effect of ♭III is not as profound, since it is typically used to prolong the primary tonic chord rather than replace it. It will almost never be the last chord in a song, but it will often appear after the IMaj7 chord, providing strong upward root motion away from tonic:

FIG. 5.27. ♭IIIMaj7 as a Modal Interchange Prolongation of Tonic

...or as a chromatic intermediary between III–7 and II–7:

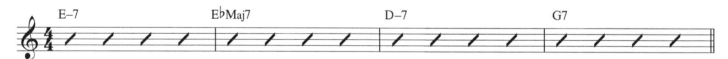

FIG. 5.28. ♭IIIMaj7 as a Chromatic Link from III–7 to II–7

...or as part of a cadential modal interchange pattern:

FIG. 5.29. ♭IIIMaj7 Starting a Cycle 4 Cadential Pattern

MODAL INTERCHANGE CHORD SCALES

The principle for deriving MI chord scales flows from the source: that is, the modal source. Unlike secondary dominants, attempts to derive the chord scale by mixing chord tones and tensions from the major key signature will often give unmusical results. Take IV–7 for example:

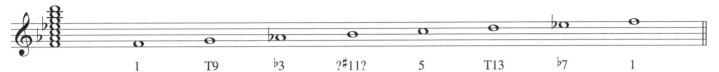

FIG. 5.30. Chord Scale for IV–7 from C Ionian Source—a Questionable Choice

The odd augmented second in the middle of the scale makes it unsuitable for chord voicings or stepwise passages. What to do?

The complete sound of modal interchange chords can be reliably discovered by treating them as displacements of the parallel source scale that is operating behind the scenes. Recognizing the Aeolian scale as the source for IV–7, we get a Dorian chord scale: no avoid notes, no awkward altered intervals.

FIG. 5.31. Chord Scale for IV–7 from Aeolian Source

This approach works for all MI chords. In cases where multiple sources produce the same chord, there is room for creative choice. For example, there is a subset of all MI chords that share major 7 quality: ♭VII, ♭III, ♭VI, and ♭II. They are often found in combination with one another, creating brief episodes of *constant structure*.[19] To reflect their similarity, they are all expressed with a Lydian chord scale, whether they sound alone or in a patterned string in a progression. The Lydian chord scale also provides an important connection to the major modality: in every case, ♯11 is diatonic to the key. Here they are in C major.

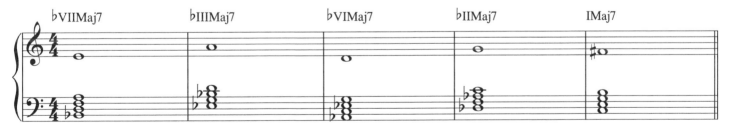

FIG. 5.32. ♯11 of Each Chord in the Treble Clef Is Diatonic to C Major.

It is fascinating that this cadential pattern, with the very dark ♭IIMaj7 from the parallel Phrygian, carries the DNA of III VI II V root motion; it is expressed in the ♯11 of each chord. The progression in figure 5.32 generally ends with a continuation of the constant structure, creating a Lydian tonic color: IMaj7(♯11). Lydian tonic is very often used at the end of jazz performances, and is a prominent feature in many Brazilian tunes as well.

---

19   Phrases in which all the chords are of the same quality. See chapter 10, "Constant Structure."

In some instances, the most appropriate chord scale for a modal interchange chord will be the result of a compromise between the minor source scale and the major scale of the parent key. When scale degree 3 (Mi) of the parent key is harmonized with IV–, the result is the quality IV–(Maj7). Here, the appropriate chord scale is F melodic minor, which includes scale degree 3 of the key as well as the modal notes ♭6 and ♭7 of the source scale.

FIG. 5.33. F Melodic Minor: the Chord Scale for IV–(Maj7) in the Key of C Major

Similarly, the appropriate chord scale for ♭VII7 in a major key is Lydian ♭7.

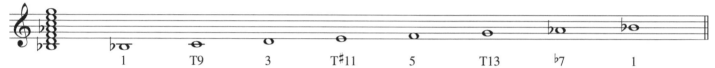

FIG. 5.34. Chord Scale for ♭VII7 in C Major

Note that the tensions of this chord scale are identical to the tonic triad of the key. The available tensions reinforce ♭VII7's function as a cadence chord that strongly suggests resolution to IMaj7.

ANALYSIS OF MODAL INTERCHANGE

Modal interchange chords are described by their intervallic distance from the tonic and by their chord quality. It is also helpful to indicate their function as subdominant minor (SDM) or tonic minor (TM).

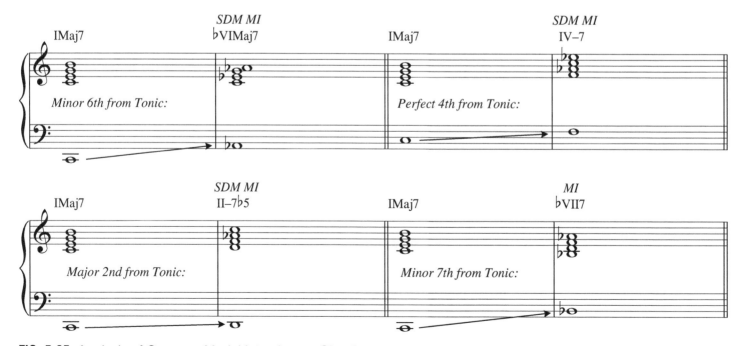

FIG. 5.35. Analysis of Common Modal Interchange Chords

This is a simple addressing system that facilitates transposition and reinforces the concept that these chord choices are still related to a *single tonal center*.

Summary of Important Aspects of Modal Interchange

- It adds a momentary minor sound to major key music

- It can be used to:

    - change the mood of a passage

    - harmonize chromatic melodies

    - emphasize, reinforce, or subvert a lyric

    - add variety to a diatonic passage

    - change or embellish the bass line

    - create alternate cadential patterns

Subdominant minor chords are the most common modal interchange chords: Aeolian mode is the most common *modal source* of subdominant minor modal interchange chords: II–7b5. IV–, IV–7, IV–6, bVI, and bVIMaj7.

- Either bVII, bVII6, or bVII7 is often used as a linking chord between bVI and I for smooth bass motion.

- One or two chords in a progression will provide the most effective contrast without losing the major modality.

- Major key chords can theoretically be used in a minor key environment, but minor keys already have a rich chord vocabulary due to their multiple modal sources.

CHAPTER 6

Blues in Jazz

Jazz harmony is drenched in blues. The richly chromatic jazz vocabulary owes much to late 19th century European concert music, and yet the predominant form in which it finds its expression is the 12-bar blues. From Louis Armstrong through Lester Young to Charlie Parker, Miles Davis, John Coltrane, and beyond, the standard for jazz credentials has been the ability to create an expressive world within the confines of the shortest form of all. What makes blues so flexible, with the potential to be utterly simple or dauntingly complex? This chapter will look at blues harmonic practices and point the way to understanding the numerous varieties of blues.

Pentatonic Melody + Diatonic Harmony = Blues

We can begin with a fundamental observation about blues harmony: it springs from the combination of minor pentatonic melodies over tonic, subdominant and dominant major chords. This results in a unique hybrid melody-harmony relationship that depends on familiar functional relationships, but goes beyond the constraints of a pure major key system.

In this example, a minor pentatonic figure is repeated over a I IV V triadic accompaniment. Look at the rich melodic/harmonic color that results.

FIG. 6.1. Minor Pentatonic Melody over I IV V Progression Creating I7, IV7, and V7

Notice especially that as a result of the melody-harmony relationship, *all three chords now have a ♭7, giving them dominant quality*. The result would be much the same even if the accompaniment were just open-fifth voicings. The changing set of chord tones and tensions that arises from repeated melodic statements over changing roots forms the basis for blues harmony.

Blues harmony works in a different way than conventional diatonic harmony. Although some of the gestures and points of connection are the same, a crucial difference is that there is *no single modal source* that defines blues tonality. No conventional scale yields I7, IV7, and V7. Similarly, blues melody is an independent layer with its own set of defining pitches. The interaction between these two layers creates the characteristic tensions that define the sound of blues. One of the great innovations of African-American performers was to apply this syncretic result to more traditional diatonic songs. Altering melodic pitches to create "blue" notes in the melody puts an individual stamp on a song and opens the door to new choices for tensions in chord voicings.

"THE" BLUES SCALE

The minor pentatonic scale is the basic melodic pitch set in simpler blues songs. Although it is a minor scale, it is still the fundamental sound of major key blues melodies. This is critical, because its use creates a new set of rules for what sounds acceptable on a tonic or subdominant chord. When sounded against I7, IV7, and V7, it creates a particular combination of chord tones and tensions on each chord.

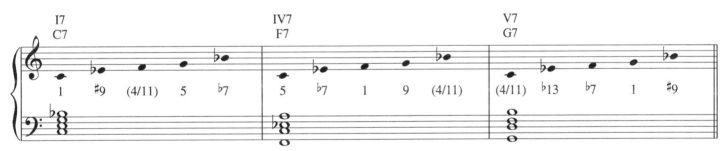

FIG. 6.2. Tensions Resulting from C Minor Pentatonic Scale on I7, IV7, and V7

The ♯9 on the I7 chord and the 9 on IV7 are characteristic of the vast majority of blues. The melody-harmony relationships created by the melding of the minor pentatonic melodic layer with the constant chord qualities of the harmonic layer form a unique harmonic idiom: non-diatonic to any standard Western scale or mode, but still functional and completely clear as to tonal center.

In many jazz blues, the minor pentatonic scale is not used exclusively. The highly inflected performance practice of blues singers and instrumentalists often involves bending pitches, especially the 3 and 7, in a way that blurs the distinction between major and minor. On the tonic I7, the tension between major 3 in the accompaniment and ♯9 in the melody allows a performer or arranger to emphasize or de-emphasize the major quality of a tune by using one or the other more liberally, or by bending the ♯9 upward toward the major 3. The same possibility exists on the V7 chord: the player has the freedom to use major 3 of the scale to create a major 13 on V7, or ♭3 to create ♭13. In fact, in many blues performances (those by B.B. King, for example), it makes more sense to think of the scale this way:

FIG. 6.3. Blue Note Approach on Scale Degree 3

Things get even more interesting with the inclusion of an important "blue" note: ♭5. In a conventional setting, it would be an intensely dissonant tone against any of the three basic chords: a tritone against the tonic, ♭2 on the subdominant, and major 7 on the dominant chord! But in blues, the dominant quality of the chords and the melodic strength of the blues-inflected pentatonic scale allow for much greater tension. In addition, similar to what often occurs with scale degree 3, the practice of bending the pitch of ♭5 microtonally to approach 5 makes this note stylistically acceptable, even when played or sung on a strong beat. Our scale is starting to sound more like this:

FIG. 6.4. Blue Note Approaches on Scale Degrees 3 and 5

Often in a blues performance, there is no clear, conventional third or fifth degree in the melody. Instead, flexible pitch areas will lean more toward 3 or ♭3, 5 or ♭5, at the whim of the performer. The accompanying instrumental harmony is unambiguous, allowing these expressive pitches to sound against a solid background.[20]

An important scale variation that sounds more clearly major was used in early New Orleans jazz and by many "classic" blues singers. It was also used extensively by boogie-woogie pianists and became a primary part of the sound of New Orleans R&B. It can be described as a "blues major pentatonic" scale.

FIG. 6.5. C Blues Major Pentatonic Scale

In these styles, the V7 chord is often arpeggiated, and ♭5 and ♭7 are important expressive pitches, so really the full scale is more like this:

FIG. 6.6. A More Complete Blues Scale

At this point, we are pretty close to all twelve notes! (Of course, the music sounds much more centered than the scale resources would suggest, because the harmonic accompaniment is so solidly in a key.)

The elaborate harmonizations of the bebop era gave rise to blues heads that were often overtly vertical, sounding the chord scales for each chord in the highly chromatic progressions typical of the style. Any idea of a single defining scale in that context misses the point entirely.

In short, there is no single blues scale. Rather, there is a large variety of scales that share common blues characteristics. Each variety is appropriate to a particular style of blues.

"There is no single blues scale. Rather, there is a large variety of scales that share common blues characteristics. Each scale is appropriate to a particular style of blues."

---

20   The pitch bends and other subtleties that make up a blues performance are beyond the scope of a harmony book, but we urge you to immerse yourself in those elements of the style as well. The mingling of blues language with the popular song repertoire of the day is at the heart of the development of jazz and jazz harmony.

BLUES PROGRESSIONS: THE POINT OF DEPARTURE

Blues harmony is ultimately based on the familiar tonic, subdominant, and dominant functions. In its simplest form, the standard 12-bar blues progression is a set of three 4-measure phrases, each with its own harmonic rhythm and functional emphasis:

1. Measures 1–4: tonic

2. Measures 5–8: subdominant to tonic

3. Measures 9–12: dominant to subdominant to tonic

This harmonic map underlies the myriad variations that have been spun on blues progressions over the last one hundred years. No matter how complex or tangential the harmonic elaboration, this unique functional template remains a reliable touchstone that links chromatic complexity to a familiar experience.

One of the things that contributes to its power is the gradual increase in tension and release as the form progresses. Play through this basic, three-chord blues progression:

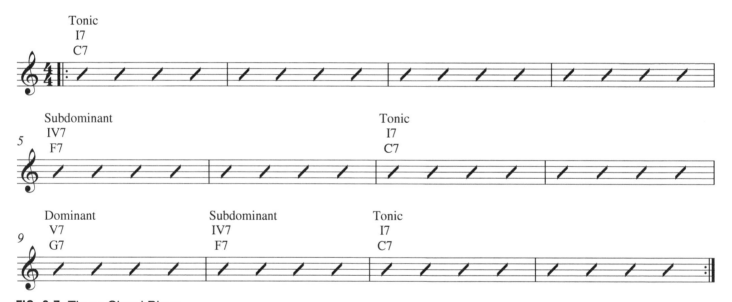

FIG. 6.7. Three-Chord Blues

The harmonic instability progressively ramps up in each phrase: first tonic, then subdominant, then dominant. Each time, the harmony relaxes back to tonic. It has proven to be a formula of enduring appeal; it is asymmetrical enough to hold the listener's interest through multiple repeats, and it provides a satisfying journey through the harmonic functions.

While the chords in a basic blues all have dominant quality, only the V7 chord has dominant function. I7 should not be confused with V7/IV. Its position in the form and its duration—occupying the entire first phrase and the last two bars of the next two phrases—help to confirm its structural importance as the tonic. Similarly, IV7 in a blues does not create an expectation to resolve to ♭VII.

It is a subdominant chord that simply has dominant color, but not a resolving tendency. As we dig into blues variations, keep in mind that the harmonic function of the I, IV, and V chords is independent of their dominant seventh quality.

> *"The harmonic function of the I, IV, and V chords is independent of their dominant seventh quality."*

The way the changes are deployed in the form—position, duration, root motion, and harmonic rhythm—all work together to create a functional progression that overrides the resolving tendency of dominant chords. This is a process that was unique to blues but is now widely applied to jazz and other styles.

Of course, there *are* many secondary dominants, including V7/IV, in jazz-blues progressions, but they are usually prepared by related II's to distinguish them from the harmonic pillars of the progression. The iconic basic structure lends itself to an almost infinite number of variations that still retain the underlying functions. In the following sections, we will use these I IV V guideposts to ground increasingly chromatic iterations of this protean progression.

STRETCHING THE BLUES

The most common variation adds a subdominant chord in measure 2 and a dominant chord in measure 12.

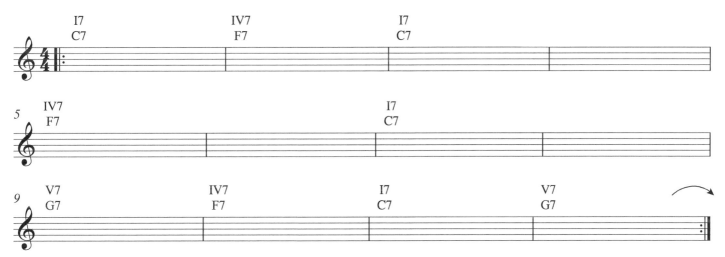

FIG. 6.8. Blues with IV7 in Measure 2

This progression is the classic blues progression played and recorded countless times since the 1950s. It is the basis for hundreds of well-known tunes from the dawn of rock 'n' roll to the present. Here are the overall dynamics of the progression:

- IV7 in the first phrase provides a little relief from four bars of tonic, but does not seriously disturb the overall stability of the phrase.

- The second phrase creates mild tension and release with plagal motion: a subdominant blues cadence.

- IV7 in measure 10 softens the return to I7. This "retreat" from the dominant is a form of retrogressive functional movement: dominant–subdominant–tonic.

The last point is subtle but important. Unlike standard popular songs from the Great American Songbook era that invariably feature dominant resolution to close the form, the harmonic tension is released more gradually than it would be with an actual dominant resolution. (V7 in measure 12 is only used on repeats. It is not part of the essential harmonic structure, it is simply a way to recharge the momentum after each chorus.)

The retrogressive harmonic motion from measure 9 to 10 is characteristic of the cadential pattern in the vast majority of standard three-chord blues. This 2-measure area of the form is particularly fertile ground for variations on the basic progression, and jazz musicians have often reharmonized these bars. Since the blues form is such a common vehicle for improvisation, creating an unusual cadential passage is one of the ways that musicians put their individual stamp on a piece. The most important variant of this cadence employs a II–7 V7 in bars 9 and 10.[21]

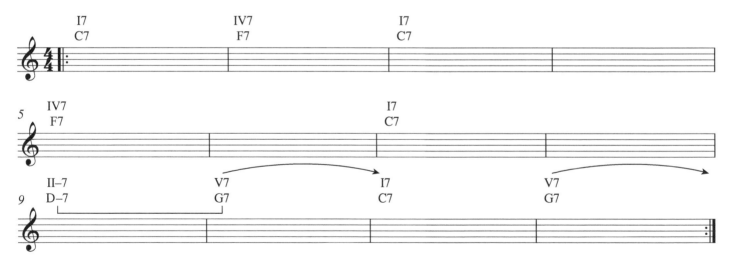

FIG. 6.9. Blues with a II V

This brings major key diatonic language into the picture. That simple replacement opens the floodgates: all the chromatic variations used in major key harmony are now

---

21   Many pre-bebop jazz and swing blues used V7/V instead of II–7. It has a more powerful, forward-driving sound and supports the blues scale (especially ♭5) more seamlessly.

in play. The next sections will apply those devices to create a wide range of jazz-blues progressions.

SECONDARY DOMINANTS/RELATED II'S AND SUBV'S

The long stretch of tonic in bars 1 to 4 builds a great deal of harmonic tension. It can be further intensified by interpolating a related II in measure 4, recasting I7 as a true V7/IV. In the last phrase, II–7 makes an inviting target for a secondary dominant. Although V7/II could be inserted alone in measure 8, it is much more common to precede it by a related II. E–7♭5 has three common tones with the tonic C7, and helps foreshadow the minor target:

FIG. 6.10. Blues with Secondary Dominants and Related II's

Adding an extended dominant series in the last two bars provides powerful momentum back to the top.

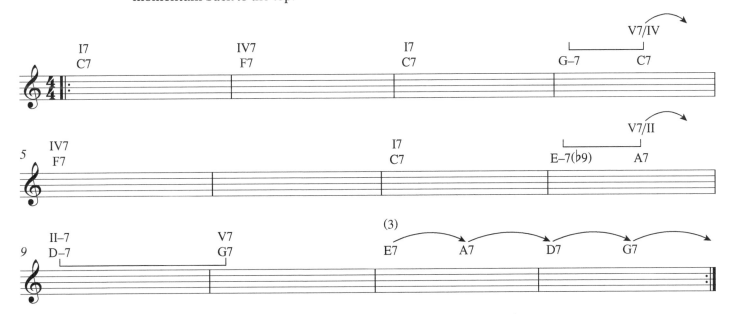

FIG. 6.11. Blues with Secondary Dominants and an Extended Dominant Turnaround

Of course, any of these secondary dominants can be replaced by a subV.

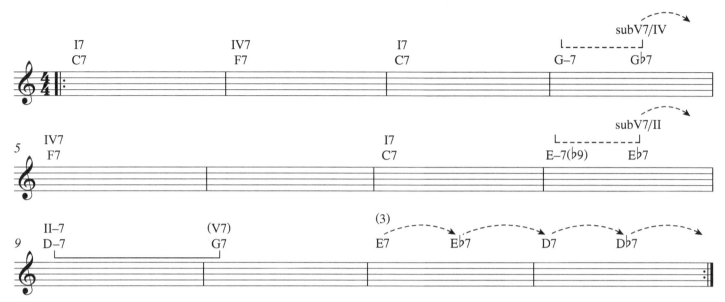

FIG. 6.12. Blues with SubV's

OTHER MAJOR KEY APPLICATIONS: BEBOP BLUES

Using major key seventh chords, adding related II's, and using modal interchange in the subdominant area can ultimately result in a progression with relentless descending chromatic root motion that retains only the barest outline of the original.

The resulting progression is similar to Charlie Parker's "Blues for Alice," among other examples. The only vestiges of a simple three-chord blues are the roots in measures 1, 5-6, and 11. Neverthelesss, it retains its structural identity as a blues, because it has:

- 12-bar form

- Tonic chord in measure 1

- Alternate tonic chord in measure 3

- Subdominant chords in measures 5 and 6

- Tonic substitute in measure 7

- Turnaround in measure 9-10

- Tonic chord in measure 11

In figure 6.13, the parentheses around the analysis of A♭7 in measure 3 highlights its deceptive resolution to a related II chord, instead of the expected dominant V7. Similarly, in measure 11, E♭7 does not resolve to the subdominant II–7. Instead, it has an alternate resolution to another secondary subV. The arrows tell the important story: dominant resolutions with mixed root motion.

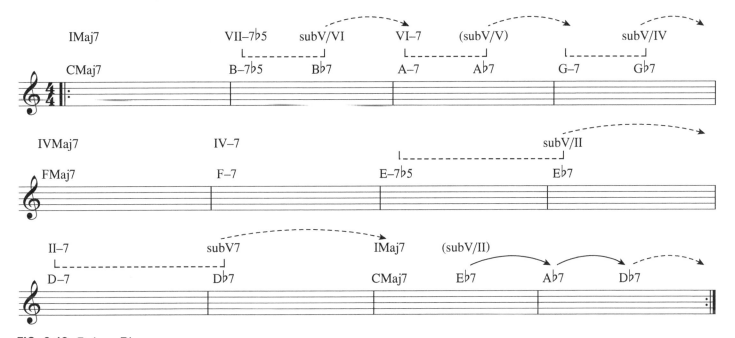

FIG. 6.13. Bebop Blues

Antonio Carlos Jobim wrote a very creative blues reharmonization in the A section of his famous composition "Wave." Figure 6.14 analyzes a similar progression shown here in the key of C major.

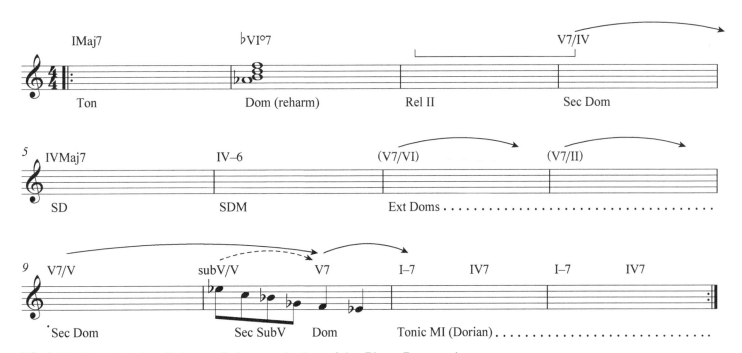

FIG. 6.14. Analysis of an Extreme Reharmonization of the Blues Progression

Jobim uses almost every trick in the book to filter the blues through a Brazilian lens:

- A lyrical melody that differs markedly from the typical AAB phrase structure of blues

- An initial tonic that is diatonic to the major key

- ♭VI°7 in measure 2 hints at V7(♭9), and chromatically approaches the G–7 in measure 3

- Subdominant minor modal interchange in measure 6

- An extended dominant series from measure 7–10

- An interpolated subV/V in measure 10

- A tonic Dorian modal vamp in measures 11–12

When played in a bossa nova rhythmic style, it is almost unrecognizable as a blues. The only obvious hint is the blues minor pentatonic figure in measure 10. Back to the source!

16-BAR BLUES AND OTHER FORMS

Although 12-bar blues is the iconic form, 8-bar or 16-bar versions do appear occasionally. The extended 16-bar form is usually achieved by repeating the turnaround changes from bars 9 and 10. Herbie Hancock's "Watermelon Man" (figure 6.15) and Joe Henderson's "Step Lightly" (figure 6.16) are two examples.

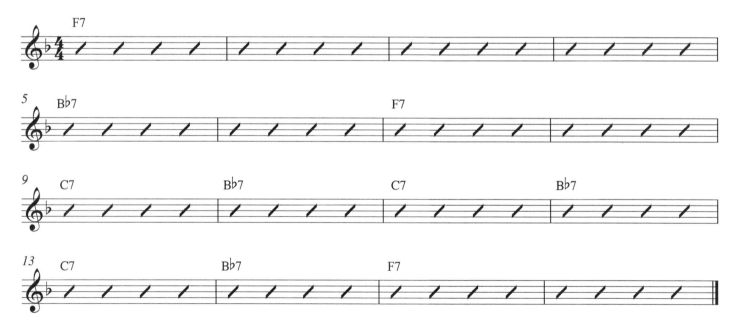

FIG. 6.15. Changes for Herbie Hancock's "Watermelon Man"

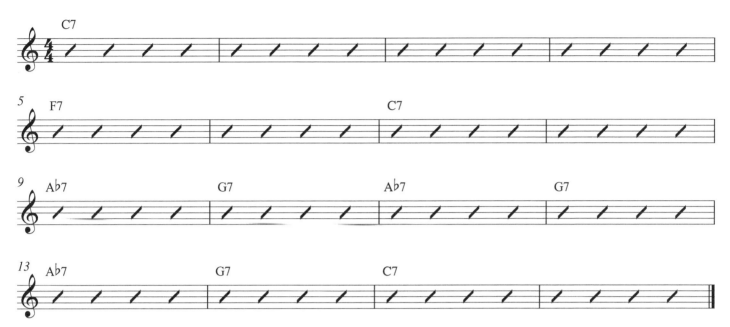

FIG. 6.16. Changes for Joe Henderson's "Step Lightly"

MINOR BLUES

Although less common in contemporary practice, minor key blues are important variants of the basic blues form. Minor blues can be a pure Aeolian version of the classic progression. Here is one in C minor:

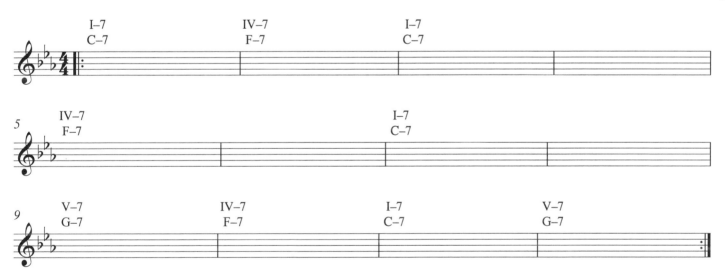

FIG. 6.17. Basic Aeolian Blues

Minor blues often contain some version of a subdominant–dominant turnaround in measures 9–10. John Coltrane's "Equinox" is a good example of a blues with Dorian voicings on the I–7 and IV–7 chords, then a powerful subV/V to V7 resolving back to tonic.

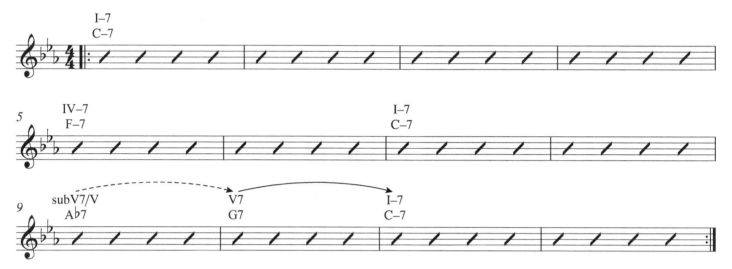

FIG. 6.18. Minor Blues with SubV/V in Measure 9

SubV/V sounds to many ears simply like ♭VI7, and in practice, this is how players usually think of it. Still, it is useful to consider how to approach the chord. ♭VI7 could use a straight Mixolydian chord scale, while subV/V implies Lydian ♭7. In fact, Coltrane hammers at the ♯11 of A♭7 in the melody, clearly sounding the Lydian ♭7 chord scale choice.

As always, there are many variations on this basic progression. John Carisi's "Israel" and Frank Foster's "Simone" are good examples of minor blues that employ secondary dominants and other devices. "Stolen Moments" by Oliver Nelson has a non-functional turnaround with a long string of constant structure quartal voicings, extending the form to sixteen bars. Charles Mingus's "Goodbye Porkpie Hat" is perhaps the ultimate expression of minor key complexity, putting constant structure, extreme modal interchange, and highly deceptive resolutions in the service of an almost purely pentatonic melody.

FOR FURTHER STUDY

Have fun analyzing these blues tunes. They are progressively more complex harmonically, but they all have the essential functional template and 12-bar form that characterize blues progressions.

Bloo-Zee

By Tom Hojnacki

FIG. 6.19. "Bloo-Zee," Major Key Blues

The All–Nighter

By Tom Hojnacki

FIG. 6.20. "The All–Nighter," Minor Key Blues

FIG. 6.21. "Bopston Blues," Bebop Blues

CHAPTER 7

The Diminished Seventh Chord

The diminished seventh chord (°7) is one of the most exotic and beautiful harmonies that equal temperament has to offer. This chord type has a completely symmetrical structure. It is constructed of thirds, but it is the only seventh chord in which all of the thirds are of the same size. This makes it something of an anomaly in the asymmetrical environment of the major/minor key system.

FIG. 7.1. Interval Structure of the Diminished Seventh Chord: Stacked Minor Thirds

SPELLING ISSUES

Because of the symmetry of the chord, spelling all of the intervals literally as a minor 3, °5, and °7 can sometimes be confusing.

FIG. 7.2. Technically Correct Spelling of G♭°7

In the case of C♭°7, precise spelling becomes impossible, as our system of notation does not allow for a triple flat. For this reason, the diminished seventh chord is the only chord type in which enharmonic spelling is deemed acceptable. One will see C♭°7 spelled with the 3, 5, and 7 spelled enharmonically in different ways. This version is acceptable:

FIG. 7.3. Basic Spelling of C♭°7

...as is this:

FIG. 7.4. Simplified Enharmonic Spelling of C♭°7

In practice, even the roots of diminished seventh chords may be spelled enharmonically, either to reflect the direction of the root motion or for ease of reading. Depending on context, C♭°7 might be rendered as B°7.

THE DIMINISHED SEVENTH CHORD IN PROGRESSIONS

Although it has its origin in minor key harmony as the chord built on the leading tone, the diminished seventh chord is rarely used as a primary dominant function in jazz harmony. Instead, the diminished seventh chord type has three general uses in jazz harmony, almost always in the context of major key:

1. As a *secondary dominant function* (ascending diminished)

2. As a descending chromatic approach chord (passing diminished)

3. As an *embellishing sound* (auxiliary diminished) for the IMaj7 and V7 chords in a major key

It is a uniquely flexible chord type with many possible outcomes when it appears in a progression, so take plenty of time to understand and absorb each process. Refer to the repertoire list and study questions at the end of the chapter to see how diminished chords function in practice. Please note that because of the multiple functions of diminished seventh chords, our practice is to refer to them in analysis by their root address in the key (e.g. I°7, ♭III°7 or V°7.)

1. SECONDARY DOMINANT FUNCTION: THE ASCENDING DIMINISHED SEVENTH

V7/VI and ♯V°7

Its origin as a leading tone chord in minor key means that a diminished seventh chord can be used in place of a dominant seventh chord in a progression to achieve the same functional result. It acts as VII°7 of the target chord. In figure 7.5, G♯°7 stands in for V7/VI; it is functioning as the VII°7/VI. You can clearly see the two tritones resolving inward, and the *ascending* half-step root motion.

FIG. 7.5. Analysis of ♯V°7 Progressing to VI–7

We analyze ascending diminished chords by their root in the key. In this case, the root is ♯5 (*Si*), so it is ♯V°7.

Chord Scale for ♯V°7

Throughout this book, we have stressed that diatonic tensions are the most effective way to reinforce a given tonality. The same concept applies to diminished seventh chords. Just as with secondary dominants, diminished chord scales are created with chord tones plus tensions and avoid tones from the prevailing key. Following this model, let's compare chord scales for V7/VI and ♯V°7.

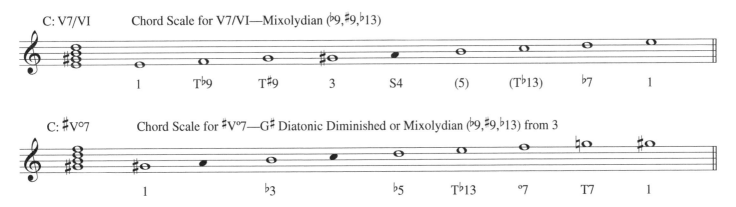

FIG. 7.6. Chord Scale Equivalence for V7/VI and ♯V°7

The diatonic diminished chord scale for ♯V°7 is simply a displacement of that of V7(♭9)/VI. Although ordered differently, the notes are identical. Note these relationships between the two scales:

- The note A is the root note of the chord of resolution. It is avoided harmonically in both scales.

- The root of V7/VI (E natural) appears in ♯V°7 as the available diatonic T♭13.

- In the chord scale for V7/VI, C natural (T♭13) is available if B natural is omitted from a voicing.

- In the chord scale for ♯V°7, C natural is not available, since it is a half step above the chord tone B natural.

In order to avoid confusion in situations with complex enharmonic spelling (e.g., C=♭4 in figure 7.4), our convention is to leave avoid tones in diminished chord scales unlabeled.

V7/III and ♯II°7

The same relationship exists between V7/III and ♯II°7 as does between V7/VI and ♯V°7. The ♯II°7 functions as the VII°7/III.

FIG. 7.7. Simliarity Between V7/III and ♯II°7

A comparison of the chord scales for V7/III and ♯II°7 further reveals the relationship.

Again, they contain exactly the same notes, ordered differently.

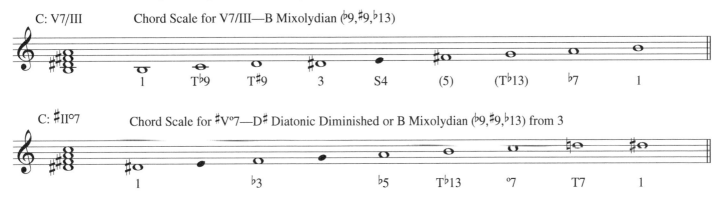

FIG. 7.8. Chord Scale Equivalence for ♯II°7 and ♯II°7

Another way for ♯II°7 to move is to IMaj/3. III–7 and IMaj/3 are both *tonic* function family chords. This alternate resolution retains that functional expectation.

FIG. 7.9. ♯II°7 Progressing to I/3

This outcome for a diminished chord still hinges on tritone action. In this case, D♯ and A resolve inward to E and G.

V7/II and ♯I°7

The ♯I°7 will perform the same function in a progression as the V7/II.

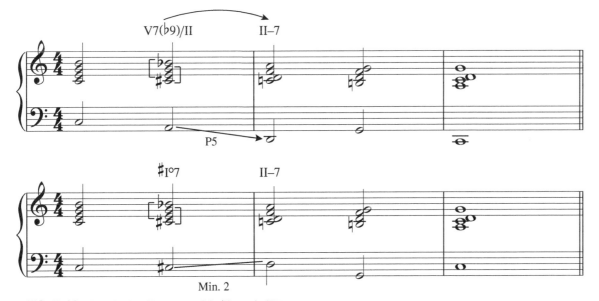

FIG. 7.10. Similarity Between V7/II and ♯I°7

The tritones in the two chords are identical; the bass motion is quite different. As with ♯V°7 and the other ascending diminished chords, this provides more variety and casts any tensions in a different relationship to the root.

The C♯ diatonic diminished chord scale is identical in pitch content to the A Mixolydian (♭9, ♯9, ♭13) scale.[22]

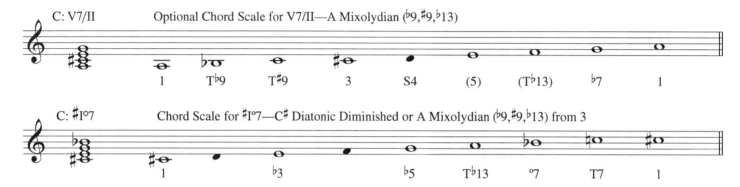

FIG. 7.11. Chord Scale Equivalence for V7/II and ♯I°7

V7/V and ♯IV°7?

♯IV°7 does not perform the same function as V7/V in the standard repertoire.[23]

Its most typical resolution is to the second inversion of the I chord (IMaj/5).

FIG. 7.12. ♯IV°7 Progressin to I/5

For this reason, ♯IV°7 might best be thought of as an inversion of ♯II°7. Compare its chord scale with that of ♯II°7. Aside from an enharmonic spelling, the scales have identical pitch content.

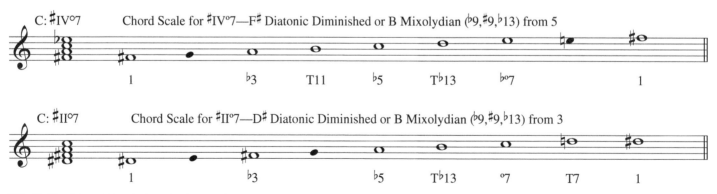

FIG. 7.13. Chord Scale Equivalence for ♯IV°7 and ♯II°7

---

22   See chapter 2 for chord scales for V7/II.

23   ♯IV°7 does occasionally move to V7. Older standards such as "The Birth of the Blues" and "Paper Moon" make use of the progression ♯IV°7 resolving to V7, but the ♯IV°7 chord appears on a weak metrical stress and does not give the aural impression of the dominant preparation V7/V.

An Alternate Diatonic Chord Scale for ♯IV°7

The interval structure of diminished chords leaves room in certain cases for an additional diatonic tension: tension Maj7. The following is an alternative diatonic chord scale for ♯IV°7:

FIG. 7.14. Alternate Chord Scale for ♯IV°7 Including TMaj7

This chord scale is of particular interest in a blues, as 1, ♭3, 4, and ♭5 of the blues scale have a strong expressive melodic relationship with ♯IV°7. Figure 7.15 shows measures 5 through 8 of a jazz blues.

FIG. 7.15. Measure 5–8 of a Blues with ♯IV°7

To recap and contrast, secondary dominant seventh chord progressions are notable for strong bass root motion by *descending* perfect fifth (cycle 5):

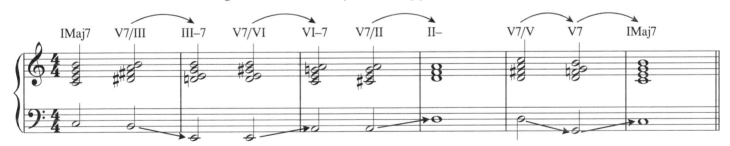

Root Motion in Bass Line: Strong Descending P5ths or Ascending P4ths

FIG. 7.16. Progression with Secondary Dominants. Descending Cycle 5 Root Motion

Diminished seventh chords with secondary dominant function are notable for dramatic *ascending* chromatic root motion (cycle 2).

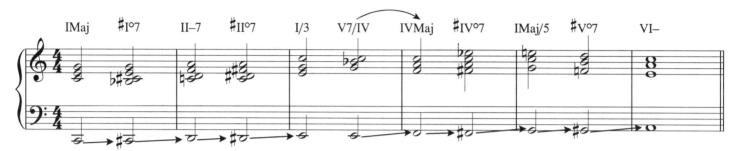

FIG. 7.17. Progression with Ascending Diminished Chords. Ascending Cycle 2 Motion

Diminished Chords and Symmetry

Unlike dominant sevenths, a diminished chord contains not one, but *two* tritones, making it a highly unstable structure.

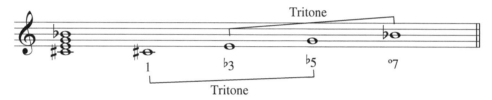

FIG. 7.18. Two Tritones in a Diminished Seventh Chord

Because tritones can resolve inward or outward, diminished seventh chords have many possible resolutions. These are the eight major and minor targets for C#°7. The arrows in the example show which tritone is resolving to the root and third of the target chord. Don't worry about the enharmonic spellings; concentrate on the half and whole steps.

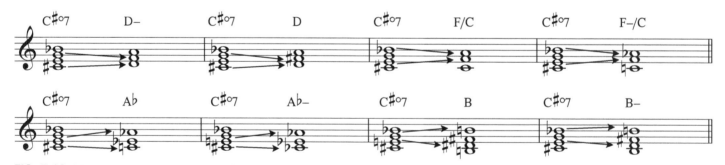

FIG. 7.19. Multiple Resolutions for a C#°7 Chord

Note that the target chords taken as a group are each a minor third apart: the roots are D, F, A♭, and B, respectively. This reflects the symmetrical structure of the diminished chord itself.

2. THE °7 CHORD AS A DESCENDING CHROMATIC APPROACH CHORD: PASSING DIMINISHED

In this section we will look at a different kind of diminished operation: *descending approach*. In all of the following common chord progressions, the diatonic goal chord II–7 is preceded by a chromatic approach chord.

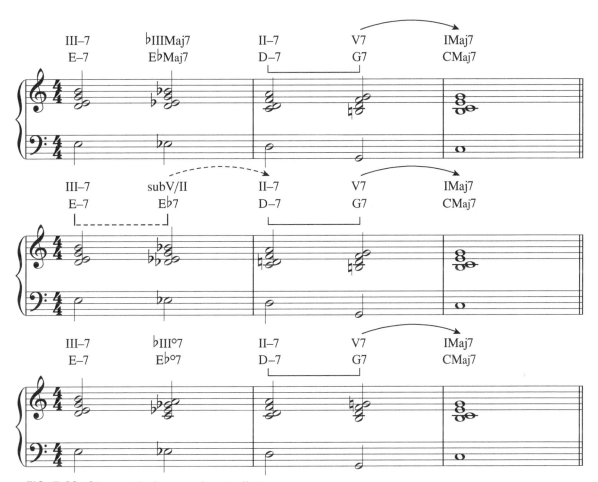

FIG. 7.20. Chromatic Approaches to II–7

As the last phrase shows, another common use of diminished seventh chords is as a *descending chromatic approach chord* to a diatonic goal. The most common of these is ♭III°7. It typically progresses to II–7. Unlike the ascending diminished chord, which functions like a secondary dominant, the descending diminished does not depend on the tendency of the tritone for its resolution, but rather on the powerful melodic tendency of descending half-step motion (as in a substitute dominant or modal interchange chord) and a connection of common tones with the goal chord.

FIG. 7.21. ♭III°7 Progressing to II–7

Context is important in identifying the function of a diminished chord. ♯II *resolves* upward from II- to III- (or less frequently to I/3) whereas ♭III *progresses* downward from III- to II- (or less frequently to V7/5). The harmonic mechanisms are different—tritone resolution vs. chromatic parallelism and common tone connection.

Chord Scale Options for ♭III°7

If we examine the chord scales for ♯II°7 and ♭III°7 we can see that the pitch content is identical, although enharmonically spelled. In the key of C:

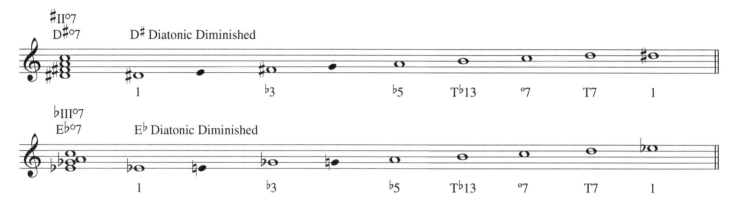

FIG. 7.22. ♯II°7 Is Enharmonically Equivalent to ♭III°7

So the chord scales for ♯II°7 and ♭III°7 are essentially the same. However the E♭ to G♭ spelling between the root and ♭3 of ♭III°7 suggests another possible chord scale option.

FIG. 7.23. Optional Chord Scale for ♭III°7

The pitch F is diatonic to the key of C and makes tension 9 available as a part of the chord as well. This gives ♭III°7 yet another tone (F) that is common with the goal chord II-7.

Varied Melodic/Harmonic Options

The ♭III°7 chord allows for an additional melodic option compared to other ways of approaching the II-7 chord. If we compare the chord scales for the descending chromatic approach chords based on scale degree ♭3, we can see that each represents a different set of diatonic melodic options:

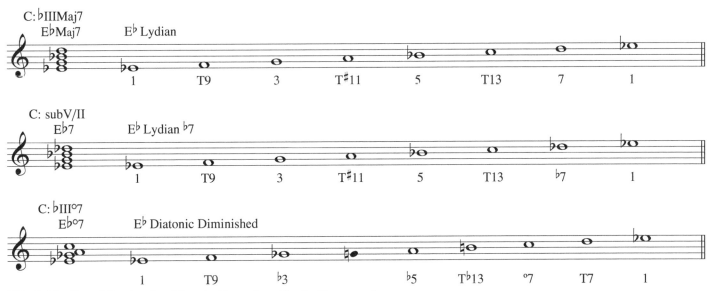

FIG. 7.24. Chord Scales for Chords Based on Scale Degree ♭3

♭IIIMaj7 and sub/II each have their own unique flavor, but only ♭III°7 will allow for a consonant use of scale degree 7 (*Ti*).

FIG. 7.25. T♭13 on ♭III°7

♭VI°7

This function is rare, but is found in some tunes in the repertoire as a descending chromatic approach chord to the related II–7 of the V/IV. See Jobim's "Corcovado" or "Wave" for further study.

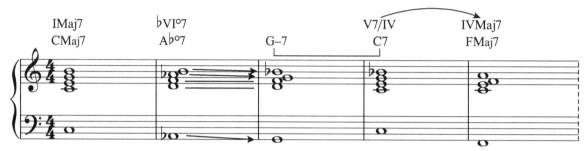

FIG. 7.26. ♭VI°7 as a Chromatic Approach Chord

Once again, the chord scale consists of chord tones, diatonic tensions, and diatonic avoid tones from the parent key.

FIG. 7.27. Chord Scale for ♭VI°7

♯IV–7♭5

The minor7♭5 chord has been treated in previous chapters as a related subdominant chord for V7/III and an integral part of the minor key II V progression. Despite its tritone, it doesn't have primary or secondary dominant function in the vocabulary of jazz harmony. We deal with it here because the –7♭5 chord built on scale degree ♯4 can play a special descending linear role in chord progressions in much the same way that ♭III°7 and ♭VI°7 do. ♯IV–7♭5 occurs on a strong stress in the meter and serves as the point of departure for a progression of descending chromatic root motion. It is often used in this way to launch a final coda in arrangements. It shares an important common tone, Do, with IV–7. The remaining chords also share common tones or move in parallel stepwise motion:

FIG. 7.28. ♯IV–7♭5 Initiating a Chromatic Progression Toward IMaj7

One way to think of this function is as a modal interchange chord from the parallel Lydian scale. This helps make sense of the chord's usual appearance as a "deceptive" resolution of V7.

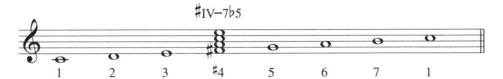

FIG. 7.29. Lydian Modal Source for ♯IV–7♭5

The chord consists of the tonic function VI triad superimposed over the ♯4 root. It avoids scale tone 4, which would define it as subdominant. Not *quite* tonic, yet *not* subdominant, the ♯IV–7♭5 floats between these two functions and precipitates motion downward, usually to IV–7, IV–6, or IV7, subdominant minor modal interchange chords built on scale degree 4. Its associated chord scale is Locrian, the fourth mode of the Lydian source scale. See Cole Porter's "Night and Day" for an idiomatic example of its use in a tune.

3. EMBELLISHING CHORDS: AUXILIARY DIMINISHED SEVENTH CHORDS

Auxiliary diminished chords are created by lowering the 3, 5, and 7 of IMaj7 or V7. I°7 is used to alternate with I6 or IMaj7 for a mild pulsation of color without abandoning the tonic. It can also create a surprising delayed resolution to the IMaj chord. The lowered tones are usually resolved upward to the regular chord tones of the function.

FIG. 7.30. I°7 Delaying Final Resolution to IMaj6

T7 as a melodic tone on I°7 has been a popular color with composers over the years. See Richard Rodgers' and Lorenz Hart's "Spring Is Here" for further study. The unresolved I°7 chord with tension 7 in the lead has become a popular feature of contemporary jazz composition and performance.

Chord Scales for I°7

The chord scale for I°7 is created by spelling the chord tones, and then connecting them with scale tones that are diatonic to the parent key. The following are both possible diatonic chord scales for I°7 in C major. Neither is a mode of any other conventional scale.

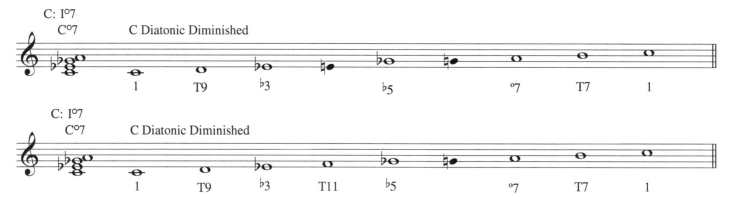

FIG. 7.31. Diatonic Chord Scales for I°7

V°7

Similar to I°7, the V°7 chord is used to *prolong* or *embellish* dominant function, as in Herman Hupfeld's "As Time Goes By" or George Gershwin's "How Long Has This Been Going On?"...

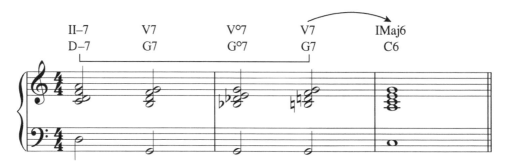

FIG. 7.32. V°7 Alternating with V7

...or this well-worn blues cliché.

FIG. 7.33. Elaboration of V7 Using V°7

Again, its chord scale consists of chord tones and diatonic tensions, befitting its role as a diatonic approach chord.

FIG. 7.34. Chord Scale for V°7

DIMINISHED APPROACH

This book is at heart about the structural functions of jazz harmony—the root-oriented chords that we think of as the changes of the tune. However, there is one interesting idiomatic use of diminished seventh chords in jazz that we can't neglect to mention. It is not a structural harmonic phenomenon but rather an embellishing device. This is the practice of harmonizing passing tones with diminished seventh chords, or *diminished approach technique.* Consider the following passage. Each note labeled *pt* (passing tone) approaches a stable chord tone of the prevailing C6 harmony.

FIG. 7.35. Melodic Analysis of C Major Scale Accompanied by C6

Let's harmonize each of the passing tones in the melody with B°7 or VII°7/I.

FIG. 7.36. Harmonization of C Scale with Diminished Approaches to Chord Tones

The functional root of the passage is still C, but by harmonizing the passing tones with diminished chords we get an undulating effect that effectively retonicizes C6 each time it occurs. Diminished approach technique creates a more active harmonic surface within the context of a single chord, in this case C6. This technique was pioneered by Milt Buckner and popularized by George Shearing.

The Symmetric Diminished Scale

Throughout this chapter we have put a premium on embedding functional diminished seventh chords in the key by using only diatonic tensions. However, the use of nondiatonic tensions on diminished chords can have a startling dramatic effect.

If we extend a C♯°7 chord in such a way that each tension is a major ninth above a chord tone, the result is C♯°7 (Maj7, 9, 11, ♭13); the chord scale for this structure is called the *symmetric diminished* scale. The interval structure of this scale is completely regular: whole step, half step, whole step, half step, whole step, half step, whole step, half step. It is also called an *octatonic* scale because it has eight different pitches rather than the seven we see in major and minor scales (*heptatonic*) or the five pitches in pentatonic scales.

FIG. 7.37. Symmetric Diminished Scale on C♯°7

Symmetrical structures from this chord scale can be used for dramatic effect over a functional diminished seventh chord. In measure 2 of figure 7.35, we can see all of the basic chord tones of C♯°7 spelled out in the tenor voice. Superimposed above the chord tones are minor seventh chords drawn from the symmetric diminished scale. These combinations produce all of the colorful tension combinations inherent in the scale. The nondiatonic tensions 9 and 11 really give this chord an acidic bite. Use with caution!

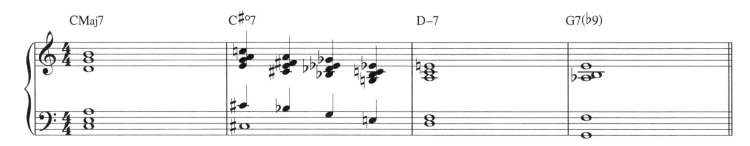

FIG. 7.38. Symmetric Diminished Scale Voicings Applied to ♯I°7

The symmetric diminished chord scale is not diatonic to any key. It is often deployed as an optional chord scale for special situations where its vibrant color is desired as contrast to a more diatonic passage.

Now that you've had the tour, let's try some analysis. You should be able to find all of the different diminished functions that we've discussed (ascending, descending, and auxiliary) in the following tune, "Diminishing Returns." In addition, you should be able to distinguish the major key diatonic functions from secondary dominants, related II's, substitute dominants, and modal interchange chords. The second half of the bridge changes key. Modulation is discussed in chapter 8.

Diminishing Returns

By Tom Hojnacki

FIG. 7.39. "Diminishing Returns"

Diminishing Returns

By Tom Hojnacki

FIG. 7.40. "Diminishing Returns" Roman Numeral Analysis

RECOMMENDED LISTENING

Richard Rodgers, "Spring Is Here" (I°7)

Fats Waller, "Ain't Misbehavin'" (♯I°7, ♯II°7)

Charlie Parker, "Now Is the Time" (♯IV°7)

Cole Porter, "Night and Day" and Bill Evans, "Tiffany" (♭III°7)

Antonio Carlos Jobim, "Corcovado," "Wave" (♭VI°7)

George Gershwin, "How Long Has This Been Going On?"

Herman Hupfeld, "As Time Goes By" (V°7)

Modulation

Since the advent of equal-tempered tuning, modulation has been one of the techniques that composers have employed to create contrast within compositions. Eighteenth and nineteenth century European composers used it as a principal device to articulate structure in their longer form compositions. Schubert, Schumann, Brahms, Fauré, and Debussy all used modulation to distantly related keys to create emotionally affecting changes of color within shorter song forms. The practice filtered into the compositional technique of American songwriters in the twentieth century on a more compressed scale within the confines of the short chorus. In turn, jazz composers have left their own imprint on the use of modulation, and in so doing, created some expressive and challenging vehicles for improvisation.

So, what is modulation? We say that a modulation has occurred when the listener senses arrival at a new tonal center: the note we have thought of as *Do* changes. In this chapter, we'll discuss the expressive possibilities of moving from one key to another and the basic processes for modulation that occur in the standard repertoire: direct modulation, pivot modulation, and transitional modulation.

AESTHETIC EFFECTS

Modulations create one of two basic aesthetic effects: a brightening or heightening of intensity, or a darkening or relaxation of intensity. The intensity with which these two musical effects register on the listener is dependent on the number of common tones from one key to another. Keys that have many common tones are referred to as *closely related*. Those with few common tones are *distantly related*.

The circle of fifths is a convenient tool for measuring these effects. We will use the key of C major as our point of reference and express the relationships as Roman numerals so that we can commute this understanding into other keys.

Parent Tonic

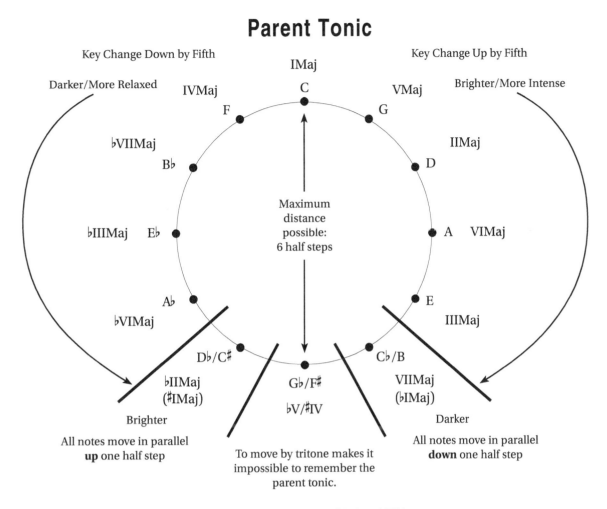

FIG. 8.1. Aesthetic Effect of Movement Around the Circle of Fifths

If we move around the circle by fifths in a sharp direction (clockwise), lining up the pitches of the scales in parallel, we can observe that even though there are many common tones between the keys, each of the principal tonal degrees 1, 4, and 5 is eventually raised by one half step. This creates a successive feeling of brightening, with III major the most extreme example. So, to move from C major to the *closely* related key of G major creates some brightening, but to move from C major to the *distantly* related key of E major will create a more exciting contrast.

I Major	C:	C	D	E	F	G	A	B	
V Major	G:	C	D	E	F♯	G	A	B	(4 is raised)
II Major	D:	C♯	D	E	F♯	G	A	B	(1 and 4 are raised)
VI Major	A:	C♯	D	E	F♯	G♯	A	B	(1, 4, 5 are raised)
III Major	E:	C♯	D♯	E	F♯	G♯	A	B	(1, 2, 4, 5 are raised)

FIG. 8.2. Moving in a Sharp Direction

If we move around the circle by fifths in a flat direction (counterclockwise), the effect is one of relaxation or darkening. The principal tonal degrees 1, 4, and 5 are retained with each successive move, maintaining a strong connection with the parent key. The scale degrees 2, 3, 6, and 7 are lowered successively, creating a graduated darkening.

I Major	C:	C	D	E	F	G	A	B
IV Major	F:	C	D	E	F	G	A	B♭
♭VII Major	B♭:	C	D	E♭	F	G	A	B♭
♭III Major	E♭:	C	D	E♭	F	G	A♭	B♭
♭VI Major	A♭:	C	D♭	E♭	F	G	A♭	B♭

FIG. 8.3. Moving in a Flat Direction

In the most distantly related keys, this phenomenon begins to break down. Moving directly from IMaj to ♭IIMaj creates a sense of brightening, since every tone is one half step higher: in effect, it sounds like ♯IMaj. This upward parallelism overrides the pattern of darkening as the pendulum swings further from the home tonic.

I Major	C:	C	D	E	F	G	A	B
♭II Major	D♭:	D♭	E♭	F	G♭	A♭	B♭	C
♯I Major	C♯:	C♯	D♯	E♯	F♯	G♯	A♯	B♯

FIG. 8.4. I Major to ♭II or ♯I Major. ♭II is enharmonically equivalent to ♯I.

Similarly, moving directly from I major to VII major creates a darkening, as all tones move *down* in parallel by one half step. Conversely, its effect is that of ♭I major.

I Major	C:	C	D	E	F	G	A	B
VII Major	B:	B	C♯	D♯	E	F♯	G♯	A♯
♭I Major	C♭:	C♭	D♭	E♭	F♭	G♭	A♭	B♭

FIG. 8.5. I Major to VII or ♭I Major. VII major is enharmonically equivalent to ♭I Major.

MECHANISMS FOR KEY CHANGE: DIRECT MODULATION

Direct modulation usually occurs at the beginning of a phrase or a new section of the song form such as the bridge. The new tonality is often established by an unambiguous progression such as I VI II V or II V I. This can be called a "confirming cadence." A tonic chord with a very long duration can also serve to confirm the new tonal center. New contrasting melodic material often coincides with the change of key.

The Shadow of a Memory

By Tom Hojnacki

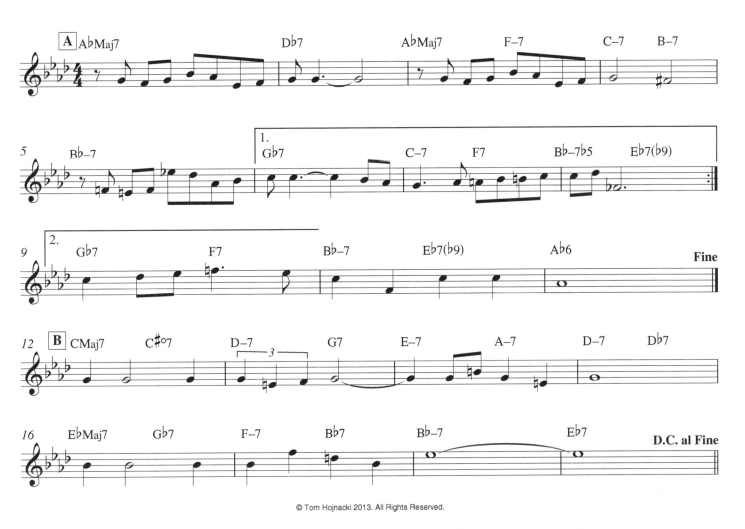

FIG. 8.6. "The Shadow of a Memory," Direct Modulation from A♭ Major to C Major in Measure 12

In the ballad in figure 8.6, "The Shadow of a Memory," the A section is in the key of A♭. At the bridge (measure 12), the tune changes key without prior warning to C major, a distantly related key (four fifths in a sharp direction on the circle of fifths). In measure 16, the melody and chord changes shift directly up a minor third to the key of E♭ major (three fifths in a flat direction) bringing us one fifth above A♭ for the return to the A section.

Duke Ellington's "Prelude to a Kiss" and "Do Nothin' till You Hear from Me" have bridges that begin with a direct change of key and a melody that contrasts with the A section.

In other compositions, an exact sequential repetition of material from a previous section is used. The change of key creates musical variety; the transposed melody maintains musical unity. Figure 8.7 is a bluesy jump tune in ABA form that uses this device.

FIG. 8.7. Exact Melody-Harmony Sequence Causing Modulation

The B section, beginning at measure 9, is a literal transposition of the A section. The change from a C to an F tonality at the bridge is the variation that creates structural contrast. Jerome Kern's "Long Ago and Far Away," Todd Dameron's "Good Bait," and Thelonious Monk's "Bemsha Swing" are good examples of tunes from the standard repertoire that belong to this category.

KEY CHANGES FROM MAJOR TO MAJOR

The following standards include changes from one major key to another. Analyzing, studying, and memorizing the melodies and chord progressions of these tunes will help you to appreciate the affective qualities of different key relationships.

1. Modulation in a *sharp* direction:

   • "I Can't Get Started" modulates to II major at the bridge.

   • "Emily" modulates to VI major in the B phrase.

   • "How My Heart Sings" modulates to III major in measures 13–16.

- "Prelude to a Kiss" and "If You Could See Me Now" modulate to III major at the bridge.

- "Body and Soul" modulates to ♯I major at the bridge.

- "Joy Spring" modulates to #1 major for the second A section and again at the bridge.

2. Modulation in a *flat* direction:

- "What's New?" modulates to IV major at the bridge.

- "How High the Moon" modulates to ♭VII major in the second phrase and then again by the same distance in the third phrase.

- "Joy Spring" modulates to ♭VII major twice sequentially in the first four measures of the bridge.

- "Hi-Fly" modulates to ♭VII major in measures 5–8.

- "Long Ago and Far Away" modulates to ♭III major at the bridge.

- "Do Nothin' till You Hear from Me" modulates to ♭VI major at the bridge.

- "Sophisticated Lady" modulates to ♭I major at the bridge (enharmonically, VII).

THE PIVOT MODULATION

Direct modulation is dramatically striking because of the immediate contrast it creates. It often coincides with the beginning of a new phrase or section within the song form. As listeners, we have become conditioned to expect a musical variation at these junctures in the standard song forms. The contrast offered by a direct modulation fulfills that expectation nicely.

The *pivot modulation* is much subtler. A *pivot chord* is one that functions in both the parent key as well as that of the new key, acting like a bridge between the two tonalities. Because the shift from one key area to another occurs more smoothly, the listener experiences the contrast of the modulation, but is often unaware *by what means* the shift has taken place. Secondary and substitute dominants are particularly useful as pivot chords because their resolving tendency is so clear. Resolution can be to either a major *or* a minor target, and it can be by half-step *or* perfect fifth, so they potentially act as pivots to a variety of different key areas.

In figure 8.8, the melody and chord changes establish G major as the parent
tonality of the tune. In measure 4, F♯–7♭5 to B7 prepares the listener to expect an E-
chord on the downbeat of measure 5. The diatonic tensions ♭9 and ♭13 of the B7 chord
help further to telegraph that outcome. However, as B7 is also the dominant function
chord in E major, it pivots seamlessly into the EMaj7 chord in measure 5. The dual
analysis of B7 reflects its identity in both keys. The I VI II V progression and melody
diatonic to E major in measures 5–6 confirm that E, rather than G, is our new tonal
center.

FIG. 8.8. Progression with Deceptive Resolution of V7/VI as Pivot Chord

Subdominant function chords are also used as pivot chords. In figure 8.9, the modal interchange chords IV–7 ♭VII7 in the key of C major also function as the II V in the key of E♭ major. The ♭VII7 usually returns to I, but instead is used here to pivot to a key a minor third higher. Just as it was used to move from C to E♭ (measures 8–9), the B♭7 chord can be used to pivot once more back into C major (measures 12–13).

FIG. 8.9. C Major Progression with SDM IV–7 ♭VII7 as Pivot to Key of ♭III

Modal interchange chords I–7 IV7 (from the parallel Dorian source) are widely used to form an effective pivot II V into a new key one whole step below the parent tonality. The listener first perceives the chords as a modal shift. But, because the intervals in the chords are identical to II V of the next key, the shift to the new tonality has a smooth inevitable feeling facilitated by the cycle 5 root motion of the II V progression. Compositions that employ this device often feature sequential melodies that provide musical unity to balance the variety provided by the changes of key. Figure 8.10 employs this device in measures 3–4 and 7–8.

FIG. 8.10. Dorian Modal Interchange Pattern as Pivot to Key of ♭VII. Deceptive Resolution of V7/III as Pivot to Key of III.

Nancy Hamilton and Morgan Lewis's "How High the Moon" (the basis for Charlie Parker's "Ornithology") or John Lewis's "Afternoon in Paris" contain clear examples of this pivot device.

TRANSITIONAL MODULATION

Chains of descending cycle 5 and/or cycle 2 resolutions of II V patterns can create moments within a phrase in which there is no clear reference to the parent tonality or the eventual new tonality. During these moments the listener is carried along by a strong progressive pattern that creates a sense of motion or transition toward a new goal key. In figure 8.11, "Lithe and Lovely," we have a mid-tempo bebop tune in AABA form.

Lithe and Lovely

TRACK 12

By Tom Hojnacki

FIG. 8.11. "Lithe and Lovely," Extended Dominant Series as Transition Back to Original Key

The A section is in the key of F. The B section moves directly to the key of Db major in measures 13–17. In measures17–20, we lose our sense of Db to the strong forward harmonic motion. The series of II V's constitute an extended dominant string that implies successive unresolved key centers. The passage is eventually resolved across the section break. See figure 8.12 for a Roman numeral and graphic analysis.

FIG. 8.12. "Lithe and Lovely," Analysis of Transitional Extended Dominant Series

In measure 17, it is possible to hear the first two chords in relation to the key of D♭ as I–7 and IV7 from the parallel Dorian scale. (C♯ is enharmonic to D♭.) However, the subsequent chords in the phrase bear no functional relation to D♭ whatsoever. Instead, we are carried along by the power of the cycle 5 root motion and the descending chromatic guide tones until we return to the parent key of F major.

KEY CHANGES FROM MAJOR TO MINOR

Within major key tunes there are two typical shifts to minor keys. The most common is a change to the submediant, or relative minor (e.g., C major to A minor). This relationship can be heard in "God Bless the Child," "Georgia on My Mind," and "There Is No Greater Love." Although this can be accomplished by direct key change, the key of the relative minor is most often introduced through the use of the V7/VI as a pivot chord. Shifts to the mediant III minor (e.g., C major to E minor) are somewhat less common; Tadd Dameron's "Soultrane," Charlie Parker's "Yardbird Suite," or Benny Golson's "Stablemates" are good examples.

MINOR KEY TUNES

For structural contrast, minor key tunes often change key to the relative major (e.g., C minor to E♭ major). Chapter 4 contains a detailed discussion of this phenomenon. "Black Orpheus," "My Funny Valentine," and "You Don't Know What Love Is" are classic examples from the repertoire. Although less common, analogous movement between different minor keys exists within some tunes in the repertoire. In figure 8.13, pivot modulations to closely related minor keys are a structural feature of this progression.

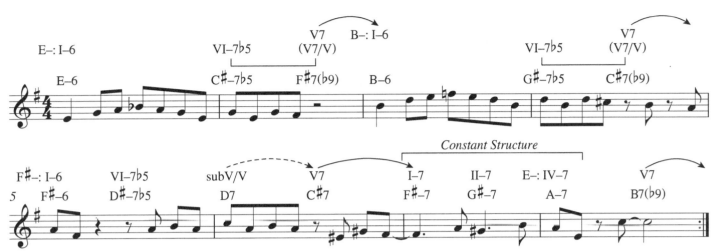

FIG. 8.13. Deceptive Resolution of V7/V as a Pivot to Modulate Down a Perfect Fourth

Bronislaw Kaper's "Invitation" (direct modulation up a minor third) and Benny Golson's "Whisper Not" (two pivot modulations up a perfect fifth and a transitional modulation down a major second) are minor key tunes that modulate to other minor keys.

THE KEY OF THE MOMENT

A chord progression will sometimes momentarily imply a contrasting key without definitively establishing a new key center. The mechanism is often a non-diatonically related II V pattern inserted in a tonal passage or an extended dominant string. These key-of-the-moment or "tonal interchange"[24] passages represent a higher level of chromaticism than modal interchange or secondary dominant function but do not represent a true or complete modulation. They point temporarily to a different tonal center without a confirming cadence, then return immediately to the primary key. In figure 8.14, measures 3–4 imply the key of A♭ major without resolving to its tonic chord.

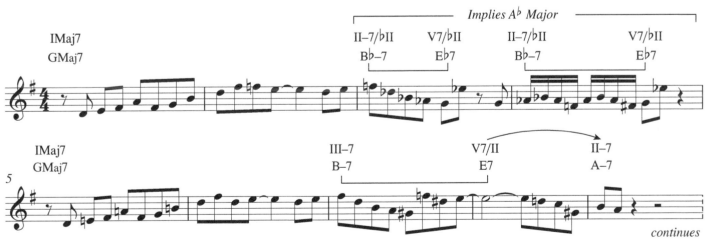

FIG. 8.14. Temporary Tonicization of A♭ in Measures 3–4

See "Darn That Dream," "Out of Nowhere," and "Just Friends" for examples of this phenomenon.

---

24   Thanks to our colleague Steve Rochinski for this term.

MULTIPLE LOCAL MODULATIONS

Some tunes in the repertoire make use of multiple modulations within short spans. In these tunes, both the harmony and melody are sequential in nature, offering multiple transposed repetitions of a single melodic/harmonic motive. The relationships between keys are often organized around a specific interval. The intervallic design of the key changes can be completely symmetrical or may change for the sake of variety.

KEY CHANGES ORGANIZED BY HALF STEP

In the following example, three direct modulations take place. The intervallic relationship between each of the new keys is a minor second. Notice how the exact sequential repetitions of the melody are supported by the three transposed sequential repetitions of II–7 V7 IMaj7.

FIG. 8.15. Sequential Descending Half-Step Modulations

While each key change provides a contrast, the continuity between keys is facilitated by the guide tones (3 and 7 of each chord), which remain common as each direct modulation occurs.

FIG. 8.16. Voice Leading of Sequential Descending Half-Step Modulations

Sonny Rollins's "Airegin" and Billy Strayhorn's "Daydream" contain examples of this pattern.

KEY CHANGES ORGANIZED BY WHOLE STEP

In the next example, the first changes of the bridge create a direct modulation up a half step from C to Db major. Then, transposed repetitions of the melody create a descending sequence supported by the II–7 V7 IMaj7 progression. This time the defining interval between keys is a whole step (Db, B, A).

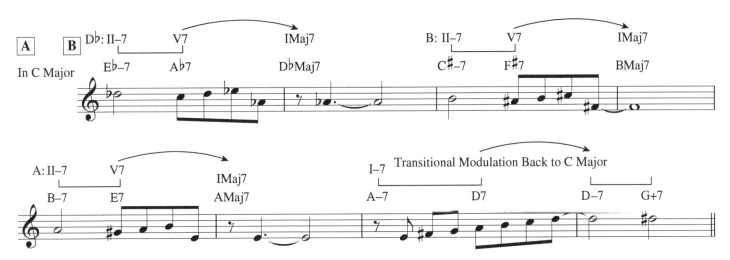

FIG. 8.17. II V's Modulating Down by Whole Steps

While the seventh measure of the phrase implies yet another change of key down a whole step, this time to G, the II V (A-7 D7) progresses instead to D-7 G7 changing up the pattern. This creates a transitional modulation back to the parent key of C. The key changes in this example are facilitated by common tone root motion (D♭Maj7 to C#-7, BMaj7 to B-7, AMaj7 to A-7). See Ray Noble's "Cherokee," Miles Davis' "Tune Up," or Horace Silver's "Metamorphosis."

KEY CHANGES ORGANIZED BY MINOR THIRD

The chord progression in the next example is completely symmetrical. Here the key changes are organized around the interval of a descending minor third. Minor thirds divide the octave into even quarters.

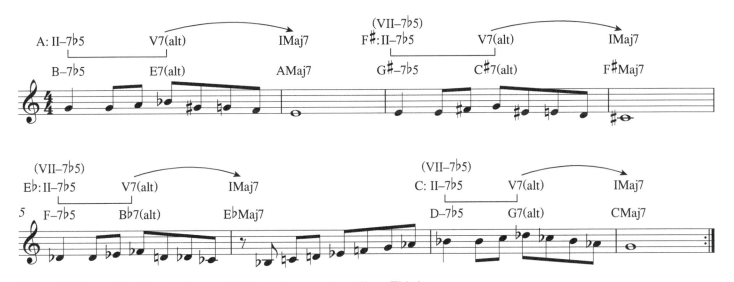

FIG. 8.18. Deceptive Resolutions of II V's in Descending Minor Thirds

See Benny Carter's "When Lights Are Low" and Kenny Barron's "Sequel."

KEY CHANGES ORGANIZED BY MAJOR THIRD

After the initial move to IV at the beginning of the bridge, this passage changes key three times. Each change moves by the interval of a major third. In a passage such as this, common tones from key to key are few, making this particular progression a perennial challenge for improvisers.

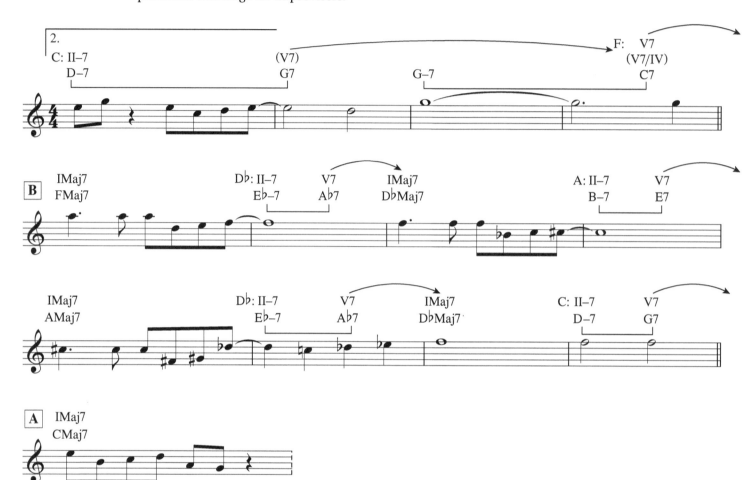

FIG. 8.19. Modulations by Descending Major Third

See Richard Rodgers' "Have You Met Miss Jones?" and Alexander Borodin/Robert Wright/George Forest's "Baubles, Bangles, and Beads."

COLTRANE CHANGES

We'd be remiss if we didn't at least mention the chord progression that John Coltrane pioneered with his tunes "Giant Steps" and "26-2" and employed in his famous reharmonizations of "Body and Soul" and "But Not for Me." The "Trane Changes" compress the direct modulation into a smaller temporal span than in any of the examples shown previously. The modulations are organized around a symmetrical division of the octave into major thirds.

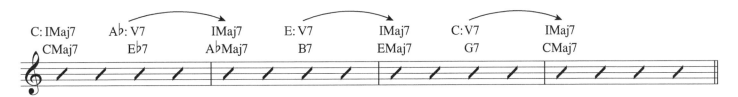

FIG. 8.20. "Trane Changes": Symmetrical Division of the Octave by Major Thirds

The progression can be completely symmetrical and circular as in the example above, or it can come to rest in the third measure. A new II V in the fourth measure breaks the intervallic pattern and allows the pattern to commence anew on a different starting tonic.

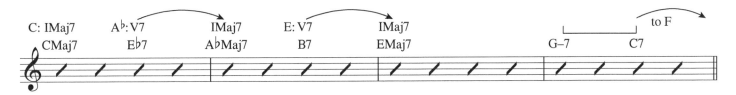

FIG. 8.21. Incomplete Symmetrical Division of the Octave

While some tunes that employ this key scheme are organized around a central tonic chord, the equal division of the octave by organizational interval and the relentless changes of key suggests a triumvirate of tonics where pre-eminence is only decided by primacy. In fact, "Giant Steps" establishes new key centers a descending major third apart in measures 5 and 9, thus dividing the octave symmetrically, then continues by reversing the direction of the modulations and halving the harmonic rhythm to reiterate the cycle 3 organization. This has led some theorists to refer to this sort of harmonic organization as a *multi-tonic system*. A number of other musicians, such as Charles Lloyd and Pat Metheny, have written tunes with a similar design. Here is one last example of "Trane Changes." Here, the cycle 3 pattern of modulation is embedded in the larger II V I pattern of the phrase.

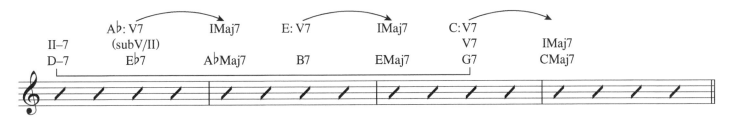

FIG. 8.22. "Trane Changes" Embedded within a II V I Progression

For further study, see "Countdown," John Coltrane's famous reimagining of Miles Davis' "Tune Up."

CHAPTER 9

Modal Harmony in Jazz

One of the the principal themes in this book has been the balance between tension and release in music. We have explored this duality thoroughly in the minor key and major key functional worlds. In both those contexts, the concept of *dominant resolution* has been central, with the tritone as the primary engine that powers the forward movement of diatonic harmony. But there is another harmonic paradigm that can animate a musical situation: *succession of modal colors.*

Modal jazz has been part of the scene for more than fifty years. It emerged as a framework for fresh compositional and improvisational strategies, partially as a reaction to the endpoint complexity of bop and post-bop harmonies and melodic practices. Many players were beginning to feel handcuffed by the melodic ornamentations and complex reharmonizations of standard tunes that were developed to a very high level by Charlie Parker, Dizzy Gillespie, John Coltrane, Art Tatum, and Lennie Tristano. Miles Davis and others felt that this extreme virtuosic approach had run its course, and they were searching for a harmonic concept that offered fewer impediments to their melodic flights.

As early as 1950, some musicians were already experimenting with extended passages based on a single chord. Improvising over a single chord or scale (or very few) was a radical re-thinking of the entrenched tradition of interpreting standard popular songs of the day. This new approach was explored by many musicians in more depth over the next few years; its most prominent initial expression was in Miles Davis's album *Kind of Blue*. The influence of this recording was profound, although it was certainly not the first example of modal music by well-known jazz artists.

As a result, a new body of repertoire began to emerge: original tunes with passages or sections that exploited a single mode, often with *no significant chord changes at all.* This trend continues to the present day. The jazz repertoire now includes a large number of tunes with significant modal sections in the form.

"Modal" can mean many things. As we use the term in this chapter, it describes music that has one or more of these characteristics:

- a very limited set of chords, all of which are derived from a single scale

- a lack of functional harmony, especially dominant resolution and II V I patterns

- limited use of the chord that represents the relative Ionian scale

- slow harmonic rhythm

- repetitive oscillation between two chords

- chord scale voicings over a pedal point, usually the tonic

In the entire jazz repertoire, only a handful of relatively obscure tunes use just a single mode as a source for diatonic chords. The overwhelming majority instead have one section that expresses a modal tonic. This open, single-color region is then paired with more conventional tonal passages, cyclical II V's, or constant structure patterns.[25] This basic structure provides contrast and dramatic pacing for improvisers that is different than that in the American Songbook repertoire. The tension between relatively static modal passages and forward-moving tonal passages is an effective means of organizing a composition. Bobby Timmons' "Moanin'," Cedar Walton's "Bolivia," Wayner Shorter's "Yes and No," and Joe Henderson's "No Me Esqueça" ("Recorda Me") are prime examples of this approach.

The other common device is to base each phrase or section on a different scale (often using just the tonic from that scale), as in Miles Davis's "So What" and Herbie Hancock's "Maiden Voyage." The movement between the various tonal centers and scale qualities gives the music contrast and momentum.

MODES AND MODAL PROGRESSIONS

When discussing chord scales, modes are associated with specific diatonic chords and are treated as momentary *displacements* of the major scale. In this chapter, we will explore something very different: sections or whole pieces based on one of these "displaced" scales.

Changing the focal pitch of a major scale moves the familiar tonic, subdominant, and dominant chord functions to different and potentially confusing scale degrees. This shift calls all our reliable functional relationships into question. What is the role of a dominant chord when it is no longer V7? What happens when III–7 becomes the tonic chord?

For this reason, when discussing modal **music**, as opposed to individual chord/scale relationships, we must abandon our emphasis on functional families. Instead, modal music is organized around a different principle: it is based on a tonic scale with a unique intervallic structure and harmonic tendencies.

---

25   Non-functional harmonic phrases consisting of a single chord quality, e.g., all minor sevenths. See chapter 10.

> *"Modal music is based on a tonic scale with a unique*
> *intervallic structure and harmonic tendencies."*

When we examine the modes in detail, we will find that, besides their differing moods or "colors," each one has harmonic strengths and weaknesses that must be managed and exploited. We will explore how modes are used in jazz as the tonal center of a piece, rather than just a momentary chord scale.

Although diatonic chord scales are in fact modes (displacements) of a major or minor scale, the emphasis here is quite different. Now the focus will be on *modal systems*: chord progressions and melodies with a clear tonal center, diatonic to a single scale other than the major or composite minor. The Dorian, Phrygian, Lydian, Mixolydian, and Aeolian scales can each be employed as a modal system.

We have spent a lot of time analyzing the chromatic options present in functional harmony: secondary dominants, substitute dominants, diminished chords, and modal interchange. What can substitute for this rich chromatic vocabulary in the reduced harmonic spectrum in modal jazz? The short answer is: no substitute is needed; the *sound of the mode itself* is intrinsically satisfying. Our ears are captivated by the unique flavor and unusual balance of tone tendencies in each mode, so chromatic variation is not as necessary. Across an entire tune, transposition of the mode to other pitch levels and juxtaposition with other modal colors provide contrast that captures our attention and creates momentum in time.

Modal music has a well-defined tonal center, but it is notable for the *lack* of dominant resolution in the harmony. Dominant chords may occasionally appear, but they function very differently. This is a puzzle. What takes the place of dominant resolution as a defining force in creating a clear sense of tonal center?

ESTABLISHING THE MODAL TONIC 1: REPETITION

Modal jazz differs stylistically from rock and pop harmony of the 1960s through the early 21st century. The rock and pop harmonic style is often reminiscent of modal English and Celtic folk songs, with clear elements of movement away from and back to the tonic. There is often one chord that stands in for the V7, and it plays a similar role in the release of tension upon the return to tonic. In contrast, the great majority of modal jazz tunes contain long passages with just a single chord. *Prolonged repetition of the tonic chord* is one way of maintaining modal equilibrium. This differs substantially from diatonic harmony with its variable harmonic rhythm, strong directional root motion, ebb and flow of harmonic tension, and wide range of functional substitutions.

Of course, too much repetition is boring for listener and player alike. When confronted with a lead sheet that says simply "16 bars of C7," we have to find ways to animate the unchanging chord. Rhythmic comping is part of the answer, but creative *voicings* of the chord are crucial as well. In figure 9.1, stepwise motion in the upper voices is used to sound all seven notes in the mode without ever leaving the chord.

C Dorian:

FIG. 9.1. A Voicing of the C Dorian Tonic Chord

Figure 9.1 fully expresses the underlying Dorian scale in just two voicings: after the root, 9, 5, 11, and 13 are sounded first, they then relax into a more clear-cut version of C–7(11). This technique of voicing in adjacent fourths is ubiquitous, but it is especially prevalent in modal jazz. Quartal voicings gives a fresh, open sound to a chord. Because of their non-tertian structure, they are inherently ambiguous and do not carry the implication of chord *change* when supported by a tonic pedal or ostinato.

ESTABLISHING THE MODAL TONIC 2: MELODY

Just as in functional music, the melody also helps to create forward motion and clarify moments of closure in a phrase or section. Modal jazz melodies can incorporate blue notes or other chromatic variations, but they generally rely on repeated references to the tonic or fifth, often contrasted with the pitches that define the mode. The tunes listed at the end of the chapter all contain melodies that help define the central pitch in the mode.

PROTO-PROGRESSION: REPETITION AND CONTRAST

Modal tunes and sections always contain liberal amounts of the I chord, especially at the beginning of a phrase. There is no alternate tonic function: only the I or I– chord will do. Non-tonic chords that contain the characteristic pitch are sometimes used to provide harmonic movement or contrast. They can be thought of as "character chords" or "color chords," and they often *alternate* with the tonic in two-chord patterns, as in this C Phrygian example:

FIG. 9.2. Classic Phrygian Harmonic Pattern

The tonic is defined and reinforced through repetition and contrast. The oscillation between tonic and color chords is a heightened version of the stepwise voicing patterns we illustrated in figure 9.2. The main effect is to sound the tonic effectively, but the changing root motion provides a rudimentary form of chord progression. It does not have the variety or the asymmetric harmonic rhythm that usually characterizes functional progressions, but the sense of departure from and return to the tonic is clear.

Depending on the harmonic rhythm, these same non-tonic chords can be used to effect a more significant departure from and return to the I chord. Some jazz tunes deploy these character chords at cadential points in the phrase to create a rise and fall of harmonic tension that is analogous to diatonic progressions. When used in this way, we can describe them as "cadence chords." Phrases that more dramatically depart from and return to the stable tonic can be said to contain *cadential patterns*. As such, they often follow familiar models.

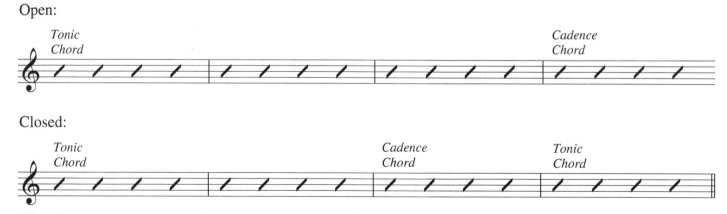

FIG. 9.3. Functional Models for Open and Closed Modal Phrases

Although there are certainly other ways to treat modal harmonic rhythm, these are reliable templates. The first is open-ended, with a characteristic chord propelling the listener forward to the next phrase; the second is closed-ended, with a feeling of finality.

These modal chord pairs are often deployed in diatonic tunes that contain a great deal of modal interchange; measures 6 and 7 of Miles Davis's "Nardis" are a clear example of ♭IIMaj7 (a Phrygian reference) being used to complete a phrase. The A section of Chick Corea's "Crystal Silence" could be characterized as "composite modal." It has a predominant tonic color (Aeolian) with a variety of cadence chords from several different modes, each returning to the tonic I–7.

In the next sections, we will look at the modal tonic scales and get acquainted with their unique characteristics. We will apply these observations to phrases and sections, showing how repetition, duration, harmonic stress, and rhythm can work together.

INTRODUCING THE MODES

The scales used in modal jazz fall into two general categories: those with a major 3rd and those with a minor 3rd. We will call these categories modal *families*. This allows for useful comparisons among a number of similar modes. The point of reference for major scales is the Ionian; for minor scales, it is Aeolian. Other modes can be understood as variations on these primary types.

The note that distinguishes each scale from the other members of its family is called the *characteristic pitch* or *character note*. For example, C Aeolian and C Phrygian share the same interval structure except for their second degree. The minor second in Phrygian is its characteristic pitch.

You will notice that –7♭5 chords are absent from all the following discussions. Along with dominant seventh chord, they are problematic, because of their strong potential to resolve away from the modal tonic. Except in the case of a Mixolydian tonic (I7), dominants are used very sparsely within a phrase and kept separate from the chord that represents the relative Ionian.

The examples in these sections all have a tonal center of C. Depending on their family, they are notated with a C major or C minor key signature and accidentals, as necessary. A traditional major or minor key signature is generally the clearest way to communicate the tonal center and major or minor modality. Many writers use an "open" key signature (no sharps or flats) regardless of the tonal center. A score can also include an indication of the predominant mode, for example "D Mixolydian."

Here are the tonic modes in a generally accepted order of brightest to darkest.

Lydian

FIG. 9.4. Lydian Tonic Scale with ♯4, the Characteristic Pitch

- Family: major. Even brighter than Ionian: a "super major" scale.

- Characteristic pitch: ♯4

- Tonic chord: IMaj7(♯11)

- Cadence chords: II7, VII–7

- No avoid notes on the tonic chord

- Subjective effect: bright, clear, balanced

- Problems: II7 tends to resolve to VMaj7, tonicizing the relative Ionian. Similarly, IMaj7 can create a plagal cadence to VMaj7. No IV chord for root motion contrast with IMaj7.

Standard Lydian Harmonic Phrases

Although the Lydian mode would seem like a prime candidate for use as a modal system—highly stable tonic chord, cadential chords that move stepwise—Lydian progressions are almost non-existent in the jazz repertoire. It is quite common to hear Lydian tonic *modal interchange* (especially at the end of tunes), but full-fledged Lydian *progressions* are virtually non-existent.

Nevertheless, it is possible to create progressions that hew to a Lydian tonic. Figure 9.5 has several of the hallmarks of stable modal progressions: there are long periods of CMaj7 at the beginning and end and few changes, and the characteristic II7 returns immediately to I.

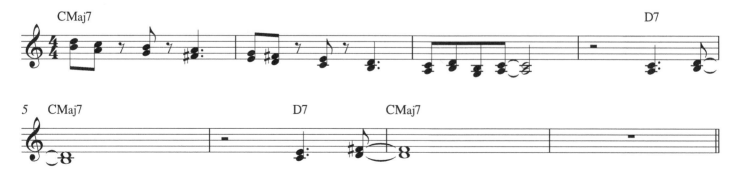

FIG. 9.5. Lydian Melody and Progression

Characteristic Lydian phrases like the one above potentially have a strong resemblance to a functional harmonic pattern: IVMaj7 V7. This similarity can pull the ear away from the ostensible Lydian tonic, down a fourth to the relative Ionian. Repetition of the tonic and appropriate distribution of other chords in a phrase are used to maintain the tonic. Otherwise, phrases like this can occur:

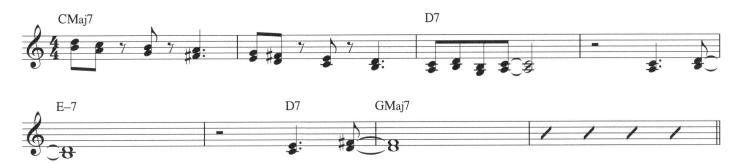

FIG. 9.6. Ineffective Lydian Progression

The melody alone is strongly Lydian in character and the phrase starts on CMaj7, but that is not enough. The similarities to harmonic resolutions in G major—deceptive resolution of D7 to E-7 and dominant resolution to GMaj7 at the end—ultimately establish G as the tonal center. Sing the root, G, and you will hear that it feels like home base.

The potential to stray from the intended tonic exists in any purely modal tune. Many contemporary pop and rock writers consciously exploit this ambiguity to create tunes that move fluidly back and forth between two or more modal tonic areas. That potential certainly exists in jazz too, but for clarity, we will show examples that unquestionably sound a single mode. These are the factors that help accomplish that goal:

1. Repeated iteration of the I chord

2. Appearance of the I chord at the beginning and end of phrases or sections

3. Avoidance of the relative Ionian tonic chord

4. Only chords derived from the mode

5. No dominant resolution down a fifth

6. Relatively slow harmonic rhythm

Mixolydian

FIG. 9.7. Mixolydian Tonic Scale with the Characteristic Pitch ♭7

- Family: major. One degree darker than Ionian, due to the minor 7th

- Characteristic pitch: ♭7

- Tonic chord: I7, I7sus4

- Cadence chords: V–7, ♭VIIMaj7

- Subjective effect: solid, robust

- Problems: Minimal

Standard Mixolydian Harmonic Phrases

V–7 and ♭VIIMaj7 both contain the characteristic pitch of the mode: ♭7. They are good chords to use in cadential positions in a harmonic phrase.

The tonic chord in Mixolydian is I7: dominant in quality, but with tonic function. It is often embellished with tensions 9 and 13 to more fully sound the mode. Here is our open-ended template with tensions on the tonic chord and both cadence chords:

FIG. 9.8. Open-Ended Mixolydian Phrase Voiced with Tensions

The cadence chords can be reversed and the effect will be pretty much the same. Either descending fifth (G–7 to C7) or stepwise (B♭Maj7 to C7) root motion are satisfying as cadential movements. V–7 to I7 has the advantage of including both the character note and root motion that mimics traditional dominant resolution.

Here is an effective closed Mixolydian phrase:

FIG. 9.9. Closed Mixolydian Phrase Voiced with Tensions

As we saw in the Lydian examples, the dominant chord can potentially resolve to other chords in the mode, tonicizing away from the modal tonic.

Example 9.10 turns C Mixolydian on its head by using familiar patterns from F major: the first and last chords are IMaj7 in F and there are two V7sus4 to IMaj7 resolutions. The resolution of C7 to FMaj7 resets the tonic, and it is very difficult to shake the sense that the tonal center has shifted to F major intead of C Mixolydian.

FIG. 9.10. Ineffective Mixolydian Harmonic Phrase

Regarding other possibilities for chord patterns, root motion by thirds *away* from the tonic is generally weak: e.g., C7 to E–7♭5 or C7 to A–7. These sound like inversions of the tonic chord rather than true progression in a modal system. (III–7♭5 is further compromised by the fact that it readily tonicizes FMaj7.) These other diatonic chords are sometimes called *linking* or *transitional* chords. They are theoretically available, but in practice, they are vanishingly rare. When they do appear, they are generally brief in duration, and they approach stronger chords by stepwise motion.

Dorian

FIG. 9.11. Tonic Dorian Scale with Characteristic Pitch Major 6

- Family: minor. One degree brighter than Aeolian due to the major 6

- No avoid notes on the tonic chord

- Characteristic pitch: 6

- Tonic chord: I–7

- Cadence chords: II–7, IV7, ♭VIIMaj7

- Subjective effect: hopeful, yearning, smooth, cool

- Problems: I–7 IV7 ♭VIIMaj7 tonicizes ♭VII

Standard Dorian Harmonic Phrases

The bright major 6 is the characteristic pitch in a Dorian scale. I–6 is a common variation on the tonic I–7 that sounds the mode more explicitly. VI–7♭5 is not a good candidate for expressing a stable tonic because of the diminished fifth above the root. It has strong potential to resolve away from the modal tonic to the relative Ionian on ♭VII.

Since I–7 does not contain scale degree 6, other chords that sound this pitch provide a strong contrasting color and fully reveal the sound of the mode. II–7, IV7, and ♭VIIMaj7 all fit this description. Of the three, IV7 is probably the strongest, due to the plagal root motion when it returns to I–7. Figure 9.12 is an open-ended harmonic phrase with a walking bass line and IV7 at the end of the phrase.

FIG. 9.12. Open-Ended Dorian Harmonic Phrase

Note the immediate return to I–7 to reconfirm C as the tonal center. Any other movement (especially to ♭VIIMaj7 or V–7) risks modulating away from C Dorian. Once again, clear modal progressions never contain phrases that operate like II V I in a related mode.

Here is a closed phrase using II–7 instead.

FIG. 9.13. Closed-Ended Dorian Harmonic Phrase

Like II–7, ♭VIIMaj7 also has the stepwise motion that characterizes many modal progressions.

FIG. 9.14. Open-Ended Dorian Phrase with ♭VIIMaj7 in Cadential Position

The ♭VIIMaj7 chord can be extended down by a third to create V–7(9). With 9 in the top of a voicing, the Dorian major 6 is still prominent, and the powerful root motion by fifth gives this chord strong impetus back to the tonic:

FIG. 9.15. The Same Phrase with V–7(9) Substituted for ♭VIIMaj7

In the last two examples, note the voicings in measures 1–2. As noted above, moving through the chord scale of the tonic in this way is typical of modal jazz performance practice.[26] It does not create harmonic progression, and the secondary voicings on weaker beats serve to fully sound the mode without creating dense vertical stacks. In general, it is better to avoid tritones in these passing voicings, but many variations exist in practice.

Aeolian

FIG. 9.16. Tonic Aeolian Scale with Characteristic Pitch ♭6

- Family: minor. The default minor scale

- Characteristic pitch: ♭6

- Tonic chord: I–7

- Cadence chords: IV–7, V–7, ♭VII7 (especially when preceded by ♭VIMaj7)

- Subjective effect: dark, strong, clear

- Problems: IV–7 ♭VII7 tonicizes ♭III, the relative Ionian

Standard Aeolian Harmonic Phrases

As the natural minor mode, Aeolian has a wide variety of possible progressions. IV–7 to I–7 works as a simple plagal pattern to create tension and release. More complex phrases that contain IV–7 ♭VII7 I–7 and ♭VIMaj7 ♭VII7 I–7 also create a strong feeling of completion. They combine the benefits of stepwise root motion

---

26   Miles Davis's "So What" and John Coltrane's "Impressions" (based on the formal/harmonic structure of "So What" with a melody borrowed from Morton Gould's "Pavane") are excellent examples of this practice.

and exposure of the character note. Figure 9.17 avoids the "phantom II V" dilemma by giving IV-7 and ♭VII7 a consistent harmonic rhythm with the tonic chord, and separating them across a cadential phrase point. Finally, there is no reference to the relative major E♭, and the return to I-7 brackets the phrase with tonic chords.

FIG. 9.17. Effective Aeolian Passage

Although V-7 does not contain the characteristic pitch (even as a tension, where it would clash harshly with the root), the strong descending-fifth root motion is reminiscent of resolution from a V7 chord, although obviously without the tritone. Here is a straight eighth-note example using an open-ended phrase model with V-7.

FIG. 9.18. Open-Ended Aeolian Phrase with V-7

As in all the other modes, the -7♭5 chord is almost never found. Despite containing the characteristic ♭6 scale degree and being adjacent to the tonic, the diminished fifth above the root is inconsistent with the perfect fifth chord structure that is associated with modal music. Its inversion, IV-6, is much more common and combines important features of ♭VII7 and IV-7.

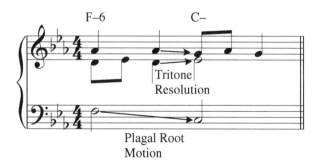

FIG. 9.19. IV-6: Stronger Root Motion Than II-7♭5

Although tritone resolution is definitely at work, it is supported by a strong intervallic root motion back to I, so the modal tonic is not compromised.

Phrygian

FIG. 9.20. Tonic Phrygian Scale with Characteristic Pitch ♭2

- Family: minor. One degree darker than Aeolian

- Characteristic pitch: ♭2

- Tonic chord: I–7

- Cadence chords: ♭IIMaj7, ♭VII–7

- Subjective effect: stark, somber, brooding

- Problems: ♭IIMaj7 or ♭III7 to ♭VIMaj7 can tonicize ♭VI

Tonic Phrygian Voicings

Modal progressions usually feature long stretches of the tonic chord. Phrygian has a very distinctive characteristic pitch, but its ♭9 relation to the root presents special difficulties not shared by the other modes. When exposed as a tension on a conventional tonic chord, it creates a harsh dissonance.

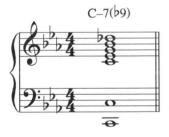

FIG. 9.21. Dissonant Voicing of Phrygian Tonic Chord

To circumvent this problem, the tonic chord is often voiced as I7sus4(♭2). The non-tertian structure and the lack of the minor third mitigate the effect of the minor ninth against the root. Here are three typical voicings:

FIG. 9.22. Tonic Phrygian Voicing with ♭2 and sus4

A related strategy is to use a series of quartal voicings over a tonic pedal or ostinato.

FIG. 9.23. Stepwise Quartal Phrygian Voicings

The open quartal sound and stepwise parallel structures subsume the ♭2 scale degree into an overall Phrygian texture. Often, only two or three of the possible voicings are used, freely reordered as necessary.

Standard Phrygian Harmonic Phrases

As in the other models we have shown, this example contains liberal amounts of the tonic chord. It also has IV–7 for variety, and the characteristic ♭IIMaj7 chord at a climactic point.

FIG. 9.24. Effective Phrygian Passage

Notice that neither the chords nor the melody reveal the Phrygian character until the final bar. Up until that point, this could just as easily be an Aeolian passage. This ambiguity can be a useful creative tool. When the tune doesn't "show its hand" right away, the uncertainty captures and holds our interest.

A slightly less common cadence chord is ♭VII–7. It is a little more subtle than ♭IIMaj7: it lacks the characteristic half-step root motion, and is identical in quality to the I–7 chord. Still, it is a unique harmonic function that clearly signals Phrygian when used in a progression. In figure 9.25, it is expressed as ♭VII–6, but the melody completes the chord scale.

FIG. 9.25. ♭VII– As a Cadence Chord

Locrian

- Family: minor. Darkest possible version

- Characteristic pitch: ♭5

- Tonic chord: I–7♭5

- Cadence chords: none

- Subjective effect: unbalanced, super-dark, circular

- Problems: Diminished fifth renders the tonic chord very unstable; a contradiction in terms. Every other chord in the mode sounds more stable.

There are fleeting instances of a sustained –7♭5 chord being used as an accompaniment to a melodic figure (e.g., "Inner Urge" by Joe Henderson), but as a modal system with movement to and from a stable tonic, Locrian tunes (or even phrases) simply do not exist in the repertoire. Experiment if you must, but...

Tunes for Analysis

Check out the compositions that follow to see the concepts from the chapter at work.
As you listen or play through them, ask yourself:

- Which mode or modes are at work in each?

- What other harmonic techniques do you see?

- What is the form of each tune?

- Where in the form do modal cadences occur?

- What are the cadence chords?

- How does the melody contribute to the modal sound?

- What kind of voicings are used?

- Do tensions contribute to the modal sound?

The Slip-Up

By Joe Mulholland

FIG. 9.26. "The Slip-Up"

Moonlight on Spot Pond

TRACK 14

By Joe Mulholland

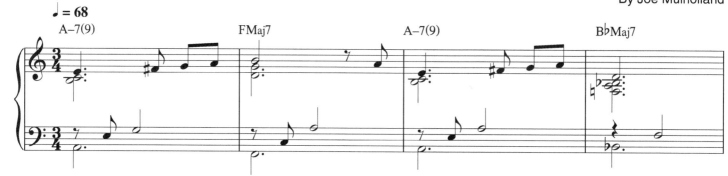

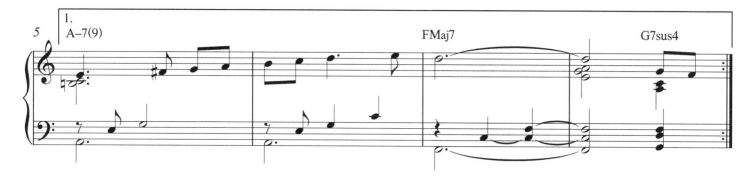

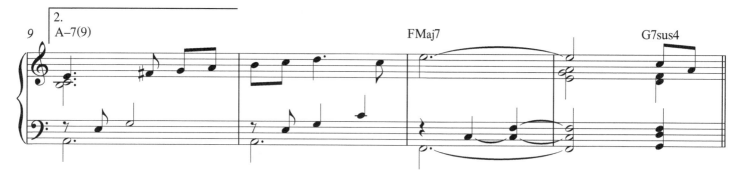

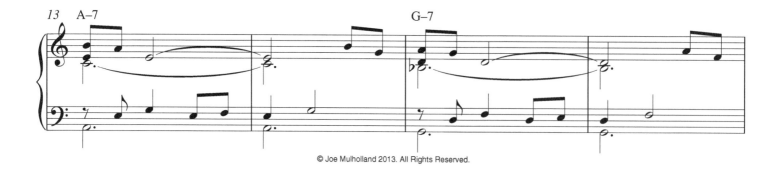

FIG. 9.27. "Moonlight on Spot Pond"

CHAPTER 10

Outside of the Box: Constant Structure Progressions

Throughout this book, we have been looking at ways of expanding the diatonic universe. Many of the techniques we have explored involve chromatic variations of familiar "inside" harmonic events: for example, secondary dominants as alterations of diatonic chords. This chapter will take that idea a step farther and bring us to the far edge of functional harmony. The chord qualities will be comfortingly familiar, but their relationships in some cases will be new and different. First, a partial definition: constant structure progressions employ a single chord quality.

At first glance, one could make the case that these four-bar phrases are examples of constant structure:

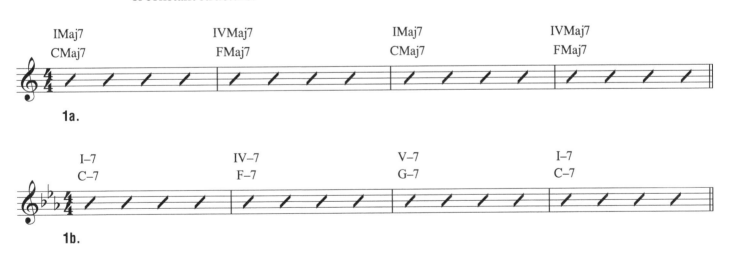

FIG. 10.1. Major and Minor Diatonic Progressions

But the Roman numeral analyses show that they are easy to explain as diatonic progressions, one in C major and one in C natural minor. A basic principle of analysis is that the simplest explanation is the best. Listen to these progressions and then find the tonic note in your voice or on your instrument; there is no doubt that they are clearly centered on C and are functional in their respective modalities. Figure 10.1a is clearly a tonic-subdominant vamp; figure 10.1b is a tonic-subdominant-cadential chord pattern typical of Aeolian modal tunes.

A more subtle example of the same phenomenon involves a mix of diatonic and modal interchange chords:

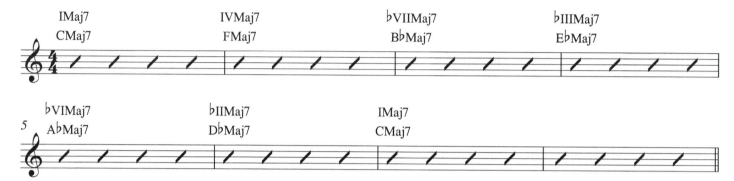

FIG. 10.2. C Major Progression with Extensive Modal Interchange

The modal interchange is extensive, maybe even extreme, but the tonic IMaj7 at the beginning and the end anchors the progression in C major; the IVMaj7 in measure 2 helps confirm it. The DbMaj7 is a common Phrygian cadence chord. When it is followed by IMaj7, it emphasizes the return to C as a tonic center. At a moderate to fast tempo, there is no sense that we have left the key of C major.

So let us not complicate our thinking by over-interpreting subsets of familiar functional progressions. For our purposes, if a passage can reasonably be interpreted as being functional in a key, it needs no special analytical tool to unlock its workings.

Compare the passages above to the final eight measures of Joe Henderson's "Inner Urge."

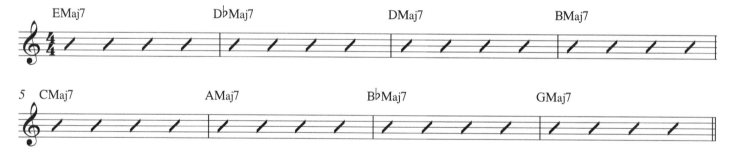

FIG. 10.3. Patterned Constant Structure Progression

Roman numeral analysis breaks down because no key can accommodate all these chords. The only thing linking them is their consistent chord quality and their motivic root motion: descending minor thirds and ascending minor seconds, in a repeating pattern. This suggests a more precise definition: *constant structure progressions are organized, non-functional harmonic phrases employing a single chord quality.*

> *"Constant structure progressions are organized, non-functional harmonic phrases employing a single chord quality."*

Organized means that the progressions are not merely random; there is some principle or device that imposes order on the changes. The mechanically regular root motion in figure 10.3 is one of the hallmarks of constant structure passages. Although it is not always present, an intervallic pattern helps the ear make sense of the non-diatonic collection of chords. Some of the chords in passages like this may happen to be diatonic, but if a phrase composed of identical chord qualities cannot be cleanly analyzed using familiar functional categories, it merits the constant structure label.

Extended constant structure passages like the one in "Inner Urge" are more common in jazz compositions from the late 1960s onward. In standard tunes, it is much more typical to see constant structure in the form of chromatic approaches to functional harmonic goals in a progression. This is really localized parallelism rather than true constant stucture comprising the important chords in a progression.

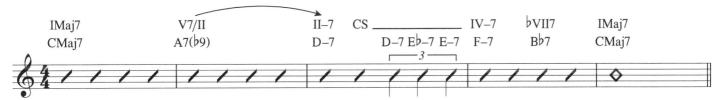

FIG. 10.4. Minor Seventh Constant Structure Chromatic Approach to IV–7

Constant structure is a powerful tool for composition, since it can temporarily suspend the clear sense of key before a return to functional relationships. Figure 10.5a is clearly in C major and sounds as though it will continue in that key, barring a deceptive resolution or other unexpected outcome. Figure 10.5b cannot be pinned down to any particular tonality despite its identical diatonic melody.

FIG. 10.5A. Diatonic Melody Harmonized Conventionally

FIG. 10.5B. Same Melody Harmonized with Constant Structure Major Sevenths

Because they are non-functional, harmonies like 10.5b are often created to add an element of surprise or ambiguity to an otherwise tonal section. They commonly merge back to the diatonic through a familiar pivot chord relationship.

Finally, constant structure can be tied to the melody. Instead of an intervallic root motion pattern, a familiar melody can provide the sonic anchor that helps the listener to accept a non-functional progression. The relationship to the melody can be based on a fixed interval, like a major ninth:

FIG. 10.6A. Constant Structure Major Sevenths, Matched Harmonic and Melodic Rhythm

...or it can vary freely:

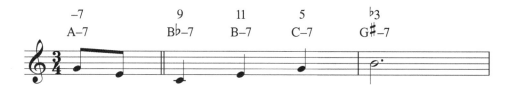

FIG. 10.6B. Same Melody with Constant Structure Minor Sevenths

Summary of Constant Structure Passages

These are the most common uses of constant structure passages:

1. Chromatic approach to a diatonic chord (the first two measures of John Coltrane's "Moment's Notice")

2. Extended root motion by a single interval, especially half steps (the bridge to Thelonious Monk's "Well You Needn't"), minor thirds, or perfect fourths

3. Root motion creating an intervallic pattern, either regular, additive, or subtractive

4. Tying the chords to the melody, either in a parallel relationship (the last two measures of the A section of Michel LeGrand's "Watch What Happens," the first two measures of Benny Golson's "Along Came Betty"), contrary motion, or multiple harmonizations of a single pitch

EXERCISES

1. Write all the major seventh chords (including modal interchange) that could harmonize this pitch in the key of C, and label the melody/harmony relationship:

FIG. 10.7. Major Seventh Possibilities Against Scale Degree 5

2. What organizing principle is at work in this constant structure harmonization of two nearly identical phrases?

FIG. 10.8. Patterned Minor Seventh Harmonization of a C Major Melody

"The Same Sky" uses constant structure in some phrases as a compositional
element. What other concepts from previous chapters are embodied in this tune?

The Same Sky

TRACK 15

Joe Mulholland

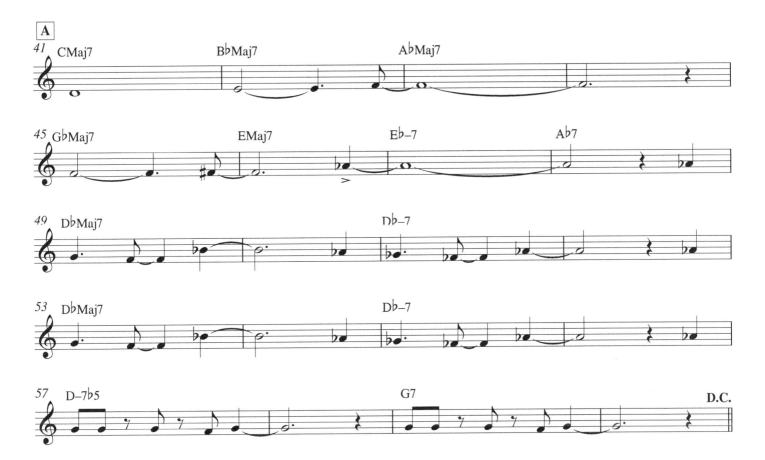

FIG. 10.9. "The Same Sky" with Constant Structure Passages

RECOMMENDED LISTENING

Jazz tunes that feature constant structure:

- Joe Henderson, "Black Narcissus" and "Inner Urge"

- Jimmy Heath, "A Sound for Sore Ears"

- Hal Galper, "Triple Play"

- Pat Metheny, "Timeline"

CHAPTER 11

Jazz Voicings

A comprehensive treatment of jazz voicings would fill a book of its own. There are so many possibilities depending on the instrument, ensemble, and style that we mostly leave it up to you to take the theoretical ideas we present here and apply them in the way that suits you best.

Nevertheless, there are six categories of voicings that are fundamental to the sound of jazz in the last fifty years and merit a closer look:

1. 3-note voicings: guide tones and roots

2. 4-note voicings: guide tones, roots, and an added tension

3. 5-note voicings: 4-way close voicings and roots (with or without tension substitutions)

4. *Polychord* voicings: tertian stacks in which the tensions form an independent triad over the essential chord

5. *Hybrid* voicings: triads or seventh chords consisting of tensions and upper chord tones, sounded over a root

6. *Quartal* voicings: arrangements of chord tones and tensions based mostly or completely on perfect fourths

These are *not* new types of chords, merely interesting arrangements of familiar ones. Any song can be arranged and played using these techniques without changing the essential identity and function of the chords.

3-NOTE VOICINGS

The 3-note voicing is the most essential expression of the chord symbol. Since the most important information about a chord's identity is carried in its root, 3, and 7, the perfect 5 can be omitted without losing the essential sound of the chord.

FIG. 11.1. Basic 3-Note Voicing

The 3-note voicings provide a smooth background accompaniment to a melody when the upper tones are voice-led smoothly. Movement by common tone, by step, or at the most a third will ensure this. When realizing a chord progression with 3-note voicings, the cycle of root motion determines the voice leading procedure from one chord to the next.

When root motion is by cycle 5, the 3 of a chord will move to the 7 of the next chord and vice versa.

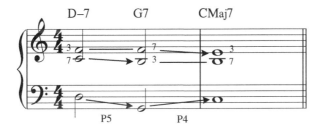

FIG. 11.2. Cycle 5 Root Motion, 7 moves to 3, 3 to 7

When root motion is by cycle 2, the most efficient voice leading is via parallel motion. Chord 7's will connect to 7's and 3's to 3's.

FIG. 11.3. Cycle 2 Root Motion, Parallel Voice Leading

When root motion is by cycle 3, efficient voice leading can move in either direction. At least one voice will have to move by a third:

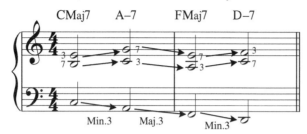

FIG. 11.4. Cycle 3 Root Motion, Variable Direction, No Common Tones

The following progression contains all three cycles of root motion. The upper two voices of the chords create lines that move efficiently by conjunct motion.

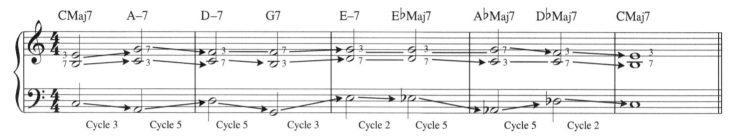

FIG. 11.5. Mixed-Interval Root Motion, 3's and 7's in the Treble

These melodic lines are called *guide tone lines* because the 3's and 7's are the most meaningful tones and guide the ear through the chord progression. If 7sus4, Maj6, or min6 chords appear in a progression, 4 is substituted for 3 and 6 replaces 7.

ADDING A TENSION TO CREATE A FOURTH VOICE

To add more color, a tension can be stacked above a 3-note voicing. As always, the choice of tension is determined or limited by the chord's function.

- When the 3 is the uppermost note of the voicing, add 13.

- When the 7 is the uppermost note, add 9.

- When the appropriate tension is unavailable, the chord's 5 (or an optional tension) may be substituted to maintain the texture. This ensures a linear connection in the new fourth voice.

FIG. 11.6. Progression from Figure 11.5 with Added Tensions above Guide Tones

5-NOTE VOICINGS

A fuller voicing results from *4-way close* technique. Over roots in the bass, all four notes of the chord are voiced as close together as possible. The starting position is arbitrary.

FIG. 11.7. 4-Way Close Voicings of CMaj7

The voice leading procedure for 4-way close technique is identical to that of the 3-note voicings on the preceding pages; thus, the same guide tone lines will appear in these examples along with the root and 5. When the root motion is cycle 5, connect the common tones between the chords and move the remaining notes downward by step. Once again, 3 will connect to 7 and vice versa.

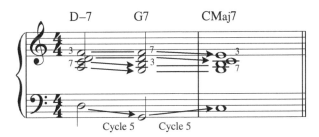

FIG. 11.8. II V I Pattern with 4-Way Close Voicing

When the root motion is cycle 2, move all voices in parallel motion:

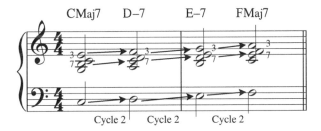

FIG. 11.9. Cycle 2 Progresssion, 4-Way Close Voice Leading

When the root motion is cycle 3, connect the common tones between chords and move the last note by step. Because of the abundance of common tones that occur in cycle 3 progressions, the guide tones will migrate from voice to voice:

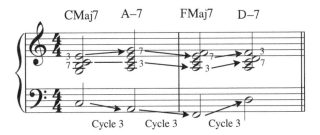

FIG. 11.10. Cycle 3 Progresssion, 4-Way Close Voice Leading

TENSION SUBSTITUTIONS ON 4-WAY CLOSE VOICINGS

If the root is present in the bass, the root in the upper voices of a 4-way close voicing is redundant. It can be replaced by tension 9, when available.

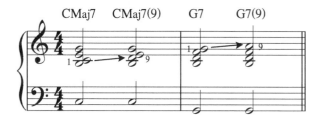

FIG. 11.11. Tension Substitution: 9 for 1

The 5 is a non-essential chord tone and can be replaced by tension 13, when available:

FIG. 11.12. Tension Substitution: 13 for 5

Or both tensions can be substituted:

FIG. 11.13. Tension Substitution: 9 for 1 and 13 for 5, When Available

Voicings with tension substitution are a mainstay of jazz comping, whether on guitar, piano, organ, or vibraphone. Take the time to discover as many variations as you can.

POLYCHORD VOICINGS

Polychord voicings consist of a lower structure that contains only chord tones of the basic function and an upper-structure triad or seventh chord drawn from its chord scale.

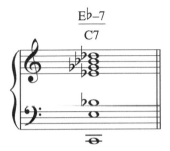

FIG. 11.14. C7(alt), Polychord Voicing

The upper structure contains at least one tension. (Harmonic avoid notes are not included in either structure, for obvious reasons.) Polychord construction offers the conceptual advantage of combining two easily understood objects to create something richer and more resonant.

Polychord symbols are usually written as an upper-structure chord symbol separated from the lower-structure chord symbol by a horizontal line as in figure 11.14.

CONSTRUCTING POLYCHORDS

Let's create a polychord voicing for IMaj7 in the key of C. The lower structure will consist of the chord tones of CMaj7. Now we need to select a triad from the chord scale that contains at least one available tension and no harmonic avoid tones. This eliminates any triad that contains the avoid tone S4. So, D–, F, and B° are not options:

FIG. 11.15. Triads with Avoid Notes Eliminated

Of those remaining, CMaj and E– offer no tensions, but GMaj contains 9. Its remaining tones are the 5 and 7 of the lower structure, so G is a good choice for an upper-structure triad.

The upper-structure triad can be positioned as desired. Omitting the 5 from the lower structure makes the overall sonority of the voicing less dense.

FIG. 11.16. Polychord Voicings for CMaj7, with and without the 5 in Lower Structure

A– also seems a viable choice for an upper-structure triad as it contains 13, but the fact that it contains the root of the lower structure makes it problematic. If its 3rd is positioned anywhere other than a half step above the lower structure, it creates the interval of a minor 9 with the 7 of the chord:

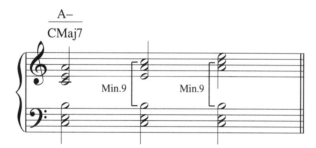

FIG. 11.17. Difficulties with Polychord Voicing Containing the Root of IMaj7

As you'll recall from earlier chapters, this is generally deemed too dissonant to be acceptable on a tonic function chord.

CMaj7 as the IV chord in G major does not present these problems. With a Lydian chord scale and no avoid notes, there is a greater number of available upper-structure triads. These are all voicings of CMaj7, differing only in the amount of doubling and tensions.

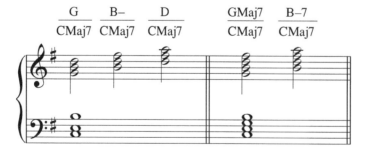

FIG. 11.18. Polychord Voicings for IVMaj7

D7/CMaj7 is omitted because the top note of the D7 upper structure creates a dissonant minor 9 with the major 7 of the basic chord.

Dominant Polychords

Chord scales on other chord qualities yield other upper-structure possibilities. Let's look at the altered dominant scale as an example.

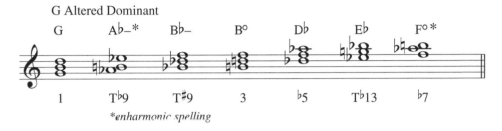

FIG. 11.19. Upper-Structure Resources from the Altered Dominant Scale

Aside from GMaj and B°, which only replicate lower-structure tones, the other five triads all offer one or more tensions and make fine upper-structure choices. Each combination yields a slightly different color from the chord scale.

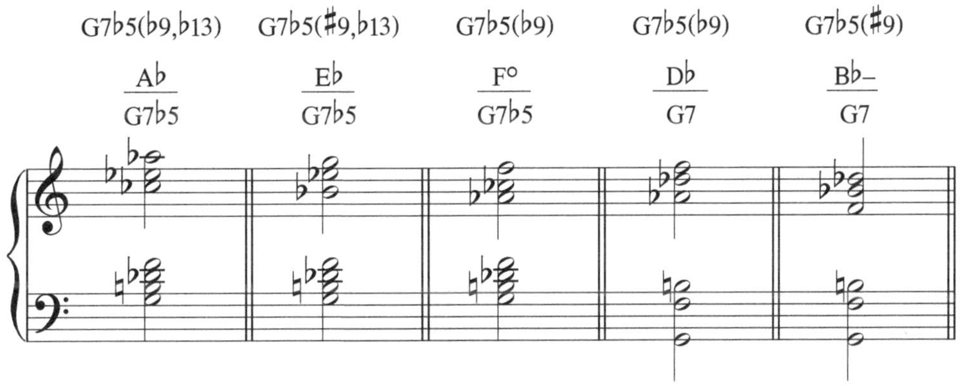

FIG. 11.20. Polychord Voicings for G7(alt)

Consistent polychord voicings create a dense, complex texture with great potential for chromatic voice leading in the upper structure. In figure 11.21, optional chord scale colors for all the chords except II–7 and IMaj7 have been used for this purpose.

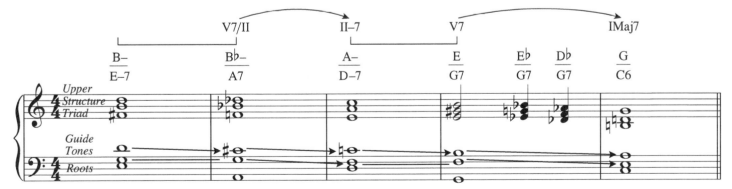

FIG. 11.21. III VI/II II V I Progression Voice-Led with Polychords

- The upper structures are voice-led as an independent layer above the guide tones.

- The guide tones provide the essential voice leading.

- The roots move in typical cycle 5 pattern.

- The analysis symbols reflect the fundamental chord functions.

Polychord Summary

- Polychords are voicings with tensions in the upper structure grouped as triads or seventh chords above the essential chord tones.

- Harmonic avoid notes are omitted from the voicing.

- Diatonic tensions are often altered to add color or work around an avoid note.

- The lower-structure may be in close position or spread.

- The upper-structure tones may be close-voiced, spread, or inverted as desired.

- The perfect 5 is often omitted, but can be included if it does not interfere with tensions such as ♭13 or ♯11.

- Polychord voicings are expressed as an upper-structure chord symbol over the lower-structure chord symbol, separated by a horizontal line: $\frac{A\flat}{C7}$.

HYBRID VOICINGS AND INVERSIONS

Hybrid voicings, sometimes called slash chords or ambi-chords, typically omit the 3 and emphasize one or more tensions instead. Hybrid voicings consist of a chord root and three or more tones selected from the "upper structure" of the extended chord.

"Hybrid voicings consist of a chord root and three or more tones selected from the 'upper structure' of the extended chord."

The result is a voicing that can be described as a triad or seventh chord "grafted" onto an apparently unrelated root: for example, G over C, with the chord symbol G/C. Typically the root is separated from the upper-structure tones by more than an octave, emphasizing the impression of independence between the two components of the voicing. In an ensemble, the bassist will hold down the root, allowing the pianist or guitarist to play higher up in the branches, so to speak.

Compare these three voicings of CMaj7: the first is a basic root position voicing, the second a polychord, and the third a hybrid.

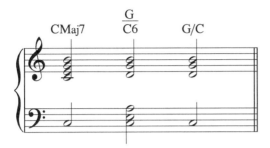

FIG. 11.22. 4-Way Close, Polychord, and Hybrid Voicings for CMaj7

Hybrid voicings give an arrangement a little more "air," or transparency. They are the flip side of polychords: whereas polychords have all the chord tones and tensions, hybrids are a "low-calorie" voicing, missing that tasty 3. Without the definitive major or minor third, a chord has an ambiguous quality (hence the term "ambi-chord"). But tonality results from *all* the notes in a tune operating in relation to one another. The overall collection of tones in a passage effectively suggests the missing notes to the ear. In fact, root motion alone is enough to strongly suggest functional identity in a good progression. The characteristic tensions associated with each chord provide further confirmation of that identity.

Constructing hybrid voicings is straightforward. Here is the process for IMaj7 in the key of C:

1. Extend the chord to the 13th, using harmonic analysis to determine the available tensions and avoid note.

FIG. 11.23. Chord Scale for IMaj7 in C Major

2. Drop the root an octave.

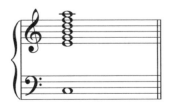

FIG. 11.24. CMaj7 with the Root Isolated in the Bass

3. Eliminate the 3.

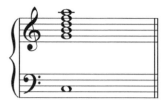

FIG. 11.25. Same Voicing without a 3

4. Eliminate the avoid note, S4:

FIG. 11.26. S4 Eliminated

5. Identify a triad or seventh chord in the upper structure and name the voicing.

G/C

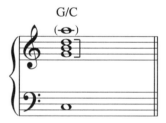

FIG. 11.27. Upper-Structure Available Triad over Root

G7/C was *not* an option, since F is a harmonic avoid note on the tonic chord. The 13 could have been included in the upper-structure voicing, creating G(add9)/C.

G(add9)/C

FIG. 11.28. Upper-Structure Triad with Added 9 (13 of the Chord)

This increases the level of color and tension, and it would ideally be matched by other voicings of similar density in a passage.

In context, the upper structures are usually arranged to create efficient voice leading between successive chords. Here is a IMaj7 VI-7 IVMaj7 V7sus4 progression in C major, using seventh chords voiced as hybrids.

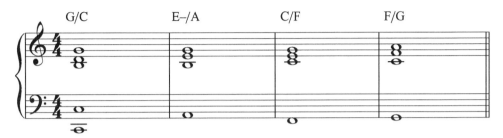

FIG. 11.29. I VI IV V Progression Voiced with Hybrids

Hybrid Chord Symbols and Analysis

Hybrid chord symbols appear similar to inversions, but inversions have a chord tone in the bass, like CMaj7/E. Hybrid chord symbols place an *apparently* unrelated triad or seventh chord over the root: G/C, or G-7/C. This can be a little confusing to read, since the root comes last in the chord symbol, but with practice, you will be able to interpret them quickly and accurately.

Analyzing hybrid progressions is simple, with a little detective work. Focus on the root first, then deduce the full chord quality that is implied by the tensions in the upper structure. Let's follow the evidence in this C major example:

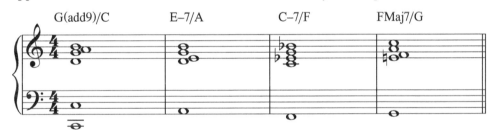

FIG. 11.30. C Major Progression with Modal Interchange Voiced with Hybrids

Measures 1, 2, and 4 are diatonic: despite the missing 3's, they function as IMaj7, VI-7, and V7sus4. Let's look at measure 3.

1.   The F in the bass in measure 3 tells us that C-7/F is some kind of a IV chord.

2.   The C at the bottom of the upper structure is a perfect 5, so it is not -7♭5.

3.   E♭, G, and B♭ are ♭7, 9, and 11. Only minor 7, dominant, and 7sus4 chords have those notes in their chord scales.

4.   IV-7, a modal interchange chord, is a very familiar minor subdominant chord preceding V7. So although F7sus4 is a possibility, C-7/F functions most clearly as F-7, IV-7.

Hybrid Voicings of Modal Interchange Chords

The upper structure of each hybrid voicing comes from the chord scale of the function it represents, thus:

- Modal interchange chords that are major seventh in quality (♭IIMaj7, ♭IIIMaj7, ♭VI Maj7, and ♭VIIMaj7) have a Lydian chord scale.

- Modal interchange chords that are minor seventh in quality (I–7, IV–7, and V–7) have a Dorian chord scale.

- Modal interchange chords that are dominant seventh in quality (♭VII7 and ♭VI7) have a Lydian ♭7 chord scale.

Here are hybrid voicings of the most common modal interchange chords in C major:

FIG. 11.31. Hybrid Voicings of Common Modal Interchange Chords

Things to note about these voicings:

- They have four-note upper structures, but triads are also an option.

- V–7 is indistinguishable from V7sus4, but neighboring voicings or a melody that contains B♭ would suggest the missing note.

Dominant Hybrids

Dominant chords present a wide variety of possible hybrid voicings. When deciding the upper structure from a diatonic Mixolydian chord scale, it's best not to think of scale degree 4 as an avoid tone, but rather as a substitute for the 3: sus4.

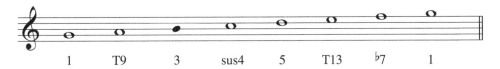

FIG. 11.32. Chord Scale for V7sus4

Since a 7sus4 chord will function syntactically as a dominant, this approach yields three viable hybrids within the Mixolydian scale:

FIG. 11.33. Hybrids Using Sus4 as a Substitute for Dominant

A more colorful solution is to apply the altered dominant chord scale to either the primary or a secondary dominant. Either ♭5 ♭7 ♭9 alone (D♭/G in C) or two successive upper-structure groups will create an altered dominant sound.

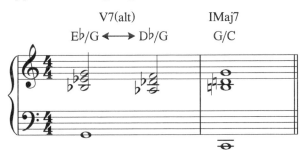

FIG. 11.34. Altered Dominant Hybrid Combination for G7

E♭/G is technically an inversion, but when paired successively with D♭/G, the upper structures sound all the tones of the G7 altered chord scale except B natural, the major 3.

Odds and Ends

While the primary formula for creating the *ambi-sound* is to omit the third of the chord, there are a few combinations that have a hybrid-like sonority but actually contain thirds. These are:

FIG. 11.35. Hybrid Voicings for Less-Common Chord Qualities

The first two voicings can be used as colorful tonic chords and the third as a dominant function chord that includes T♭9 and T13.

Pat Metheny, Michael Brecker, and Richie Beirach and the Yellowjackets are just a few of the artists who use hybrid voicings extensively in their compositions. The following summary will help you decipher hybrids in tunes you encounter, regardless of style.

Hybrid Summary

- Hybrids are specific voicings of familiar chord qualities.

- The root is *always* in the bass.

- The 3 is almost always omitted.

- Upper-structure pitches—5, 7, 9, 11, and/or 13—comprise the rest of the voicing.

- Upper-structure tones are usually voiced at least an octave above the root.

- Hybrids are notated as an upper-structure triad or seventh over the root, separated by a diagonal line: GMaj7/C.

- Hybrids are analyzed from the root.

- Major seventh chords can be expressed by a major triad (for IMaj7) or a Maj7 chord a twelfth above the root (for ♭IIMaj7 and other Lydian chord scales).

- Minor seventh chords can be expressed by a minor triad or minor seventh chord a twelfth above the root.

- Dominant 7 chords can be expressed in three ways:

    - by a minor seventh chord a twelfth above the root,

    - a major triad a diminished twelfth above the root, or

    - an augmented triad a diminished twelfth above the root.

Exercise

Voice this progression using hybrid voicings by putting roots in the bass and upper structures in the treble.

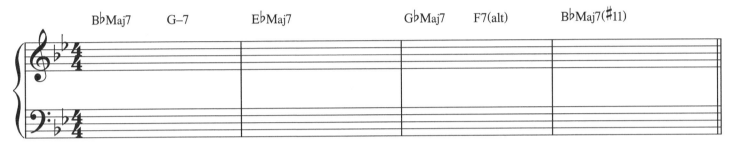

FIG. 11.36. Progression in B♭ Major to Be Voiced Using Hybrids

QUARTAL VOICINGS

Yet another conceptual option is to arrange chord tones and available tensions vertically in fourths: *quartal* voicing. Voicings that consist mostly of fourths have a particularly powerful, percussive quality that has been an idiomatic feature of jazz harmony for the last fifty years or so. Like hybrids, quartal voicings can be ambiguous and depend partly on context for the ear to interpret them in a key. Stacked fourths are perfectly regular, and therefore inherently ambiguous. Consider this stack of fourths:

FIG. 11.37. Stacked Fourths

Depending on the underlying bass note, the voicing could suggest:

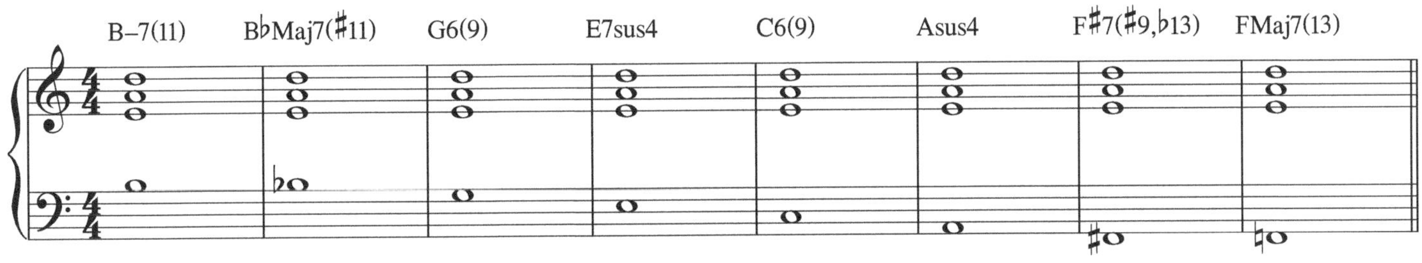

FIG. 11.38. Stacked Fourths over Different Roots: Eight Different Chords

In each instance, the presence of a root creates intervallic relationships with the stack of fourths that allow identifiable chord tones and tensions to emerge.

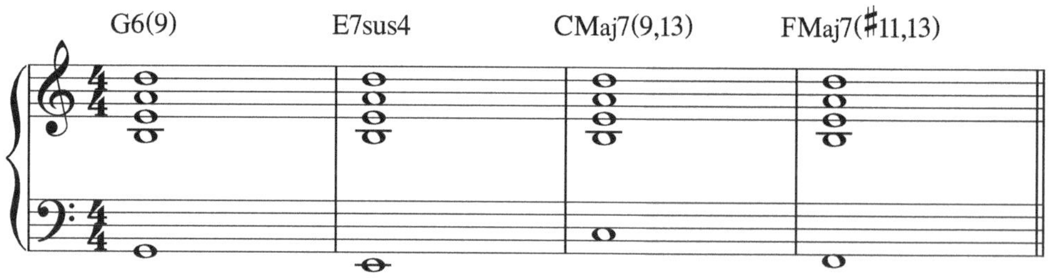

FIG. 11.39. Four Notes in Fourths over Different Roots: Four Different Chords.

Adding another fourth to the stack adds a little more aural information.

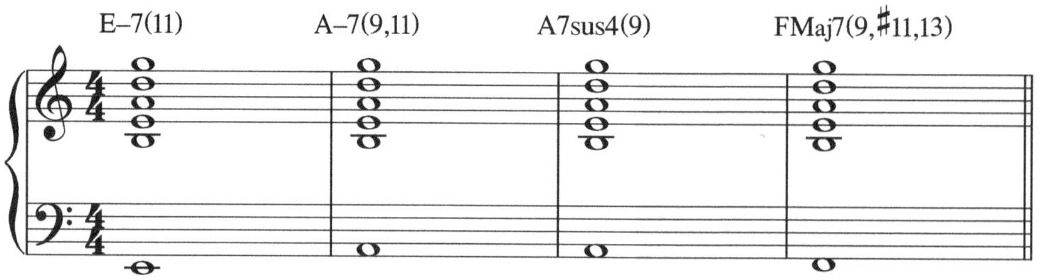

FIG. 11.40. Five Notes in Fourths over Different Roots: The Same Four Chords More Fully Expressed.

Quartal voicings can be especially challenging to pin down. However, we can give a clear starting framework and describe some of the principles that are in common use. This will allow you to understand examples you encounter and begin to build voicings that work for you.

Building Quartal Voicings

1. The root is critical.

   The root of the chord is essential to give a quartal voicing its identity. It can be included in the quartal stack or in the bass.

2. Look for 3's, 6's, and 7's.

   These are the chord tones that carry the most harmonic information; if possible, include all of them in the voicing. The perfect fourth between scale degrees 3 and 6 or 7 and 3 is the ideal jumping-off point for a quartal voicing. Adding another fourth will yield 9 or 13.

C6(9)

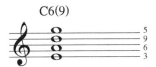

FIG. 11.41A. Fourths Starting with the 3 of a C Chord

CMaj7

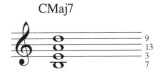

FIG. 11.41B. Fourths Starting with the 7 of a C Chord

In some voicings, the 3, 6, and 7 are higher in the voicing, but in general, the closer they are to the bottom of the stack, the more clearly they signal the chord quality. Because diatonic chords are *not* perfectly symmetrical, they cannot all be expressed by a rigid system of perfect fourths. To create a minor 6 chord, the *augmented* fourth from ♭3 to 6 creates the two defining chord voices. Continue building perfect fourths above the 6 to round out the voicing: (1) ♭3 6 9 5. The root can be doubled on top by adding another fourth to the stack. Or one can "shorten" the last fourth and top the stack with a major third for a minor(Maj7) voicing that includes T9 and T13.

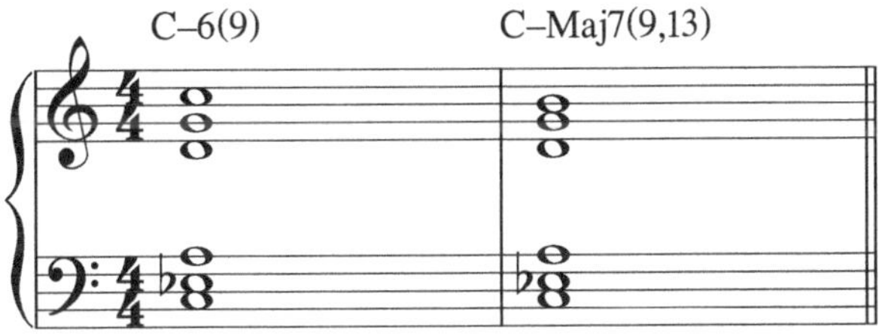

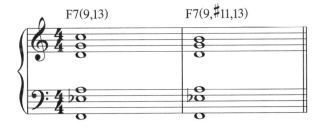

FIG. 11.42. C–6/9, Using an Augmented Fourth in the Bass and Doubled Root. C–(Maj7) with a Major Third on Top.

Changing the root creates dominant 7 voicings.

F7(9,13)   F7(9,♯11,13)

FIG. 11.43. Same Upper Notes Creating Quartal Voicings for F7

For 7(♯9), the diminished fifth from 3 to ♭7 (enharmonically an augmented fourth) defines the guide tones. Add a perfect fourth to get ♯9, then a diminished fourth (major third) at the top of the voicing to complete the chord quality: (1) 3 ♭7 ♯9 5. *Or* continue to stack fourths for a voicing that includes T♭13 and T♭9. Add a final fourth for a complete altered dominant voicing.

FIG. 11.44. C7(♯9) and Further Quartal Extensions Adding Tensions

Exercise

Create quartal voicings for these chords. The root is in the bass. Build a stack of fourths above the given note in the treble clef. Use your ear to determine how many fourths can be piled up before the chord sound is compromised. When these are thoroughly understood, continue on to the other diatonic chords. Choose the chord tone or tension from which to start and see what you come up with. How high can you stack 'em?!

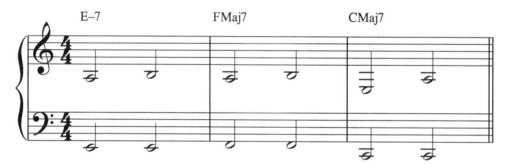

FIG. 11.45. Build Quartal Voicings for Diatonic Sevenths

VOICING SUMMARY

As we stated at the outset, an exhaustive study of voicings would fill a book on its own. There is much more to discover, such as drop 2, drop 2 and 4, mixed interval voicings, and clusters. Jazz players are constantly looking for that "lost chord."

We wish you the best as you set out on your own personal search! For further exploration of this topic, we recommend *Modern Jazz Voicings* by Ted Pease and Ken Pullig, also published by Berklee Press.

FOR FURTHER STUDY

"Smooth Sailing" is a medium-tempo tune that has been arranged using techniques from this chapter: guide tones, 4-way close, hybrids, polychords, and quartal voicings. Listen or play through it, then answer these questions:

- In measures 1–4, name the chord tones that are in the treble clef. Draw ties between the common tones.

- In measures 5–8, supply a complete chord symbol, including tensions where appropriate.

- In measures 9–12, add hybrid chord symbols, consistent with the example in measure 9.

- In measures 13–16, add polychord symbols, consistent with the example in measure 13.

- In measures 17–20, indentify the chord tones and tensions in each quartal voicing.

- What is the form of the tune?

- Where are the deceptive resolutions? What purpose do they serve?

- Do a complete harmonic analysis of the tune.

Smooth Sailing

TRACK 16

Joe Mulholland

FIG. 11.46. "Smooth Sailing" with Voicings. Note that the melody is performed in octaves.

Smooth Sailing

Joe Mulholland

FIG. 11.47. "Smooth Sailing" Lead Sheet

The Standard Deceptive Resolutions of V7

The following progressions are often employed as phrase extensions at the ends of tunes to create a final extended ending or coda. The jazz half cadence in the first measure of each phrase creates a strong expectation of resolution to the IMaj7 chord. This expectation is thwarted by the appearance of an unexpected chord on the downbeat of the next measure. Because each of these moves is tonally logical, they have come to be regarded as *standard deceptive resolutions* that will extend what seems like an obviously closed-ended phrase. In addition to extending a phrase or section of a composition, these deceptive resolutions and subsequent progressions can be used to create interludes in arrangements, or to facilitate modulation to distantly related keys.

Figure A.1 is the traditional deceptive cadence. The move to VI– is logical because its third is the tonic note of the key and VI–7 is a tonic function chord. The deceptive cadence is generally followed by a full jazz cadence to bring the piece to a close. When used mid-song, the progression can continue in any fashion.

FIG. A.1. Deceptive Cadence: V7 to VI–7

Figure A.2 is the *extended turn-around* ending. The move to III–7 is logical because it is a member of the tonic function family. The cycle 5 progression III–7 V7/II II–7 V7 may be repeated multiple times before a final cadence to IMaj7. III–7 can be treated diatonically or as a related II by adding non-diatonic tension 9 for a bright lift. III–7♭5 can also be used in this progression.

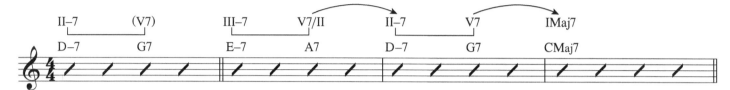

FIG. A.2. V7 to III–7, Starting an Extended Turaround

Figure A.3 is often heard as an ending for slow ballads. The move to ♯IV–7♭5 is logical because its 3, 5, and 7 are the tonic function VI– triad in the key, and the tritone in V7 resolves to the upper two voices in the chord. The descending move from V7 to ♯IV precipitates a descending chromatic bass line that eventually cadences on IMaj7. ♭III°7 can be replaced by subV7/II or ♭IIIMaj7; subV7 can be replaced by ♭IIMaj7.

FIG. A.3. V7 to ♯IV–7♭5 Triggering a Chromatic Descent to Tonic

Figure A.4 is another popular ballad ending. The move to ♭IIMaj7 on a strong metrical stress is quite shocking but there is a thread of tonal logic: its 7 is the tonic note in the key. This creates a surprising delayed resolution to IMaj7, completed by the Phrygian cadence. Think of it as a *very* dark "Amen cadence."

FIG. A.4. V7 to ♭IIMaj7: Delayed Resolution to IMaj7

Figure A.5 is a wonderful deceptive resolution. It is tonally logical because the 3 and 7 of ♭VI are the highly stable tonic and fifth scale degrees in the key. ♭VIMaj7 then moves down by fifth to ♭II and ♭II to IMaj7 by half step: a strong progression for a final ending. ♭VIMaj7 may also progress to I directly or by way of ♭VII.

FIG. A.5. V7 to ♭VIMaj7

In figure A.6, V7 moves unexpectedly but logically to the tonic minor modal interchange chord ♭III. The subsequent cycle 5 root motion to ♭VI and ♭II leads then to a satisfying subdominant minor cadence to I.

FIG. A.6. V7 to ♭III: Tonic Modal Interchange, Then Constant Structure Approach to I Maj7

Figure A.7 is unusual. The move from V7 to ♭VII is facilitated by common tones *Re* and *Fa*. The inclusion of ♭VII completes the cycle 5 series of parallel minor modal interchange chords of a Maj7 quality.

FIG. A.7. V7 to ♭VIIMaj7: Cycle 5 Constant Structure Approach to IMaj7

Non-Resolving Dominant Seventh Chords

Dominant seventh chords normally form a peak of harmonic tension that creates an expectation of resolution; that resolution may be fulfilled, delayed, or subverted. But jazz benefits from the synergy between European tonal practices, African influences, and specific instrumental practices. It is a living language that evolves as it absorbs ideas from a wide variety of musical sources. In keeping with this flexible tradition, dominant chords have come to have other uses besides their usual role in tension-resolution patterns. This appendix describes the contexts in which dominant 7 *quality* chords can operate without dominant *function*: non-dominant dominants!

Special Function Dominants

In a clearly-defined tonal area, the primary dominant V7 and its subV7 will *always* create the expectation of resolution: either down a fifth or down a half step, respectively. The situation is not always so clear-cut with secondary dominants and secondary subV7's. Certain contexts or patterns create an environment in which these chords do *not* resolve or do not have an expectation of resolution. Dominant chords in these situations can be called *special function dominants* or *color chords.*

There can be debate about whether these non-resolving patterns constitute a disguised form of deceptive resolution. We encourage you to explore this ambiguity on a case-by-case basis.

Some of them are familiar from earlier chapters:

IV7, the blues subdominant, is an integral part of jazz language and is widely used or substituted in major key progressions where a bluesy flavor is desired. It typically returns to IMaj7 or I7. Progression to ♭IIIMaj7, ♭VI, or ♭VII are also common.

- Duke Ellington, "Warm Valley"

- Clifford Brown, "Tiny Capers"

- Peter DeRose and Bert Shefter, "The Lamp Is Low"

- Anne Ronnell, "Willow Weep for Me"

- Walter Gross, "Tenderly"

- Tadd Dameron, "If You Could See Me Now"

♭VII7 is a subdominant minor modal interchange chord. With VII-7♭5 as a related II-7 and the appropriate harmonic rhythm, it will occasionally function as subV7/VI, but it more often appears on a weak rhythmic stress, then progresses back to IMaj7 or I7. It is often preceded by IV-7.

- Benny Golson, "Killer Joe"

- Benny Goodman/Edgar Sampson/Clarence Profit/Walter Hirsch, "Lullaby in Rhythm"

- Charlier Parker, "Yardbird Suite"

- Thelonious Monk, "I Mean You"

Others appear at first glance to be secondary dominants or secondary subV's, but context, metric position, and non-resolution will blur their functional identity.

Although not common in mainstream jazz harmony, II7 can act as a brighter subdominant, in effect a II chord from the parallel Lydian. It appears in a weaker metric position of the phrase than its identical twin V7/V. It most clearly functions as II7 when it immediately progresses to IV or back to I. Although there is some ambiguity due to the presence of a V7 chord, the following tunes are sometimes analyzed as containing II7:

- Measures 3–4 of Billy Strayhorn's "Take the 'A' Train" and Plater/Bradshaw/Johnson's "Jersey Bounce," measure 8 of Chick Corea's "Bud Powell"

- Jimmy Van Heusen/Johnny Burke, "But Beautiful"

- Michel Legrand, "Watch What Happens"

- Antonio Carlos Jobim, "The Girl from Ipanema"

- Louis Alter, "Do You Know What It Means to Miss New Orleans"

♭III7 could function as a bluesy alternative to ♭IIIMaj7 or as part of a constant structure passage. It is not a feature of the American Songbook repertoire.

III7 is not commonly found, but can function as a constant structure chord (especially in tunes with a I7 blues tonic), or as a reharmonization of I+7. It typically progresses to IVMaj7.

♭VI7 can be thought of as an altered subdominant minor chord. It usually departs from and returns to IMaj7 or I-7.

- Fred Hamm/Dave Bennett/Bert Lown/Chauncey Gray, "Bye-Bye Blues"

- Duke Ellington, "Sweet Zurzday"

- Thelonious Monk, "I Mean You"

- Herbie Hancock, "Canteloupe Island"

VII7 can function as a reharmonization of the tonic auxiliary diminished, I°7. When used as such, it is sometimes preceded by a related II-7♭5. It returns to IMaj7.

- Dizzy Gillespie, "Groovin' High"

- Antonio Carlos Jobim, "Meditation"

- Jazz harmonizations of Victor Schertzinger and Johnny Mercer's "I Remember You" and Victor Young's "Stella By Starlight"

Finally, any combination of these chords and/or other dominants in a *non-resolving* constant structure pattern.

Summary of Special Function Dominants

- any dominant chord other than V7 or subV7 that does not resolve down a fifth or down a half step

- either a Mixolydian or Lydian dominant chord scale is appropriate.

JOE MULHOLLAND

Joe Mulholland is an Associate Professor and the Chair of the Harmony Department at Berklee College of Music. He is passionate about performing and teaching great popular music from the 1930s to the present. This found expression in his work as music director for Didi Stewart and Friends, an award-winning concert and event ensemble from 1985–1998. The group performed the music of Great American Songbook composers, as well as that of the next wave of great rock and pop singers and songwriters from the '60s and '70s. More than a dozen evening-length tribute shows played to sold-out houses in the Boston area. He continues to have an active freelance career as jazz instrumentalist, composer, and vocal accompanist, performing ninety nights a year with his trio, as well as with singers and other ensembles in the Boston area.

Photo by Derek Kouyoumjian

As an ensemble coach and piano instructor at Brown University, Joe found a forum for his interest in the variety of styles jazz embraces. The challenge of finding appropriate repertoire for his three-horn group led him to follow Duke Ellington's practice of writing for the strengths and weaknesses of the individuals at hand. The particular capabilities of the players imposed creative limitations that were paradoxically liberating. A year later, the first of three highly-regarded albums of original compositions and arrangements for the Joe Mulholland Sextet was recorded. Joe continued to listen hard to his band members for inspiration and technical advice, and continues to compose, now mostly for his trio. The latest recording, *Unspoken*, was released in May of 2012 and contains ten new compositions for jazz trio and quartet. In addition to his duties on the Berklee campus, Joe enjoys teaching students from around the world through his popular online course "Jazz Composition" for Berklee Music.

TOM HOJNACKI

Tom Hojnacki enjoys an unusually varied musical career. As a keyboard player, Tom has worked with the national touring productions of *A Chorus Line, Altar Boyz,* and the Big Apple Circus. He has appeared with the Prague Radio, the Claflin Hill, and the New Bedford Symphony Orchestras, and as a chamber musician in performances of the music of Brahms, Schubert, Bartok, Messiaen, and Shostakovich. As a jazz pianist, he has appeared with Billy Pierce, Joe Lovano, Jimmy Giuffre, George Garzone, the John Allmark Jazz Orchestra, the Kenny Hadley Big Band, the Cab Calloway Orchestra, the Jazz Composers Alliance Orchestra, and the singer Amanda Carr. As a conductor, he has led numerous performances of ballet, opera, musical theater, and symphonic repertoire. Tom has written over fifty compositions, including works for musical theater, orchestra, band, chorus, and various chamber ensembles. He has made a number of recordings, most notably, his *Symphony No. 1* with the Prague Dvorak Orchestra and Julius Williams, conductor, on Albany Records. Tom has taught at Dean College and the New England Conservatory of Music. He is currently the assistant chair of the Harmony Department at Berklee College of Music where he teaches theory, composition, piano, and conducting.

Photo by Jane Akiba

INDEX

♭6 scale degree, 89–91
"26-2" (Coltrane), 180

I-6 chord, chord scale for, 85
IMaj6 chord
    as tonic chord, 3, 6
    V7 chord voice leading to, 6
I°7 chord, chord scales for, 160
I7 chord, blues scales and, 133–35
I-(Maj7) chord, chord scale for, 85
IMaj7 chord
    altered to V7/IV, 41
    chord scale for, xi, 21
    diatonic 11 as harmonic avoid tone, 21
    stability of, 16, 17
    tension 9, 21
    tension 13, 21
    with tensions, 20–22
    as tonic chord, 3, 8
    V7 chord voice leading to, 5
IMaj7(♯11) chord, 129
♯I°7 chord, V7/II and, 151–52

♭IIMaj7 chord, 126–27
    chord scales for, 91–92
    deceptive resolution to, 234
II-7♭5 chord
    chord scale for, 90
    as pre-dominant chord, 90–91
II-7 chord
    altered to V7/V, 41
    chord scale for, 22
    in incomplete subdominant cadence, 19
    as member of subdominant group, 8
    as pivot chord, 174
    in plagal cadence, 19
    source scale for, 92–93
    stability of, 16
    as subdominant preparation for V7, 122
II-7 chords, related, 51–59
    related II of V7/IV, 51–52
    related II of V7/VI, 52–53
II-7 IMaj7 phrase, 19
II-7 V7 IMaj7 phrase, 19
    with ♭9, 32
    with ♭9 and ♭13, 33
    with ♭13, 33
    voicings for, 22
II7 chord
    in blues progression, 138
    as non-resolving dominant, 237
♯II°7 chord, V7/III and, 150–51

♭III°7 chord
    chord scales for, 156–57
    melodic/harmonic options, 157
♭III7 chord, as non-resolving dominant, 238
♭III(Maj7) chord
    chord scale for, 87–88
    deceptive resolution to, 235
    in modal interchange, 128
♭III+(Maj7) chord, chord scale for, 86
III-7 chord
    altered to V7/VI, 41
    chord scale for, xi, 23
    deceptive resolution to, 234
    as member of tonic group, 7, 8
III7 chord, as non-resolving dominant, 238

IV6 chord, as subdominant chord, 3–4
IV- chord, 116
    as target chord, 98
IV-7 chord
    chord scale for, 90
    modal interchange chord scales for, 129
    as pivot chord, 173
    as pre-dominant chord, 90–91
IV-(Maj7) chord, 130
IV7 chord
    in blues progression, 137–39
    blues scales and, 133–35, 136–37
    in modal interchange, 124–25
    as non-resolving dominant, 236–37
    as pivot chord, 174
    source scale for, 92, 93–94
IVMaj7 chord
    altered to IV-, 116
    altered to V7/♭VII, 41–42
    chord scale for, 23
    in incomplete subdominant cadence, 19
    in plagal cadence, 19
    as subdominant chord, 3–4, 7, 8
    as subdominant preparation for V7, 122
IVMaj7 I phrase, 19
♯IV°7 chord
    alternate diatonic chord scale for, 153–54
    V7/V and, 152
♯IV-7♭5 chord, 158–59
    deceptive resolution to, 234

V°7
    chord scale for, 161
    as embellishing dominant, 160–61
V-7 chord, 127

V7 chord
    adding chromatic tensions too, 32–33
    with ♭9, ♯9, and ♭13, 34, 65–66
    blues scales and, 133–35, 136
    chord scales for, xi, 23–24, 94–95
    deceptive resolutions of, 233–35
    as dominant chord, 5–6
    in minor key, 94–98
    optional chord scales for, 33–37
    resolution of, 5
    stability of, 16
    subdominant minor partners for, 122–23
    with T♯9, 34
    tritone in, 5, 8
    voice leading to IMaj6, 6
    voice leading to IMaj7, 5
    related II of, 51–52
V7sus4 chord, viii, 6–7
    chord scale for, 24
    functioning as dominant, 7
    functioning as subdominant, 6
V7sus4(♭9) chord, voicings, 97
V7/II chord, 40
    chord scale for, 45–46
    ♯I°7 and, 151–52
    in minor keys, 101
    related II of, 53–54
V7/♭III chord, 102–3
V7/III chord, 40
    chord scale for, 44–45
    ♯II°7 and, 150–51
    related II of, 54–55
V7/IV chord, 41
    chord scale for, 42–43
    in minor keys, 99–100
V7/V chord, 41
    chord scale for, 42–43
    deceptive resolution of, 177
    ♯IV°7 and, 152
    in minor keys, 99–100
    related II of, 56–57, 99
V7/♭VI chord, 101–2
V7/VI chord, 41
    chord scale for, 43–44
    as pivot chord, 172
    related II of, 52–53
    ♯V°7 and, 149–50
V7/♭VII chord, 41–42
V7/VII chord, 42
♯V°7 chord
    chord scale for, 149–50
    V7/VI and, 149–50

♭VI°7 chord, 158
♭VI7 chord, 104
    as non-resolving dominant, 238
♭VIMaj7 chord, 120
    chord scale for, 90
    deceptive resolution to, 235
    as pre-dominant chord, 90–91

VI-7♭5 chord
    chord scale for, 85
    as related II, 99
VI-7 chord
    altered to be dominant seventh, 39–40
    chord scales for, 24, 96–97
    deceptive resolution to, 233
    function of, 96–97
    as member of tonic group, 7, 8, 120
    stability of, 16

♭VII7 chord, 130
    chord scales for, 96–97
    as dominant function chord, 97
    in modal interchange, 123–24
    as non-resolving dominant, 237
    as pivot chord, 173
♭VIIMaj7 chord, deceptive resolution to, 235
VII°7 chord
    chord scale for, 96
    as pivot chord, 96
VII-7♭5 chord
    altered to be dominant 7th, 40
    chord scale for, 25
    diatonic function of, 52–53
    rarity of, 8, 11
VII7 chord, as non-resolving dominant, 238

Adderley, Nat, "Work Song," 104
Aeolian mode, 193–94
    characteristics, 193
    standard harmonic phrases, 193–94
    tonic scale with ♭6, 193
Aeolian scale, x
    in blues, 143–44
    chord scale for, 24
    chord scale for related II chord, 57–58
    importance in modal interchange, 119–20
    as modal system, 184
    as parallel scale, 117–18
    as source scale, 87–90, 96–97, 99
    subV/II and, 68
"Afternoon in Paris" (Lewis), 174
"Airegin" (Rollins), 178
"All-Nighter, The" (Hojnacki), 145
"Along Came Betty" (Golson), 206
Alter, Louis, "Do You Know What It Means to Miss
    New Orleans," 237
altered dominant scale, 34–36, 45
    Lydian ♭7 as replacement for, 65–67
    for V7 chord, 95
ambi-chords. See hybrid voicings and inversions
"Angel Eyes" (Dennis and Brent), 83, 104
"Anthropology" (Parker), 16n
anticipation, 59
Armstrong, Louis, 132
ascending cycle 2 pair motion, 10, 154
ascending cycle 3 pair motion, 11
ascending cycle 5 pair motion, 12–13
"As Time Goes By" (Hupfeld), 160
"At Last" (Warren), 16n
augmented 7 chord, ix

augmented sixth chords, 63–64
augmented triad, viii
"Autumn Leaves" (Kosma and Prevert), 89, 97
auxiliary diminished chords, 159–61

Barron, Kenny, "Sequel," 179
Basie ending, 59
"Baubles, Bangles, and Beads" (Borodin/Wright/
 Forest), 180
bebop blues, 135
Beirach, Richie, 224
"Bemsha Swing" (Monk), 170
Bennett, Dave, "Bye-Bye Blues," 238
"Birth of the Blues, The," 152n
"Black Nile" (Shorter), 105
"Black Orpheus" (Bonfa), 89, 96, 176
"Bloo-Zee" (Hojnacki), 145
blue notes, 134–35
"Blue Room" (Rodgers and Hart), 16n
"Blues for Alice" (Parker), 140–41
blues in jazz, 132–46
    adding to progression, 137–39
    bebop, 140–42
    blues progressions, 136–37
    blues scale(s), 133–35
    minor, 143–44
    pentatonic melody in, 132–33
    secondary dominants in, 139–40
    sixteen-bar, 142–43
blues major pentatonic scale, 135
blues scale(s), 133–35
"Body and Soul," 171, 180
"Bolivia" (Walton), 183
Bonfa, Luis, "Black Orpheus," 89, 96, 176
boogie-woogie, 135
"Bopston Blues" (Hojnacki), 146
Borodin, Alexander, "Baubles, Bangles, and Beads,"
 180
Brecker, Michael, 224
Brent, Earl, "Angel Eyes," 83, 104
Brown, Clifford, "Tiny Capers," 237
Buckner, Milt, 161
"Bud Powell" (Corea), 237
Burke, Johnny, "But Beautiful," 237
"But Beautiful" (Van Heusen and Burke), 237
"But Not for Me," 48, 180
"Bye-Bye Blues" (Hamm/Bennett/Lown/Gray), 238

cadence chords in modal music, 186–87
"Canteloupe Island" (Hancock), 238
"Captain Marvel" (Corea), 89
Carisi, John, "Israel," 144
Carter, Benny, "When Lights Are Low," 179
character chords in modal music, 186–87
"Cherokee" (Noble), 179
chord progressions
    in blues, 136–39
    of Coltrane, 180–81
    constant structure, 129, 203–9
    diatonic, 8–13

diminished seventh chord in, 148–61
    metrical stress patterns and, 14–15
    modal interchange in, 120–21
    secondary dominants in, 47, 64
chord scales
    defined, x
    for IMaj7, 21
    for II–7, 22
    for III–7, 23
    for IVMaj7, 23
    for related II–7 chords, 57–58
    for secondary dominants, 42–46
    for substitute dominants, 65–67
    for subV/I, 70
    for subV/II, 78
    for subV/III, 78
    for subV/IV, 79
    for subV/V, 79
    for subV/VI, 79
    for V7, 23–24
    for VI–7, 24
    for VII–7♭5, 25
chord-scale theory, x–xii
chord symbol nomenclature, vii
chord tones, xi
chord types, defining, vii
chromatic chord scales, x
chromaticism, 38
chromatic voice leading, 1
circle of fifths, 166–67
closely related keys, 166–67
color chords
    in modal music, 186–87
    special function dominants, 236–38
Coltrane, John, 132, 182
    "26-2," 180
    chord progression of, 180–81
    "Countdown," 181
    "Equinox," 144
    "Giant Steps," 180, 181
    "Impressions," 193n
    "Moment's Notice," 206
composite minor scale, 84
    dominant function and, 94–95
confirming cadences, 168
constant structure progressions, 129, 203–9
contrary stepwise root motion, 9
"Corcovado" (Jobim), 158
Corea, Chick
    "Bud Powell," 237
    "Captain Marvel," 89
    "Crystal Silence," 187
"Countdown" (Coltrane), 181
"Crystal Silence" (Corea), 187

Dameron, Tadd
    "Good Bait," 170
    "If You Could See Me Now," 125, 171, 237
    "Ladybird," 123
    "Soultrane," 176
"Darn That Dream," 177

Davis, Miles, 132, 182
  "Nardis," 92, 187
  "So What," 183, 193n
  "Tune Up," 179, 181
"Daydream" (Strayhorn), 178
deceptive cadence, 19
deceptive resolution
  of secondary dominants, 47–48
  of V7 chord, 233–35
delayed attack, 59
"Deluge" (Shorter), 92
Dennis, Matt, "Angel Eyes," 83, 104
DeRose, Peter, "The Lamp Is Low," 237
descending cycle 2 pair motion, 10
descending cycle 3 pair motion, 10
descending cycle 5 pair motion, 12, 153
diatonic chord progressions, 8–13
diatonic chord scales, x
diminished seventh chord, 147–65
  as descending chromatic approach chord, 148,
    155–59
  diminished approach technique, 161–62
  as embellishing sound, 148, 159–61
  interval structure, 147
  notation for, ix
  in progressions, 148–61
  as secondary dominant, 148, 149–54
  spelling issues, 147–48
  symmetric diminished scale and, 162
  symmetry and, 154
diminished triad, viii
"Diminishing Returns" (Hojnacki), 163–64
direct modulation, 166, 168–70
  half-step, 178
  minor third, 179
  whole-step, 178–79
distantly related keys, 166–67
"Django" (Lewis), 83, 100
dominant functions, minor key, 94–98
  alternative options from natural minor source
    scale, 96–97
  harmonic minor scale and, 94
  summary of functions, 98
dominant group, chord functions in, 8
dominant seventh chords, viii
  dominant to tonic motion compared with
    subdominant to tonic, 4
  harmonic function of, 3, 5–6, 182
  hybrids, 223
  non-resolving, 236–37
  tritone in, 5, 8
dominant 7♭5 chord, ix
dominant 7sus4 chord. See V7sus4
"Do Nothin' till You Hear from Me" (Ellington), 169,
  171
"Don't Go to Strangers" (Kent/Mann/Evans), 125
Dorian minor scale, 83
  as source scale, 86–87
  voicings in fourths on, 87
Dorian mode, 191–93
  characteristics, 191

standard harmonic phrases, 192–93
  tonic scale with major 6, 191
Dorian scale, x
  chord scale for, 22
  chord scale for IV-7, 90
  in modal interchange, 128
  modal interchange pattern, 174
  as modal system, 184
  as source scale, 92–94
  subV/IV and, 69
"Do You Know What It Means to Miss New Orleans"
  (Alter), 237
dual function chords, 53–54, 56–57, 58, 69–70
Duke, Vernon, "I Can't Get Started," 16n, 170

Ellington, Duke
  "Do Nothin' till You Hear from Me," 169, 171
  "Prelude to a Kiss," 49, 50, 169, 171
  "Sophisticated Lady," 171
  "Sweet Zurzday," 238
  "Warm Valley," 237
"Emily," 170
"Equinox" (Coltrane), 144
Evans, Red, "Don't Go to Strangers," 125
extended dominants, 49–50, 77
  in blues, 139–40
extended turn-around ending, 234

"Footprints" (Shorter), 87
Forest, George, "Baubles, Bangles, and Beads," 180
Foster, Frank, "Simone," 144
French sixth chord, 63–64
full dominant cadence, 19
full jazz cadence, 19

"Georgia on My Mind," 176
German sixth chord, 63
Gershwin, George
  "How Long Has This Been Going On?", 160
  "I Got Rhythm," 16n, 49, 50
  "Nice Work If You Can Get It," 49, 50
"Giant Steps" (Coltrane), 180, 181
Gillespie, Dizzy, 182
  "Groovin' High," 238
  "A Night in Tunisia," 105–6
"Girl from Ipanema, The" (Jobim), 237
"Girl Talk" (Hefti), 127
Gitler, Ira, "Swing to Bop," 21n
"God Bless the Child," 176
Golson, Benny
  "Along Came Betty," 206
  "Killer Joe," 237
  "Stablemates," 176
  "Whisper Not," 177
"Good Bait" (Dameron), 170
"Goodbye Porkpie Hat" (Mingus), 144
Goodman, Benny, "Lullaby in Rhythm," 237
Gould, Morton, "Pavane," 193n
Gray, Chauncey, "Bye-Bye Blues," 238
"Groovin' High" (Gillespie), 238

Gross, Walter, "Tenderly," 237
Gryce, Gigi, "Minority," 83, 93n
guide tone lines, 212

half cadence, 19
half-step modulation, 178
Hamilton and Lewis, "How High the Moon," 171, 174
Hamm, Fred, "Bye-Bye Blues," 238
Hancock, Herbie
    "Canteloupe Island," 238
    "Maiden Voyage," 183
    "Watermelon Man," 142
harmonic avoid notes, xi
    diatonic 11 in IMaj7 chord, 21
    S6 on ♭III+(Maj7), 86
harmonic cadence, 18–19
    deceptive, 19
    full dominant, 19
    half, 19
    incomplete subdominant, 19
    plagal, 19
    subdominant, 19
harmonic function (defined), 1, 2, 3
harmonic minor scale, 83
    dominant function and, 94
harmonic phrase, 18
harmonic rhythm, 13–18
    in 3/4 time, 17
    alternating stable/unstable harmonic and
        metric functions, 16–17
    changes in, 17
    forward motion, 16
    half note, 13, 14
    metrical stress patterns and, 14–17
    mixed-duration, 14, 17
    quarter note, 14
    summary of points, 18
    two-measure, 14
    whole note, 13, 14
Harrell, Tom, "Sail Away," 128
"Have You Met Miss Jones?" (Rodgers), 180
Hefti, Neal, "Girl Talk," 127
Henderson, Joe
    "Inner Urge," 197, 204–5
    "No Me Esqueça ("Recorda Me")", 183
    "Step Lightly," 142–43
"Hi-Fly," 171
Hirsch, Walter, "Lullaby in Rhythm," 237
Hojnacki, Tom
    "The All-Nighter," 145
    "Bloo-Zee," 145
    "Bopston Blues," 146
    "Diminishing Returns," 163–64
    "It Could Have Been the Summertime," 26–32
    "Lithe and Lovely" (Hojnacki), 174–75
    "Lucky," 59–61, 79–81
    "The Shadow of a Memory," 169
    "To the Bitter Dregs," 109–14
"How High the Moon" (Hamilton and Lewis), 171, 174
"How Insensitive" (Jobim), 96

"How Long Has This Been Going On?" (Gershwin),
    160
"How My Heart Sings," 170
Hupfeld, Herman, "As Time Goes By," 160
hybrid voicings and inversions, 218–25
    chord symbols and analysis, 221
    dominant, 223
    modal interchange chords, 222
    summary of points, 224–25
    with thirds, 224

"I Can't Get Started" (Duke), 16n, 170
"If You Could See Me Now" (Dameron), 125, 171, 237
"I Got Rhythm" (Gershwin), 16n, 49, 50
"I'll Remember April" (Raye, DePaul, and Johnstone),
    16n
"I Mean You" (Monk), 237, 238
"Impressions" (Coltrane), 193n
"In a Mellow Tone," 48
incomplete subdominant cadence, 19
"Inner Urge" (Henderson), 197, 204–5
"inside" harmony, 58, 59
"Invitation" (Kaper), 106, 177
Ionian scale, x. See also major scale
    chord scale for, 21
    as expression of IMaj7 chord, xi
    as source scale, 87
"Israel" (Carisi), 144
Italian sixth chord, 63
"It Could Have Been the Summertime" (Hojnacki)
    with chromatic tensions on V7, 37
    harmonic analysis, 28–29
    lead sheet, 26
    solo piano arrangement, 30–32

James Bond theme, 107
jazz half cadence, 18
jazz harmony
    blues in, 132–46
    constant structure progressions, 203–9
    diminished seventh chords, 147–65
    distinguishing characteristics, 1, 63
    liberal use of chromaticism in, 38
    major key, 1–81
    minor key, 83–115
    modal harmony in, 182–201
    modal interchange, 116–31
    modulation in, 166–81
    vertical emphasis of, 64
    voicings, 210–32
"Jersey Bounce" (Plater/Bradshaw/Johnson), 237
Jobim, Antonio Carlos
    "Corcovado," 158
    "The Girl from Ipanema," 237
    "How Insensitive," 96
    "Meditation," 238
    "Wave," 141–42
Jordan, Duke, "Jordu," 50
"Jordu" (Jordan), 50
"Joy Spring," 171
"Just Friends," 177

Kaper, Bronislaw, "Invitation," 106, 177
Kaper and Washington, "On Green Dolphin Street," 126–27
Kent, Arthur, "Don't Go to Strangers," 125
Kern, Jerome, "Long Ago and Far Away," 170, 171
"Killer Joe" (Golson), 237
Kind of Blue (Davis), 182
Kosma, Joseph, "Autumn Leaves," 89, 97

"Ladybird" (Dameron), 123
"Lamp Is Low, The" (DeRose and Shefter), 237
Legrand, Michel, "Watch What Happens," 206, 237
Lewis, John
    "Afternoon in Paris," 174
    "Django," 83, 100
line clichés, 106–7
    modal interchange in, 120–21
"Lithe and Lovely" (Hojnacki), 174–75
Lloyd, Charles, 181
Locrian mode, 197
    characteristics, 197
Locrian natural 9 scale, 85
Locrian scale, x
    chord scale for, 25
    chord scale for II–7♭5, 90
    chord scale for related II chord, 58
"Long Ago and Far Away" (Kern), 170, 171
Lown, Bert, "Bye-Bye Blues," 238
"Lucky" (Hojnacki), 59–61
    with subVs, 79–81
"Lullaby in Rhythm" (Goodman/Sampson/Profit/Hirsch), 237
Lydian mode, 188–89
    characteristics, 188
    standard harmonic phrases, 188–89
    tonic scale with ♯4, 188
Lydian ♭7 scale, 65–67, 73, 157
    as source scale, 94
Lydian scale, x
    chord scale for, 23
    chord scale for ♭VIMaj7, 90
    chord scale for ♯IV–7♭5, 159
    in modal interchange, 129
    as modal system, 184
    as source scale, 92

"Maiden Voyage" (Hancock), 183
major key harmony, 1–37
    diatonic chord progressions, 8–13
    extended dominants, 49–50, 77
    functional groups, 7–8
    harmonic cadence, 18–19
    harmonic phrase, 18
    harmonic rhythm, 13–18
    major scale and basic diatonic functions, 2–7
    metrical stress patterns and chord progression, 14–15
    secondary dominants, 38–49
    substitute dominants, 63–81
    tensions, 20–37
major scale. *See also* Ionian scale
    chords derived from, 3–7
    scale-tone tendencies, 2

major seventh chord, viii
major sixth chord, viii
major third modulation, 180
major triad, viii
major triad with major second. *See* sus2 chord
major triad with perfect fourth. *See* sus4 chord
Mandel, Johnny, "The Shadow of Your Smile," 93n
Mann, Dave, "Don't Go to Strangers," 125
"Meditation" (Jobim), 238
melodic minor scale, 83
    as source scale, 85–86
Mercer, Johnny, "I Remember You," 238
"Metamorphosis" (Silver), 179
Metheny, Pat, 181, 224
metrical stress patterns
    in 3/4 time, 17
    alternating stable/unstable harmonic and metric functions, 16–17
    chord progression influenced by, 14–15
    harmonic rhythm and, 14–17
    secondary dominants in, 48–49
Mingus, Charles, "Goodbye Porkpie Hat," 144
"Minority" (Gryce), 83, 93n
minor key harmony, 83–115
    dominant functions, 94–98
    line clichés in, 106–7
    scales, 83–84
    secondary dominants, 98–103
    shift to relative major, 89
    substitute dominants in, 103–6
    tonic function, 84–89
minor-major 7 chord, ix
minor 6 chord, ix
minor 7♭5 chord, viii
minor 7 chord, viii
minor third modulation, 179
minor triad, viii
Mixolydian mode, 189–91
    characteristics, 190
    standard harmonic phrases, 190–91
    tonic scale with ♭7, 189
Mixolydian scale, x
    chord scale for, 23–24
    chord scales for secondary dominants, 42–46, 101–3
    with chromatic tensions, 33–34, 100, 101–2
    from composite minor source, 95
    as expression of V7 chord, xi
    as expression of V7/V chord, 99
    as modal system, 184
    as source scale, 93
"Moanin'" (Timmons), 183
modal harmony, 182–201
    Aeolian, 193–94
    characteristics of modes, 187
    chord voicings in, 185
    defined, 183
    Dorian, 191–93
    lack of dominant resolution in, 184
    Locrian, 197
    Lydian, 188–89
    Mixolydian, 189–91
    modes and modal progressions, 183–84

Phrygian, 195–97
    proto-progression, 186–87
    tonic establishment through melody, 185
    tonic establishment through repetition, 184–85
modal interchange (modal mixture), 116–31
    ♭IIMaj7 in, 126–27
    IV7 in, 124–25
    V–7 in, 127
    ♭VII7 in, 123–24
    analysis of, 130–31
    in chord progressions, 120–21
    chord scales, 129–30
    constant structure progressions and, 203–9
    hybrid voicings, 222
    parallelism and, 117–18
    subdominant minor chords in, 119–23
    tonic, 127–28
    tonic's inviolability in, 118
modal scales, names of, x
modulation, 166–81
    aesthetic effects, 166–68
    in classical music, 166
    Coltrane changes, 180–81
    direct, 166, 168–70, 178
    in flat direction, 171
    key changes from major to minor, 176
    key changes organized by half step, 178
    key changes organized by major third, 180
    key changes organized by minor third, 179
    key changes organized by whole step, 178–79
    key of the moment, 177
    minor key tunes, 176–77
    multiple local modulations, 178
    pivot, 166, 171–74
    in sharp direction, 170–71
    transitional, 166, 174–76
"Moment's Notice" (Coltrane), 206
Monk, Thelonious
    "Bemsha Swing," 170
    "I Mean You," 237, 238
    "Round Midnight," 75, 105
    "Well You Needn't," 14, 206
"Moonlight on Spot Pond" (Mulholland), 200–201
Mulholland, Joe
    "Moonlight on Spot Pond," 200–201
    "The Same Sky," 208–9
    "The Slip-Up," 198–99
    "Smooth Sailing," 230–32
multi-tonic system, 181
"My Funny Valentine" (Rodgers and Hart), 89, 103, 107, 176

"Nardis" (Davis), 92, 187
natural minor scale, 83. See also Aeolian scale
Nelson, Oliver, "Stolen Moments," 144
"Nice Work If You Can Get It" (Gershwin), 49, 50
"Night in Tunisia, A" (Gillespie), 105–6
Noble, Ray, "Cherokee," 179
"No Me Esqueça" ("Recorda Me") (Henderson), 183

octatonic scale, 162
"On Green Dolphin Street" (Kaper and Washington), 126–27
"Ornithology" (Parker), 174
"Our Love Is Here to Stay," 48
"Out of Nowhere," 177

"Paper Moon," 152n
parallelism, 117–18
parallel stepwise root motion, 9
Parker, Charlie, 132, 182
    "Anthropology," 16n
    "Blues for Alice," 140–41
    "Ornithology," 174
    "Yardbird Suite," 124, 176, 237
"Pavane" (Gould), 193n
Pease, Ted, Modern Jazz Voicings (with Pullig), 229
Phrygian minor scale, 83
Phrygian mode, 195–97
    characteristics, 195
    standard harmonic phrases, 196–97
    tonic scale with ♭2, 195
    voicings, 195–96
Phrygian scale, x
    chord scale for, 23
    chord scale for related II chord, 57
    as expression of III–7 chord, xi
    as modal system, 184
    as source scale, 89, 91–92, 93, 97
Phrygian voicings, 97
Phyrgian scale, in modal interchange, 129
pivot chords, 171–72
pivot modulation, 166, 171–74
plagal cadence, 19
Plater/Bradshaw/Johnson, "Jersey Bounce," 237
polychords
    constructing, 215–16
    dominant, 217–18
    summary of points, 218
    voicings, 215–18
Porter, Cole, 100
"Prelude to a Kiss" (Ellington), 49, 50, 169, 171
Prevert, Jacques, "Autumn Leaves," 89, 97
Profit, Clarence, "Lullaby in Rhythm," 237
progression (defined), 8
prolongation (defined), 8
Pullig, Ken, Modern Jazz Voicings (with Pease), 229

quartal voicings, 210, 225–28
    building, 226–28

Raye, DePaul, and Johnstone, "I'll Remember April," 16n
Raye and DePaul, "You Don't Know What Love Is," 89, 176
related II–7 chords, 51–59
    in blues, 139–40
    chord scales for, 57–58
    for subVs, 74–77
    summary of points and practical considerations, 59
    of V7/II, 53–54

of V7/III, 54–55
of V7/IV, 51–52
of V7/V, 56–57
of V7/VI, 52–53
resolution (defined), 8
retrogression (defined), 8
"Rhythm Changes," 56
rock 'n' roll, 138
Rodgers, Richard, "Have You Met Miss Jones?", 180
Rodgers and Hart
    "Blue Room," 16n
    "My Funny Valentine," 89, 103, 107, 176
    "Spring Is Here," 159
Rollins, Sonny
    "Airegin," 178
    "Strode Rode," 104
Ronnell, Anne, "Willow Weep for Me," 237
root motion
    chromatic, 76–77
    defined, 9
    by fifths, cycle 5, 12–13, 16, 74–77, 211
    mixed-interval, 212
    by step, cycle 2, 9–10, 211
    by thirds, cycle 3, 10–11, 212
"Round Midnight" (Monk), 75, 105

"Sail Away" (Harrell), 128
"Same Sky, The" (Mulholland), 208–9
Sampson, Edgar, "Lullaby in Rhythm," 237
Schertzinger, Victor, "I Remember You," 238
secondary dominants, 38–49
    in blues, 139–40
    chord scales for, 42–46
    as chromatically altered diatonic chords, 39–40
    chromaticism of, 38–40
    deceptive resolution of, 47–48
    diatonic roots and targets for, 39, 42
    diminished seventh as, 148, 149–54
    French sixth chord as, 64
    harmonic function of, 39
    in major keys, 40–42
    in minor keys, 98–103
    in progressions, 47
    related II-7 chords, 51–59
    on strong metrical stresses, 48–49
    summary of points, 49
    V7/II, 40, 101
    V7/♭III, 102–3
    V7/III, 40
    V7/IV, 41, 99–100
    V7/V, 41, 99–100
    V7/♭VI, 101–2
    V7/VI, 41
    V7/♭VII and, 41–42
"Sequel" (Barron), 179
seventh chords
    as basic harmonic building block for jazz, 3
    types of, viii–ix
"Shadow of a Memory, The" (Hojnacki), 169
"Shadow of Your Smile, The" (Mandel), 93n
Shearing, George, 161
Shefter, Bert, "The Lamp Is Low," 237

Shorter, Wayne
    "Black Nile," 105
    "Deluge," 92
    "Footprints," 87
    "Yes and No," 183
Silver, Horace, "Metamorphosis," 179
"Simone" (Foster), 144
sixth chords, types of, viii–ix, 63–64
slash chords. See hybrid voicings and inversions
"Slip-Up, The" (Mulholland), 198–99
"Smooth Sailing" (Mulholland), 230–32
"Sophisticated Lady" (Ellington), 171
"Soultrane" (Dameron), 176
source scales
    Aeolian as, 87–90, 89–90, 96–97, 99
    defined, 84
    Dorian as, 92–94
    Dorian minor as, 86–87
    Ionian as, 87
    Lydian as, 92
    Lydian ♭7 as, 94
    melodic minor as, 85–86
    Mixolydian as, 93
    Phrygian as, 89, 91–92, 93, 97
"So What" (Davis), 183, 193n
"Spring Is Here" (Rodgers and Hart), 159
"Stablemates" (Golson), 176
"Stella by Starlight" (Young), 238
"Step Lightly" (Henderson), 142–43
"Stolen Moments" (Nelson), 144
Strayhorn, Billy
    "Daydream," 178
    "Take the 'A' Train," 237
"Strode Rode" (Rollins), 104
subdominant cadence, 19
subdominant chords
    from Aeolian source, 90
    dominant to tonic motion compared with
        subdominant to tonic, 4
    functions, 8
    harmonic function of, 3–4
    root of, 3–4
    subdominant to tonic motion, 4
subdominant function
    ♭6 scale degree, 89–91
    modal interchange and, 118
subdominant group, 8
subdominant minor chords (SDMs), 119–23
    as pivot chord, 173
substitute dominants (subVs), 63–81
    alternate related IIs for, 74–77
    in blues, 139–40
    chord scales for, 65–67, 78–79
    with diatonic tensions, 73–74
    in minor keys, 103–6
    related IIs for, 67–73
    subV7, 103–4
    subV/I, 73–74, 78, 127
    subV/II, 68, 78, 105–6
    subV/♭III, 105–6
    subV/III, 70–71, 78

subV/IV, 69, 73–74, 79, 104
subV/V, 69–70, 79, 104–5
subV/♭VI, 105–6
subV/VI, 71–73, 79
summary of points, 77
sus2 chord, viii
sus4 chord, viii
"Sweet Zurzday" (Ellington), 238
"Swing to Bop" (Gitler), 21n
symmetric diminished scale, 162
symmetric dominant scale, 36–37

"Take the 'A' Train" (Strayhorn), 237
Tatum, Art, 76, 182
"Tenderly" (Gross), 237
tensions, 20–37
    adding to three-note voicing, 212
    adding to V7, 32–33
    available, xi
    blues scales and, 133–35
    chromatic, 32–33, 58
    defined, ix, 1
    diatonic, 43, 73–74, 149–50
    as distinguishing feature of jazz harmony, 20
    naming of, 20
    notation of, ix–x
    substitutions on four-way close voicings, 214
"There Is No Greater Love," 176
Timmons, Bobby, "Moanin'", 183
"Tiny Capers" (Brown), 237
TMaj7 chord, 153
tonal center, 1
tonal interchange, 177
tonal music (defined), 1
tonic
    defined, 3
    establishing in modal music, 184–85
    function, 84–89
tonic chord, harmonic function of, 3
tonic group, 7
    chord functions, 8
"To the Bitter Dregs" (Hojnacki), 109–14
    harmonic analysis, 112–14
    piano arrangement, 110–11
transitional modulation, 166, 174–76
triads
    seventh chords vs., 3
    types of, viii
Tristano, Lennie, 182
tritone
    in diminished seventh chord, 154
    in secondary dominants, 39
    in V7 chord, 5, 8

tritone equivalence, 64
tritone substitution
    as characteristic jazz harmonic device, 63
    principles of, 64–65
    substitute dominants and, 65–67
"Tune Up" (Davis), 179, 181

upper-structure triads, 35

Van Heusen, Jimmy
    "But Beautiful," 237
    "Witchcraft," 107
voicings, 210–32
    five-note, 210, 213–14
    four-note, 210, 212
    hybrid, 210, 218–25
    in modal harmony, 185
    Phrygian, 97
    polychord, 210, 215–18
    quartal, 210, 225–28
    summary of points, 229
    three-note, 210, 211–12

Walton, Cedar, "Bolivia," 183
"Warm Valley" (Ellington), 237
Warren, Harry, "At Last," 16n
"Watch What Happens" (Legrand), 206, 237
"Watermelon Man" (Hancock), 142
"Wave" (Jobim), 141–42
"Well You Needn't" (Monk), 14, 206
"What's New?", 171
"When Lights Are Low" (Carter), 179
"Whisper Not" (Golson), 177
whole-step modulation, 178–79
"Willow Weep for Me" (Ronnell), 237
"Witchcraft" (Van Heusen), 107
"Work Song" (Adderley), 104
Wright, Robert, "Baubles, Bangles, and Beads," 180

"Yardbird Suite" (Parker), 124, 176, 237
Yellowjackets, the, 224
"Yes and No" (Shorter), 183
"You Don't Know What Love Is" (Raye and DePaul), 89, 176
Young, Lester, 132
Young, Victor, "Stella by Starlight," 238

More Fine Publications

GUITAR

BEBOP GUITAR SOLOS
by Michael Kaplan
00121703 Book $16.99

BLUES GUITAR TECHNIQUE
by Michael Williams
50449623 Book/Online Audio $27.99

BERKLEE GUITAR CHORD DICTIONARY
by Rick Peckham
50449546 Jazz - Book $14.99
50449596 Rock - Book $12.99

BERKLEE GUITAR STYLE STUDIES
by Jim Kelly
00200377 Book/Online Media...........$24.99

CLASSICAL TECHNIQUE FOR THE MODERN GUITARIST
by Kim Perlak
00148781 Book/Online Audio $19.99

CONTEMPORARY JAZZ GUITAR SOLOS
by Michael Kaplan
00143596 Book $16.99

CREATIVE CHORDAL HARMONY FOR GUITAR
by Mick Goodrick and Tim Miller
50449613 Book/Online Audio $22.99

FUNK/R&B GUITAR
by Thaddeus Hogarth
50449569 Book/Online Audio $19.99

GUITAR SWEEP PICKING
by Joe Stump
00151223 Book/Online Audio $19.99

INTRODUCTION TO JAZZ GUITAR
by Jane Miller
00125041 Book/Online Audio.............$22.99

JAZZ GUITAR FRETBOARD NAVIGATION
by Mark White
00154107 Book/Online Audio.............$22.99

JAZZ SWING GUITAR
by Jon Wheatley
00139935 Book/Online Audio.............$24.99

METAL GUITAR CHOP SHOP
by Joe Stump
50449601 Book/Online Audio $19.99

A MODERN METHOD FOR GUITAR – VOLUMES 1-3 COMPLETE*
by William Leavitt
00292990 Book/Online Media $49.99
Individual volumes, media options, and supporting songbooks available.

A MODERN METHOD FOR GUITAR SCALES
by Larry Baione
00199318 Book $14.99

READING STUDIES FOR GUITAR
by William Leavitt
50449490 Book $17.99

Berklee Press publications feature material developed at Berklee College of Music.
To browse the complete Berklee Press Catalog, go to
www.berkleepress.com

BASS

BERKLEE JAZZ BASS
by Rich Appleman, Whit Browne & Bruce Gertz
50449636 Book/Online Audio..........$22.99

CHORD STUDIES FOR ELECTRIC BASS
by Rich Appleman & Joseph Viola
50449750 Book $17.99

FINGERSTYLE FUNK BASS LINES
by Joe Santerre
50449542 Book/Online Audio.............$19.99

FUNK BASS FILLS
by Anthony Vitti
50449608 Book/Online Audio $22.99

INSTANT BASS
by Danny Morris
50449502 Book/CD $9.99

METAL BASS LINES
by David Marvuglio
00122465 Book/Online Audio.............$19.99

READING CONTEMPORARY ELECTRIC BASS
by Rich Appleman
50449770 Book $22.99

ROCK BASS LINES
by Joe Santerre
50449478 Book/Online Audio...........$22.99

PIANO/KEYBOARD

BERKLEE JAZZ KEYBOARD HARMONY
by Suzanna Sifter
00138874 Book/Online Audio $29.99

BERKLEE JAZZ PIANO
by Ray Santisi
50448047 Book/Online Audio $22.99

BERKLEE JAZZ STANDARDS FOR SOLO PIANO
arr. Robert Christopherson, Hey Rim Jeon, Ross Ramsay, Tim Ray
00160482 Book/Online Audio $19.99

CHORD-SCALE IMPROVISATION FOR KEYBOARD
by Ross Ramsay
50449597 Book/CD $19.99

CONTEMPORARY PIANO TECHNIQUE
by Stephany Tiernan
50449545 Book/DVD...........................$29.99

HAMMOND ORGAN COMPLETE
by Dave Limina
00237801 Book/Online Audio............$24.99

JAZZ PIANO COMPING
by Suzanne Davis
50449614 Book/Online Audio............$22.99

LATIN JAZZ PIANO IMPROVISATION
by Rebecca Cline
50449649 Book/Online Audio $29.99

PIANO ESSENTIALS
by Ross Ramsay
50448046 Book/Online Audio $24.99

SOLO JAZZ PIANO
by Neil Olmstead
50449641 Book/Online Audio............$42.99

DRUMS

BEGINNING DJEMBE
by Michael Markus & Joe Galeota
00148210 Book/Online Video.............$16.99

BERKLEE JAZZ DRUMS
by Casey Scheuerell
50449612 Book/Online Audio............$24.99

DRUM SET WARM-UPS
by Rod Morgenstein
50449465 Book $14.99

A MANUAL FOR THE MODERN DRUMMER
by Alan Dawson & Don DeMichael
50449560 Book $14.99

MASTERING THE ART OF BRUSHES
by Jon Hazilla
50449459 Book/Online Audio............$19.99

PHRASING
by Russ Gold
00120209 Book/Online Media $19.99

WORLD JAZZ DRUMMING
by Mark Walker
50449568 Book/CD $22.99

BERKLEE PRACTICE METHOD

GET YOUR BAND TOGETHER
With additional volumes for other instruments, plus a teacher's guide.
Bass
by Rich Appleman, John Repucci and the Berklee Faculty
50449427 Book/CD $24.99
Drum Set
by Ron Savage, Casey Scheuerell and the Berklee Faculty
50449429 Book/CD $17.99
Guitar
by Larry Baione and the Berklee Faculty
50449426 Book/CD...............................$19.99
Keyboard
by Russell Hoffmann, Paul Schmeling and the Berklee Faculty
50449428 Book/Online Audio............$19.99

VOICE

BELTING
by Jeannie Gagné
00124984 Book/Online Media............$22.99

THE CONTEMPORARY SINGER
by Anne Peckham
50449595 Book/Online Audio $27.99

JAZZ VOCAL IMPROVISATION
by Mili Bermejo
00159290 Book/Online Audio............$19.99

TIPS FOR SINGERS
by Carolyn Wilkins
50449557 Book/CD $19.95

VOCAL WORKOUTS FOR THE CONTEMPORARY SINGER
by Anne Peckham
50448044 Book/Online Audio $24.99

YOUR SINGING VOICE
by Jeannie Gagné
50449619 Book/Online Audio............$29.99

WOODWINDS & BRASS

TRUMPET SOUND EFFECTS
by Craig Pederson & Ueli Dörig
00121626 Book/Online Audio............$14.99

SAXOPHONE SOUND EFFECTS
by Ueli Dörig
50449628 Book/Online Audio............$15.99

THE TECHNIQUE OF THE FLUTE
by Joseph Viola
00214012 Book............................$19.99

STRINGS/ROOTS MUSIC

BERKLEE HARP
by Felice Pomeranz
00144263 Book/Online Audio...........$24.99

BEYOND BLUEGRASS BANJO
by Dave Hollander and Matt Glaser
50449610 Book/CD.......................$19.99

BEYOND BLUEGRASS MANDOLIN
by John McGann and Matt Glaser
50449609 Book/CD $19.99

BLUEGRASS FIDDLE & BEYOND
by Matt Glaser
50449602 Book/CD.......................$19.99

CONTEMPORARY CELLO ETUDES
by Mike Block
00159292 Book/Online Audio...........$19.99

EXPLORING CLASSICAL MANDOLIN
by August Watters
00125040 Book/Online Media.........$24.99

THE IRISH CELLO BOOK
by Liz Davis Maxfield
50449652 Book/Online Audio.......... $27.99

JAZZ UKULELE
by Abe Lagrimas, Jr.
00121624 Book/Online Audio...........$22.99

WELLNESS

MANAGE YOUR STRESS AND PAIN THROUGH MUSIC
by Dr. Suzanne B. Hanser and Dr. Susan E. Mandel
50449592 Book/CD $34.99

MUSICIAN'S YOGA
by Mia Olson
50449587 Book...........................$19.99

NEW MUSIC THERAPIST'S HANDBOOK
by Dr. Suzanne B. Hanser
00279325 Book...........................$29.99

MUSIC PRODUCTION & ENGINEERING

AUDIO MASTERING
by Jonathan Wyner
50449581 Book/CD.......................$29.99

AUDIO POST PRODUCTION
by Mark Cross
50449627 Book...........................$19.99

CREATING COMMERCIAL MUSIC
by Peter Bell
00278535 Book/Online Media..........$19.99

THE SINGER-SONGWRITER'S GUIDE TO RECORDING IN THE HOME STUDIO
by Shane Adams
00148211 Book...........................$19.99

UNDERSTANDING AUDIO
by Daniel M. Thompson
00148197 Book...........................$42.99

MUSIC BUSINESS

CROWDFUNDING FOR MUSICIANS
by Laser Malena-Webber
00285092 Book...........................$17.99

ENGAGING THE CONCERT AUDIENCE
by David Wallace
00244532 Book/Online Media..........$16.99

HOW TO GET A JOB IN THE MUSIC INDUSTRY
by Keith Hatschek with Breanne Beseda
00130699 Book........................... $27.99

MAKING MUSIC MAKE MONEY
by Eric Beall
00355740 Book...........................$29.99

MUSIC INDUSTRY FORMS
by Jonathan Feist
00121814 Book............................$16.99

MUSIC LAW IN THE DIGITAL AGE
by Allen Bargfrede
00366048 Book...........................$24.99

MUSIC MARKETING
by Mike King
50449588 Book...........................$24.99

PROJECT MANAGEMENT FOR MUSICIANS
by Jonathan Feist
50449659 Book........................... $34.99

THE SELF-PROMOTING MUSICIAN
by Peter Spellman
00119607 Book...........................$29.99

CONDUCTING

CONDUCTING MUSIC TODAY
by Bruce Hangen
00237719 Book/Online Media..........$24.99

MUSIC THEORY & EAR TRAINING

BEGINNING EAR TRAINING
by Gilson Schachnik
50449548 Book/Online Audio.......... $17.99

BERKLEE CONTEMPORARY MUSIC NOTATION
by Jonathan Feist
00202547 Book...........................$24.99

BERKLEE MUSIC THEORY
by Paul Schmeling
50449615 Book 1/Online Audio........$24.99
50449616 Book 2/Online Audio......$24.99

CONTEMPORARY COUNTERPOINT
by Beth Denisch
00147050 Book/Online Audio $24.99

MUSIC NOTATION
by Mark McGrain
50449399 Book...........................$24.99
by Matthew Nicholl & Richard Grudzinski
50449540 Book...........................$24.99

REHARMONIZATION TECHNIQUES
by Randy Felts
50449496 Book...........................$29.99

SONGWRITING/COMPOSING

BEGINNING SONGWRITING
by Andrea Stolpe with Jan Stolpe
00138503 Book/Online Audio..........$22.99

COMPLETE GUIDE TO FILM SCORING
by Richard Davis
50449607 Book...........................$34.99

THE CRAFT OF SONGWRITING
by Scarlet Keys
00159283 Book/Online Audio..........$22.99

CREATIVE STRATEGIES IN FILM SCORING
by Ben Newhouse
00242911 Book/Online Media........... $27.99

JAZZ COMPOSITION
by Ted Pease
50448000 Book/Online Audio $39.99

MELODY IN SONGWRITING
by Jack Perricone
50449419 Book...........................$24.99

MUSIC COMPOSITION FOR FILM AND TELEVISION
by Lalo Schifrin
50449604 Book...........................$39.99

POPULAR LYRIC WRITING
by Andrea Stolpe
50449553 Book...........................$16.99

THE SONGWRITER'S WORKSHOP
by Jimmy Kachulis
Harmony
50449519 Book/Online Audio $29.99
Melody
50449518 Book/Online Audio $24.99

SONGWRITING: ESSENTIAL GUIDE
by Pat Pattison
Lyric Form and Structure
50481582 Book...........................$19.99
Rhyming
00124366 Book...........................$22.99

SONGWRITING IN PRACTICE
by Mark Simos
00244545 Book...........................$16.99

SONGWRITING STRATEGIES
by Mark Simos
50449621 Book...........................$24.99

ARRANGING & IMPROVISATION

ARRANGING FOR HORNS
by Jerry Gates
00121625 Book/Online Audio...........$22.99

BERKLEE BOOK OF JAZZ HARMONY
by Joe Mulholland & Tom Hojnacki
00113755 Book/Online Audio............$29.99

IMPROVISATION FOR CLASSICAL MUSICIANS
by Eugene Friesen with Wendy M. Friesen
50449637 Book/CD $24.99

MODERN JAZZ VOICINGS
by Ted Pease and Ken Pullig
50449485 Book/Online Audio..........$24.99

AUTOBIOGRAPHY

LEARNING TO LISTEN: THE JAZZ JOURNEY OF GARY BURTON
by Gary Burton
00117798 Book...........................$34.99

Prices subject to change without notice. Visit your local music dealer or bookstore, or go to **www.berkleepress.com**